Praise for
Wisdom 52

"Mark Moore has masterfully transformed the ancient book of Proverbs into a practical journey that speaks directly to our modern struggles. His gift for weaving timeless biblical wisdom with contemporary insights makes this a life-changing road map for living skillfully in today's world."

—David Dummitt, pastor emeritus of Willow Creek Community Church, South Barrington, Illinois, and founder of 2\42 Community Church, Brighton, Michigan

"I am first struck by the sheer breadth of this book—most of what a Christ follower needs to focus on for transformation can be found in its weekly chapters. I highly recommend this tool for individual or group study. The questions at the end of each chapter will ignite open and probing discussion. Mark Moore has given us a gift."

—Nancy Beach, author of *Next Sunday* and *Gifted to Lead*

"Mark Moore is one of the finest Bible teachers on the planet and—better yet—one of the best men I know. His wisdom, humility, and years of experience make what you are holding a treasure. Our world needs wisdom now more than ever."

—Ashley Wooldridge, senior pastor of Christ's Church of the Valley, Phoenix, Arizona

"*Wisdom 52* is a comprehensive and practical tour de force through the real challenges our people face in relationships, work, speech, and character. Its fifteen-minute format makes profound wisdom accessible in this modern melee of diverse advice, taking us back to the bedrock of wisdom."

—Kyle Idleman, senior pastor of Southeast Christian Church, Louisville, Kentucky

"Whether you're reading this book alone or leading a discussion group, *Wisdom 52* empowers you to develop habits of godly wisdom in just a few minutes a day. I highly recommend it for leaders, discipleship groups, or anyone committed to going deeper into biblical application."

—John K. Jenkins, Sr., senior pastor at First Baptist Church of Glenarden International, Landover, Maryland, and president of Converge

"Mark Moore's deep dive into Proverbs is so practical that it literally jumps off the page and into your heart. This book has the ability to transform your personal walk with Christ and your church community as well."

—Al Robertson, author, pastor, and eldest son in the *Duck Dynasty* family

"*Wisdom 52* is an inspirational, challenging, and uniquely Christian journey through the vast experience of Solomon and his written legacy on wisdom, the book of Proverbs. Through profound biblical knowledge and his own life experiences and anecdotes, Mark Moore gives us myriad opportunities for personal spiritual introspection and development as well as guides for practical and wise daily living."

—Ronald D. Tucker, rear admiral, U.S. Navy (ret.)

"Since becoming a Christian more than thirty years ago, no one has taught me more about Jesus than Mark Moore. And now, with *Wisdom 52,* he's done it again. This book is a tour de force—rich in insight, grounded in Scripture, and full of Spirit-led guidance. More than a study in Proverbs, it's an invitation to walk closely with Jesus every single day."

—Caleb Kaltenbach, research pastor at Shepherd Church, Porter Ranch, California, and author of *Messy Grace*

"As we read the Scriptures, it is so easy for us to gain the facts and miss the wisdom. Only with understanding wisdom can we truly surrender our hearts to our heavenly Father. Mark Moore has served us well by guiding us how to draw the treasure of wisdom from the pages of the Word of God."

—Darryl DelHousaye, DMin, pastor and chancellor of Phoenix Seminary, Scottsdale, Arizona

WISDOM

52

WISDOM 52

A FIFTEEN-MINUTE DAILY GUIDE THROUGH PROVERBS

MARK E. MOORE

WATERBROOK

WaterBrook
An imprint of the Penguin Random House Christian Publishing Group,
a division of Penguin Random House LLC
1745 Broadway, New York, NY 10019
waterbrookmultnomah.com
penguinrandomhouse.com

Italics in Scripture quotations reflect the author's added emphasis.

A WaterBrook Trade Paperback Original

Library of Congress Cataloging-in-Publication Data
Names: Moore, Mark E. (Mark Edward), author
Title: Wisdom 52 / Mark E. Moore.
Other titles: Wisdom fifty-two
Description: New York, NY: WaterBrook, 2025 | Includes bibliographical references.
Identifiers: LCCN 2025021269 (print) | LCCN 2025021270 (ebook) |
ISBN 9780593603000 trade paperback | ISBN 9780593603017 ebook
Subjects: LCSH: Bible. Proverbs—Textbooks | Christian life—Biblical teaching
Classification: LCC BS1467 .M66 2025 (print) | LCC BS1467 (ebook) |
DDC 223/.706—dc23/eng/20250707
LC record available at https://lccn.loc.gov/2025021269
LC ebook record available at https://lccn.loc.gov/2025021270

Printed in the United States of America

1st Printing

The authorized representative in the EU for product safety and compliance is Penguin Random House Ireland, Morrison Chambers, 32 Nassau Street, Dublin D02 YH68, Ireland. https://eu-contact.penguin.ie

Book Team: Production editor: Jocelyn Kiker • Managing editor: Julia Wallace • Production manager: Chanler Harris • Copy editor: Kayla Fenstermaker • Proofreaders: Debbie Anderson, Emily Cutler • Editor: Susan Tjaden

For details on special quantity discounts for bulk purchases,
contact specialmarketscms@penguinrandomhouse.com.

To Barbara

EIR PATHS: TO DELIVER THEE FROM THE STRANGE WOMAN, EVEN FROM
RANGER WHICH FLATTERETH WITH HER WORDS; WHICH FORSAKETH THE GUI

An excellent wife who can find? She is far more precious than jewels.

—Proverbs 31:10

Introduction

Before we dig into the wisdom of Proverbs, I want to give you a thirty-thousand-foot view of the series and a peek behind the veil of my heart. *Wisdom 52* is the third in a series of yearlong studies. *Core 52* was the first, synthesizing the key passages in **the Word of God**. The second was *Quest 52,* tracing the contours of **the life of Jesus.**

Wisdom 52 will lead you through the Proverbs of Solomon in one year. It's the most practical guide in the series and will equip you to live out your faith in everyday life. Each is designed as a yearlong curriculum for small groups or entire churches, as well as a personal study. I've provided additional online material for each book at markmoore.org/books to augment the experience, most notably YouTube videos for each chapter, making the study more accessible for groups and more personal from me as the author.

Paradoxically, these three books were written in reverse order of my relationship with them. *Core 52* was the last to be inspired and the first to be completed. For the past twelve years, I've served as the teaching pastor at Christ's Church of the Valley in Arizona. It's the kind of church that reaches many people new to church. Thousands are giving their lives to Jesus but don't know where to begin with the Bible. *Core 52* was my attempt to make the Bible accessible to new believers by making a big book a bit more manageable and an old book a bit more relatable.

Quest 52 goes back to my days as a professor at Ozark Christian College. I wrote a textbook for my classes called *The Chronological Life of Christ,* which examines the life of Jesus in detail—every verse of all four Gospels in chronological order. It's a textbook designed for pastors and teachers but may be less helpful for the average reader. *Quest 52* focuses more on application than scholarly investigation.

Wisdom 52 is the last to be written but the earliest idea of the three. Here's the backstory: As a brash young man, I used my words for self-promotion (not a good look or an easy thing to admit). The Holy Spirit convicted me of this sin. I was using his gift of words as a weapon against those around me. To manage my mouth, I took to Proverbs, reading every proverb pertaining to the tongue and categorizing them. It's what you see in the appendix of this book under the category "Words." It was powerful, even transformational, for me. The wisdom of Proverbs gave the Holy Spirit the ammunition he needed to change how I used my words. Though I'm far from perfect, by God's grace I'm even further from who I used to be.

In the same way God used Proverbs to transform my words years ago, I realized, it had potential to transform other areas of my life. I knew the broad contours of the book—dealing with relationships, character, habits, behaviors, and money. I dreamed of one day cataloging every single proverb to make a usable template for character formation. Today is that day. The appendix, "Proverbs Arranged by Category," is the result of a two-year deep dive into Solomon's wisdom. When I shared this idea with my literary agent, Don Gates, he asked, "How many subcategories do you have?" I had never counted them. Imagine my delighted surprise when I counted fifty-four (two have since been combined). This was the next "52" book, pretty much by accident . . . or God's design. The series as a whole represents the Word of God (*Core 52*), the life of Jesus (*Quest 52*), and the life coaching of the Spirit (*Wisdom 52*).

Structure of *Wisdom 52*

Wisdom 52 is more of a life-coaching guide than a traditional devotional. Through our weekly path to transformation, its lessons are meant to be lived more than learned:

1. **Wisdom Gateway:** Opening facts, stories, and statistics.
2. **Biblical Foundations:** Core theological insights, starting with Proverbs but then radiating out through both the Old and the New Testaments.
3. **Wisdom in Action:** Practical next steps to cultivate each characteristic of wisdom in your life.
4. **This Week:** Four days of follow-up, including a passage to memorize, a biblical biography to illustrate each attribute, some New Testament passages to meditate on, and then some discussion questions for a discipleship group as well as a question for your dinner table and another for the watercooler at work or the gym.

My goal is not information but transformation. If you desire to live the good life—the life led by the Spirit of Wisdom—this book is your easiest access to implement the ancient principles of wisdom in a modern world of commotion. May this book and this series empower you to live by the Spirit for the fame of Jesus in honor of the Father.

Contents

Part 6: Wealth

Appendix
Proverbs Arranged by Category

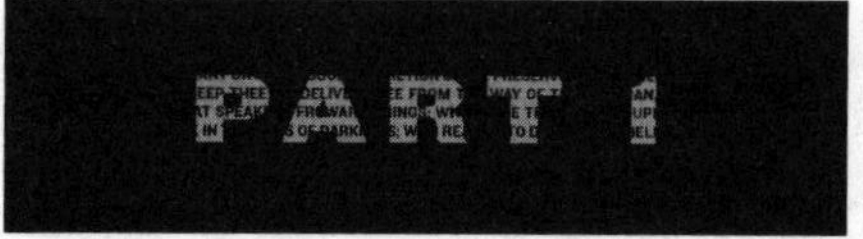

PART 1

Discernment

Wisdom

How much better to get wisdom than gold! To get understanding is to be chosen rather than silver.

—Proverbs 16:16

There is a common concept in information technology circles called the knowledge half-life. Though it has never been proven scientifically, it is often asserted that the world knowledge doubled approximately every one hundred years up to 1900. Advances in technology and science accelerated it, so by the end of World War II, human knowledge may have doubled every twenty-five years.[1] By the 1980s, that time could have been halved, doubling every twelve to thirteen years. Some experts estimated that by 2020 human knowledge would double every twelve hours! Pause to consider this staggering possibility that between dinner and breakfast, the world's database could have doubled. And with AI, our information overload could double between cups of coffee.

Despite this dizzying increase in knowledge, are we any wiser? It feels like the more we know, the less well we live. Google News leaves us shaking our heads, uttering words like "Unbelievable," "Shameful," or, perhaps less generously, "Idiots." *There seems to be an inverse ratio between knowledge and wisdom.* The more information we have, the more foolish we seem to become.

Knowledge Isn't Enough

Solomon's exhortation is more relevant today than ever: "The beginning of wisdom is this: Get wisdom, and whatever you get, get insight" (Proverbs 4:7). The value of wisdom has always been high: "How much better to get wisdom than gold! To get understanding is to be chosen rather than silver" (16:16). We could upgrade Solomon's gold and silver to plutonium since wisdom is so rare these days.

Biblical wisdom is not mere knowledge but the ability to live skillfully. Biblically, a warrior's skill with the sword, a carpenter's skill with a saw, and a chef's ability to combine ingredients thoughtfully are all considered wisdom. Wisdom is knowledge practically and skillfully applied to improve life for yourself and others.

Moses captured this idea in Deuteronomy 4:6: "Keep [God's laws] and do them, for that will be your wisdom and your understanding in the sight of the peoples." Jesus suggested the same thing in Matthew 11:19: "Wisdom is justified by her deeds." The apostle Paul echoed their sentiment: "Walk in wisdom toward outsiders, making the best use of the time" (Colossians 4:5).

The purpose of this book is to provide not theoretical truth but practical coaching. I plead with you as Solomon pleaded with his son: "Get wisdom." Chase her, embrace her, and treasure her. Only wisdom employed will be wisdom enjoyed. The life you want is on the other side of obedience to God's truth.

The Failure of Wisdom

Imagine inheriting this great kingdom—and losing it in a single decision. As the crown settled on his brow, Rehoboam inherited the nation's most robust economy and expansive borders. His father, Solomon, had gained international acclaim and accumulated wealth that was surpassed only by the number of his wives—seven hundred in total, along with an inexplicable addition of three hundred concubines (1 Kings 11:3). Excessive, to say the least.

When Solomon passed, Rehoboam took his mantle of leadership. One would think he would have been well equipped. His grandfather, David, was the shepherd-king who established the dynasty. Rehoboam's father, Solomon, had written an entire book of wisdom—yes, to Rehoboam. Twenty-two times, the book of Proverbs uses the words "my son."[2] Rehoboam had a manual of wisdom in his hands, wind at his back, and a legacy under his feet.

Nonetheless, his first act as king was to play the fool. The story is told in 1 Kings 12. A crowd flocked to his coronation, led by a rebel named Jeroboam. Their request was simple: "Lighten our tax burden." The magnificence of Solomon's kingdom had come at a heavy price. They begged for relief. At the outset of his rule, Rehoboam had a choice: Show the people kindness, which could be interpreted as weakness, or show them strength, which could be interpreted as cruelty. Two sets of advisers weighed in. The young bucks advised him to show strength: "You say to them, 'My little finger is thicker than my father's thighs' " (verse 10). Translation: Ancient Near Eastern middle finger. The elders' advice was the opposite—show humility: "If you will be a servant to this people today and serve them . . . then they will be your servants forever" (verse 7).

The elders' counsel was spurned. Rehoboam chose to flex. As a result, the ten northern tribes made Jeroboam, the opposition leader, their king, and the twelve tribes were torn apart, never to be restored. This raises the question, How could the son of the wisest man in the world be so foolish? Hold that thought

In the book of Proverbs, wisdom is *always* praised. In Ecclesiastes, however, Solomon portrayed wisdom mostly as a burden. In chapter 1, he lamented,

> I have acquired great wisdom, surpassing all who were over Jerusalem before me, and my heart has had great experience of wisdom and

> knowledge. And I applied my heart to know wisdom and to know madness and folly. I perceived that this also is but a striving after wind.
>
> For in much wisdom is much vexation,
> and he who increases knowledge increases sorrow. (verses 16–18)

Why such a different view of wisdom? Solomon gave us a clue in chapter 2: "I hated all my toil in which I toil under the sun, seeing that I must leave it to the man who will come after me, and who knows whether he will be wise or a fool? Yet he will be master of all for which I toiled and used my wisdom under the sun. This also is vanity" (verses 18–19).

Solomon knew the immense weight and complexity of leadership that awaited Rehoboam, and it vexed him. Additionally, when you trace the contours of Ecclesiastes, you see that Solomon applied his wisdom to his political career, not to his personal life. The wisdom Solomon sought from God was specifically to lead the nation: "Give your servant therefore an understanding mind to govern your people, that I may discern between good and evil, for who is able to govern this your great people?" (1 Kings 3:9).

Solomon led the nation well, but he failed to lead his family. "For when Solomon was old his wives turned away his heart after other gods, and his heart was not wholly true to the LORD his God, as was the heart of David his father" (1 Kings 11:4). That's a problem. Solomon's wives led him astray, and Rehoboam grew up with a front-row seat. Here's an unalterable rule for wisdom: Your children won't do as you say; they will do as you do.

Why did Solomon fail as a father? While this isn't an excuse, it is an explanation—David failed Solomon as a father. Though Solomon was a legitimate son, his mother's marriage wasn't. Solomon's family of origin taught him to mistreat women. He took his father's sexual exploits to an exponential level. And it wasn't just Solomon. His older brother Absalom attempted a military coup against David. David *loved* Absalom. Everyone knew it, except Absalom.

Why was David unable to express his love to Absalom? Well, that goes back to Jesse, David's dad. When God sent Samuel to Jesse's home to anoint the new king, Jesse put seven sons before him (1 Samuel 16:1–13). None of them got the nod from God. Samuel had to ask, "Do you have another son?"

"Yes," Jesse demurred, "but he's out in the field watching the sheep."

What? How could he overlook one of his sons? This lineage is a warning. Wisdom is passed from father to son through actions, not words. So, for the sake of generations to come, the call of this chapter is simple: Get wisdom by living wisely, starting in your home.

Wisdom in Action

Where do we start to acquire wisdom? "If any of you lacks wisdom, let him ask God, who gives generously to all without reproach, and it will be given him" (James 1:5). Plead with God to give you wisdom through this yearlong journey.

Perhaps your parents, regardless of your age, are an important source of wisdom in your life, or maybe God has given you other parental figures to fill that role. Pull out your phone, start a text to a parent or parental figure, and insert this into the text box: "I'm reading a book about wisdom this year. Can I ask your advice over the next twelve months about important life questions?" Press Send.

LINETH UNTO DEATH, AND HER PATHS UNTO THE DEAD. NONE THAT GO UNT
URN AGAIN, NEITHER TAKE THEY HOLD OF THE PATHS OF LIFE. THAT
YEST WALK IN THE WAY OF GOOD MEN, AND KEEP THE PATHS OF THE RIGH

This Week

- ☐ **Day 1:** Read this essay.
- ☐ **Day 2:** Memorize Proverbs 16:16.
- ☐ **Day 3:** Read the biography of Solomon (1 Kings 3) and find one thing to apply or avoid.
- ☐ **Day 4:** Meditate on Luke 21:15; Colossians 4:5; James 1:5.
- ☐ **Day 5:** Discuss.

Group Discussion

1. Who around here do you trust to give you good advice?
2. What consequences, professionally and personally, have you seen when people lack wisdom?
3. How does the biblical view of wisdom challenge the modern understanding of success?
4. In light of Solomon's failure with Rehoboam, share the wisdom you gained from your family of origin and any additions or changes you would like to make in your own home now.

Table Talk (in your home)

What are some ways we could pursue wisdom in our home?

Watercooler (at work or the gym)

Who is the wisest person you know?

MOUTH COMETH KNOWLEDGE AND UNDERSTANDING. HE LAYETH UP
DOM FOR THE RIGHTEOUS: HE IS A BUCKLER TO THEM THAT WALK UPRIGHT
PETH THE PATHS OF JUDGMENT, AND PRESERVETH THE WAY OF HIS SAINTS

Fear of the Lord

The fear of the LORD is the beginning of knowledge; fools despise wisdom and instruction.

—PROVERBS 1:7

Proverbs are short, pithy truths, similar in length to posts on social media. Social influencers know the ideal post is between forty and one hundred and twenty words (depending on the platform). Platforms like Instagram and Snapchat recognize that people prefer pictures, so they are primarily image-based. That's why social media has trended shorter and more visual. As a result, our contemporary source of "wisdom" manipulates our emotions to change our thinking rather than changing our minds to manage our emotions. But it gets worse.

"Friends" or "followers" are more like anonymous voyeurs, and their "likes" may give you a dopamine hit, but they offer no real relationships. Even more nefarious, online algorithms prioritize content that is more likely to generate engagement—sensational and salacious over true and good. These algorithms exclude opposing opinions, creating an echo chamber of ideas. As a result, social media does for you what Rehoboam's advisers did for him—nurture your vices and obfuscate God's wisdom.

This isn't a rant against social media. It is, however, a warning that our modern source of wisdom is systemically flawed, making the ancient wisdom of the Bible more needed than ever. Isn't it time to chase hard after real wisdom?

The Beginning of Wisdom

The first part of Proverbs 1:7 is repeated nearly verbatim four times (Job 28:28; Psalm 111:10; Proverbs 9:10; 15:33). This idea sounds contradictory. Why should we fear the God who loves us? After all, "perfect love casts out fear" (1 John 4:18). We need not fear for our eternity, because the God who loves us sent his Son to die for us. This does *not* mean, however, that we have no fear of God. He is, after all, awesome in the extreme.

Perhaps it would help if we used a synonym for *fear,* such as *respect, revere,* or *honor.* It's the kind of fear a child has for a father, a soldier has for a general, or an athlete has for a coach. Fear and love are often used in tandem in Scripture: "Behold, the eye of the LORD is on those who fear him, on those who hope in his steadfast love" (Psalm 33:18; see also Deuteronomy 10:12; Psalms 103:11, 17; 118:4; 147:11; Proverbs 16:6). The difference between terror and reverence is our *relationship.* God isn't some distant, capricious, and terrifying force. Rather, he's our Father, protecting, providing for, and often doting on us.

Love Wisdom

The first step toward wisdom is a healthy relationship with God. God made that pursuit easier by personifying wisdom in Proverbs, portraying her as a winsome woman who invites us to learn from her by following in her footsteps. We meet her first in Proverbs 1:20–33. She calls out in the street and implores us in the marketplace (verse 20). In Proverbs 8, she promises power to those who heed her (verses 15–16) as well as wealth and righteousness (verses 18–21). Her call culminates in Proverbs 9:1–6:

Wisdom has built her house;
 she has hewn her seven pillars.
She has slaughtered her beasts; she has mixed her wine;
 she has also set her table.
She has sent out her young women to call
 from the highest places in the town,
"Whoever is simple, let him turn in here!"
 To him who lacks sense she says,
"Come, eat of my bread
 and drink of the wine I have mixed.
Leave your simple ways, and live,
 and walk in the way of insight."

The pursuit of wisdom began in force for me in my early twenties. I had gone to Bible college to train for ministry. If you had asked me then if I was wise, I would have surely said yes (with proper Christian humility, of course). I was, after all, studying the Bible. My frontal lobes, however, weren't yet fully formed. I was at a biological disadvantage, and I had no real-life experience. That was all about to change. I got my first full-time ministry job, got married, discovered we were expecting our first baby, and got my first mortgage . . . all within three years. Inexperience quickly outpaced my false confidence.

I'm not saying knowing the Bible didn't help; it did. But it didn't directly address my real-life challenges in ministry, marriage, parenting, or home management. My greatest wisdom came not from books but from watching these men live out their faith—Dick Gibson, Chris DeWelt, and Ken Idleman showed me what wisdom looks like in action. Their wisdom seeped into my soul when I saw how they lived.

In my mid-forties, after discipling young men for twenty years, I woke up one day and realized I had something to say because of those two decades of lived experience. Wisdom takes her time, grinding slowly over decades, smoothing out the rough edges of our souls. She's not in a classroom; she calls in the street and the marketplace.

The Spirit of Wisdom

Wisdom personified in Proverbs revealed herself later in the person of the Holy Spirit. At Pentecost, Jesus poured out his Spirit on his disciples. God's people had unprecedented access to wisdom as the Spirit indwelt believers.

Paul unpacked this privilege in 1 Corinthians 2:6–16. The basic idea is this: No one knows what another person is thinking. You can't unless you get inside their head. Quoting from the prophet Isaiah, Paul asked, "Who has understood the mind of the Lord so as to instruct him?" The answer is obvious: No one can instruct God. That's true. However, in a breathtaking claim, Paul concluded, "But we have the mind of Christ" (verse 16). Astonishing!

When we give our lives to Jesus, he embeds the Spirit of Wisdom in us. That was also Jesus's experience. As a child, people noted that he "grew and became strong, filled with wisdom" (Luke 2:40). He "increased in wisdom and in stature and in favor with God and man" (verse 52). And that was just when he was a teenager.

As a man, Jesus wasn't merely wiser than Solomon; he embodied the Spirit's wisdom. He himself said as much: "The queen of the South will rise up at the judgment with this generation and condemn it, for she came from the ends of the earth to hear the wisdom of Solomon, and behold, something greater than Solomon is here" (Matthew 12:42). Paul was even more explicit: "In [Jesus] are hidden all the treasures of wisdom and knowledge" (Colossians 2:3).

If Jesus is the embodiment of wisdom, his Spirit in us grants us access to eternal wisdom: "We impart a secret and hidden wisdom of God, which

God decreed before the ages for our glory" (1 Corinthians 2:7). We may access it far too infrequently, but it is there for the taking.

Wisdom in Action

In the previous chapter, we saw that getting wisdom begins with a prayer; it did with Solomon and will with you as well (James 1:5). The answer to that prayer will likely have skin and live in your zip code, meaning God has likely answered your prayer already by putting people in your orbit who have the wisdom you need. For me, it was Dick, Chris, and Ken. What about you? Who are the people from whom you could gain wisdom through observation and osmosis? Simply being in their presence would allow you to absorb the wisdom you need for the next season of life.

You likely need at least three wisdom mentors for various areas of your life. One for character growth, one for professional growth, and one for spiritual growth. For most, their parents or a parental figure is their first character mentor. For the professional and spiritual mentors, here's what to look for: "Who is wise and understanding among you? By his good conduct let him show his works in the meekness of wisdom" (James 3:13). Begin now by writing a name in each space below. Lay the list before the Lord and ask him how you could get more face time with these people.

Character: ________________________________

Professional: ________________________________

Spiritual: ________________________________

This Week

- ☐ **Day 1:** Read this essay.
- ☐ **Day 2:** Memorize Proverbs 1:7.
- ☐ **Day 3:** Read the biography of Joseph (Genesis 41, with Psalm 105:16–22) and find one thing to apply.
- ☐ **Day 4:** Meditate on Romans 11:33; 1 Corinthians 3:19; Colossians 1:28.
- ☐ **Day 5:** Discuss.

Group Discussion

1. How does social media influence who we listen to?
2. How would you explain to a fourth grader that fear and love aren't antithetical?
3. How have you developed wisdom in various seasons of your life?
4. What practical wisdom is the Spirit trying to grow in you?

Table Talk (in your home)

What habits, decisions, or house rules show our respect, or fear, for God?

Watercooler (at work or the gym)

Who is the person you are most afraid to disappoint?

Mentors

Listen to advice and accept instruction, that you may gain wisdom in the future.

—Proverbs 19:20

Science nerd question: Who invented the lightbulb? Thomas Edison, right? He did indeed develop the first high-resistance carbon filament that could burn for hours, making the lightbulb commercially viable. However, it was Joseph Swan, before Edison, who invented an electric light using a carbonized filament in an evacuated glass bulb. Edison stood on his shoulders. Before either of them, Michael Faraday discerned the key principles of electromagnetism, paving the way for Swan and Edison.[1] The history of this simple invention turns out to involve more than one man's legacy.

Nothing that matters depends on a single person. What we have today is the result of a long line of people who have incrementally invested in others. This is true in every arena—science, education, sports, politics, religion, and more. If you want your life to matter, it matters who is in it.

The word *mentor* comes from *The Odyssey,* one of the most famous of all Greek stories. When King Odysseus sailed off to fight in the Trojan War, he left his son, Telemachus, in the care of his friend named Mentor. At key points in the story, Athena, the goddess of war, disguises herself as Mentor, advising the prince. The metaphoric meaning of Mentor, therefore, is the voice of God, preparing a young person for the battles they will face. That's very close to the biblical perspective in Proverbs. It's through mentors that we meet Lady Wisdom, who guides us through the hazards of life.

Bowling Alone

Robert Putnam's seminal work, *Bowling Alone,* traces the startling decline of civic organizations in America. Membership in local clubs on average plummeted by 58 percent between the 1970s and1997.[2] We had already been trending precipitously toward individualism when the first iPhone arrived in 2007. Smartphones put the world in our pockets but blinded us to the important people right in front of us.

This rise of individualism has resulted in crippling isolation in families. In 1970, 12 percent of children were raised in single-parent homes. By 2023, that number had doubled to 25 percent.[3] In 2014, for the first time in U.S. history, the majority of adults were single.[4] These statistics have tragic consequences for health, mental and physical. It has been widely reported by medical experts (including the surgeon general) that prolonged isolation has an equivalent impact on one's health as smoking up to fifteen cigarettes a day.[5]

The harmful effects of this trend toward individualism are compounded by another striking social trend: narcissism. Jean Twenge and Keith Campbell's research traces a startling rise in narcissism. Here is but one data point: In the 1950s only 12 percent of teens agreed with the statement "I am an important person." By the 1980s that rose to nearly 80 percent.[6] Twelve percent may not seem like much. However, narcissists tend to rise to prominence in business, sports, and entertainment. Therefore, their influence on society multiplies. It's most apparent in (social) media and entertainment. Such influencers are perilous when their allure entices us away from wisdom. The polarization of politics and cancel culture are some of the more obvious manifestations of burgeoning individualism and narcissism. We desperately need the wisdom of mentors to guide us through the malaise of culture.

Mentors Make the World Go Round

Do you know anyone who foolishly did what was right in their own eyes and suffered the consequences? Many of us could put a name next to Proverbs 12:15 (perhaps the name belongs to the person in the mirror): "The way of a fool is right in his own eyes, but a wise man listens to advice." Whether you're trying to decide who to date, which party to go to, what job to take, or which purchase to make, advice is a guardrail and guide. Sadly, most of the world ignores it.

Wise advice is as necessary for groups as it is for individuals: "Where there is no guidance, a people falls, but in an abundance of counselors there is safety" (11:14). Wisdom rarely travels alone; God's design includes guides for our journey.

Divine Appointments: God-Given Guides

Mentors are so critical that God gives them to us at birth. Parents are admonished to mentor their offspring: "Train up a child in the way he should go; even when he is old he will not depart from it" (Proverbs 22:6). God even gave explicit instructions to parents on how to do just that (Deuteronomy 6:4–9). As we grow, God puts in our path grandparents, teachers, pastors, and coaches. It's our choice to seek and heed their advice or not.

Chosen Champions: Strategic Mentoring Relationships

Other mentors we find along the way. Some seek us out (though this is rare), and others we seek out for a specific season or role. In school, we seek out a teacher; in sports, a trainer or coach; in business, a person with experience and success. The Bible is full of examples. Jethro mentored Moses (Exodus 18:13–27), who in turn mentored Joshua (Numbers 27:18–23). Eli mentored Samuel (1 Samuel 3), who in turn mentored both Saul and David (1 Samuel 9:15–27; 16:1–13). David then mentored Solomon (1 Kings 2:1–4). Elijah mentored Elisha (1 Kings 19:19–21). Naomi mentored her daughter-in-law Ruth (Ruth 1:16–18). Mordecai mentored his cousin Esther (Esther 2:7–20).

In the New Testament, mentoring is even more overt, starting with Jesus and his twelve apostles (Matthew 4:18–22). Barnabas mentored Saul/Paul (Acts 9:26–30; 11:25–26) and John Mark (Acts 12:25; 13:5, 13). Paul then mentored Timothy (Acts 16:1–5), Titus (Titus 1:4–5), Onesimus (Philemon 10–16), and Priscilla and Aquila (Acts 18:1–4). This couple in turn mentored Apollos (Acts 18:24–28).

While mentoring can seem intimidating, it's quite simple. Paul explained mentoring this way: "Be imitators of me, as I am of Christ" (1 Corinthians 11:1). Or again: "What you have learned and received and heard and seen in me—practice these things, and the God of peace will be with you" (Philippians 4:9).

Wisdom in Action

In the first two chapters, you were encouraged to identify potential mentors God might use to grow wisdom in you. Here's some sage advice on how to engage them:

- Before you ask for a mentor's time, google them. Research their story, their education, occupation, and accomplishments. Then design a question that taps into their accomplishments. It might sound like this: "On page 57 of your book, you said ______. I was wondering how to apply that to ______." This will indicate to them you are worth investing in because you know what they have to offer and are prepared to put it into practice. Now you're ready to request fifteen minutes of their time.

- Before your meeting, craft three targeted questions. Your preparation honors their wisdom. You might want to run these questions by a parent or other mentor.
- As they answer the questions, take notes (with pen and paper), particularly on how to implement their advice.
- Thank them three times for their time: when you greet them, when you leave them, and with a handwritten note after the meeting.

All of us should also be mentoring three to five individuals in areas where we have some life experience. How do we go about that? Here's some sage advice on being a mentor:

- Pray about who God wants you to pour into and invite them. It might take up to six months, but create a group of three to five, and determine a meeting rhythm (weekly, monthly, or quarterly) with a life span for the group (a year minimum). Each meeting should include discussion and prayer, but some meetings should be designated for eating, play, and work.
- Wise mentors guide the ship but let mentees chart the course with their questions.
- Give assignments, not just advice. Mentoring is *not* counseling. They aren't figuring out life; they are training for life. This requires assignments to put into practice the wisdom you provide.

Three decades of mentoring has proved that this has been one of my most important professional investments and personal joys. We all want to feel needed and valued. Mentoring is one of the most lasting ways to experience that fulfillment.

LINETH UNTO DEATH, AND HER PATHS UNTO THE DEAD. NONE THAT GO UNT
URN AGAIN, NEITHER TAKE THEY HOLD OF THE PATHS OF LIFE. THAT
/EST WALK IN THE WAY OF GOOD MEN, AND KEEP THE PATHS OF THE RIGH

This Week

- ☐ **Day 1:** Read this essay.
- ☐ **Day 2:** Memorize Proverbs 19:20.
- ☐ **Day 3:** Read the biography of Jethro (Exodus 18:13–27) and find one thing to apply.
- ☐ **Day 4:** Meditate on Philippians 4:9; 2 Timothy 2:2; Titus 2:3–5.
- ☐ **Day 5:** Discuss.

Group Discussion

1. What life lessons have you learned from your parents that have served you well?
2. Who is or has been an important mentor in your career, spiritual growth, physical health, and relationships?
3. What qualities and qualifications do you look for in a mentor? In what area of your life right now could you use a mentor?
4. Who are three to five people you could or should invest in as a mentor?

Table Talk (in your home)

Who is one leader in your life you would like to spend more time with because they make you better?

Watercooler (at work or the gym)

Who has been your most influential mentor at work?

MOUTH COMETH KNOWLEDGE AND UNDERSTANDING: HE LAYETH UP
DOM FOR THE RIGHTEOUS: HE IS A BUCKLER TO THEM THAT WALK UPRIGH
PETH THE PATHS OF JUDGMENT, AND PRESERVETH THE WAY OF HIS SAINTS

Fools

Like a dog that returns to his vomit is a fool who repeats his folly.

—Proverbs 26:11

In high school, I wanted to represent Jesus the best I could. I wasn't great at it, but one thing I tried was bringing my Bible to every class every day. I would pull it out and set it on my desk, along with my other textbooks. One day in social studies, my friend Larry reached over and picked up my Bible. He randomly turned to 2 Peter 2:22: "The dog returns to its own vomit, and the sow, after washing herself, returns to wallow in the mire."

Larry laughed out loud, mostly because he read the word *vomit* in the Bible and we were teenage boys. It sounded like nonsense to him. He didn't understand that he was unwittingly laughing at himself. This kind of derision is perfectly understandable from people who are ignorant of Scripture or don't follow Jesus. Peter, however, was applying the proverb to people who should have known better. Before reading on, consider this question: Do you have ears to hear? Could this proverb be about you?

What Makes a Fool

My friend Larry didn't know God. He wasn't a bad person. He was just uninformed. His parents were divorced, and his mom was living with another woman. His moms didn't instill faith in him, perhaps because they felt painfully condemned by the church. Consequently, when I invited Larry to church, he never felt comfortable coming. That left him in the precarious position of denying God's existence. This denial of God is the opposite of wisdom and, therefore, the epitome of foolishness.

Twice in Psalms, we read the same line: "The fool says in his heart, 'There is no God' " (14:1; 53:1). The apostle Paul argued in Romans 1:21–22 that there is no excuse for such rejection: "Although they knew God, they did not honor him as God or give thanks to him, but they became futile in their thinking, and their foolish hearts were darkened. Claiming to be wise, they became fools."

How can you know if Proverbs 26:11 applies to you? The following questions are a pretty good litmus test:

- Do you joke about things you've done that God wouldn't find funny? "Doing wrong is like a joke to a fool, but wisdom is pleasure to a man of understanding" (Proverbs 10:23).
- Do you have FOMO about passing fads or fleeting pleasures? "The discerning sets his face toward wisdom, but the eyes of a fool are on the ends of the earth" (Proverbs 17:24).
- Is it more important to you to express your opinion than to listen to mentors? "A fool takes no pleasure in understanding, but only in expressing his opinion" (Proverbs 18:2).
- Do you pride yourself on taking part in spiritual debates? "Have nothing to do with foolish, ignorant controversies; you know that they breed quarrels" (2 Timothy 2:23).

- Do you feel like (or act like) you can be "more saved" by adding good deeds to the cross of Jesus? "Are you so foolish? Having begun by the Spirit, are you now being perfected by the flesh?" (Galatians 3:3).

If these describe you, even in part, you might want to consider the danger of foolishness as described in Proverbs. Dogs lapping up their own puke is funny to teenage boys, but when humans do it, no one is laughing.

The Consequence of Foolishness

We entertain ourselves by bingeing Netflix or scrolling through Instagram. No harm in that, necessarily. However, have you noticed that a good bit of entertainment celebrates what the Bible calls folly? Folly may feel jolly, but it can be far more dangerous than it seems: "Let a man meet a she-bear robbed of her cubs rather than a fool in his folly" (Proverbs 17:12).

If you put your trust in a fool, there's a price to pay: "Whoever sends a message by the hand of a fool cuts off his own feet and drinks violence" (26:6). And if you confront a fool, you could wind up in a world of hurt: "A stone is heavy, and sand is weighty, but a fool's provocation is heavier than both" (27:3). Perhaps you've heard the adage "Don't wrestle with a pig. You'll both get dirty, and the pig will like it." Solomon offered a similar saying: "If a wise man has an argument with a fool, the fool only rages and laughs, and there is no quiet" (29:9). Whether it's a foolish employee, a wild neighbor, or an outlandish buddy, a fool leaves a wake of pain in their path.

Sometimes you find fools in a bar, and sometimes they sit on a throne. The crowns of Israel weren't immune to folly's fatal attraction. Foolishness cost Saul his kingdom when he disobeyed God's commands (1 Samuel 13:13). Amnon's foolishness robbed him of sexual self-control, leading him to rape his half sister (2 Samuel 13:14). David's decision to ignore good counsel and number his troops resulted in a plague against the nation (2 Samuel 24:10). King Asa foolishly allied himself with an enemy king, which cost him silver and gold from the temple treasury and ignited ongoing warfare (2 Chronicles 16:9). You may be unfamiliar with some of these Bible stories, but you can probably fill in some of the details from your own life experience. All of us have felt the heavy weight and high price of foolishness.

The Jesus Solution

Jesus is the first person in the New Testament to use the word *fool.* Here's what he said: "Everyone who is angry with his brother will be liable to judgment; whoever insults his brother will be liable to the council; and whoever says, 'You fool!' will be liable to the hell of fire" (Matthew 5:22). Jesus warns us not to flippantly call people fools. Yet every other use of the word *fool* in the Gospels is also from Jesus (nine in total), calling people fools!

Jesus accused the crowds of being fools if they didn't listen to his words (Matthew 7:26). He critiqued the Pharisees as fools for their hypocrisy (Matthew 23:17). He used foolishness as a parabolic description of those who weren't prepared for his coming (Matthew 25:2). Even his own followers found themselves in the crosshairs of his invective against foolishness (Luke 24:25). Why does Jesus warn us about calling people fools and then proceed to do so himself?

Matthew 5:22 doesn't warn against using the word *fool.* Rather, it warns against weaponizing words to demean or destroy others. There are times when it's kind to inform fools of their folly. Without a righteous warning, many won't recognize the she-bear they keep poking. Jesus's use of *fool* is not hypocrisy but a model of healthy confrontation.

Wisdom in Action

We want to avoid foolishness at all costs. How? Start by recognizing that your faith follows your friends and family. The weight of influence in your life must be from people of faith. If your family members are followers of Jesus, you can afford more friends who are pre-believers. Conversely, if your family doesn't share your faith, you probably need to prioritize Christian friends. You may need to do a serious audit of how much time you spend with people inside and outside the faith so that the weight of influence is tilted toward Jesus.

Think of it like a tree. The deeper the roots, the wider the limbs can spread without the tree being toppled by a storm. If your roots are deep enough in Christ and intertwined with other believers, you can withstand the ridicule of unbelievers. It's not fun, but it's vital. "God chose what is foolish in the world to shame the wise; God chose what is weak in the world to shame the strong" (1 Corinthians 1:27). You may look foolish to the world, but to be wise in God's eyes is far better.

LINETH UNTO DEATH, AND HER PATHS UNTO THE DEAD. NONE THAT GO UNT
URN AGAIN, NEITHER TAKE THEY HOLD OF THE PATHS OF LIFE. THAT

This Week

- ☐ **Day 1:** Read this essay.
- ☐ **Day 2:** Memorize Proverbs 26:11.
- ☐ **Day 3:** Read the biography of Nabal (1 Samuel 25) and find one thing to avoid.
- ☐ **Day 4:** Meditate on Matthew 7:26; 1 Corinthians 1:25; Ephesians 5:17.
- ☐ **Day 5:** Discuss.

Group Discussion

1. Just for kicks, how many synonyms can you come up with for the word *fool*?
2. What are some things the world would consider wise that the Bible would call foolish?
3. What are some healthy practices that would help you become more aware of potentially foolish behavior?
4. Based on Proverbs and the New Testament warnings, what practical steps can you take to avoid falling into foolishness, especially in spiritual matters?

Table Talk (in your home)

If you were doing something foolish, what would be the most helpful way for the people at this table to point it out to you?

Watercooler (at work or the gym)

Do you have a different idea of what counts as foolish behavior now than you did in your teens and twenties?

DOM FOR THE RIGHTEOUS: HE IS A BUCKLER TO THEM THAT WALK UPRIGH
PETH THE PATHS OF JUDGMENT, AND PRESERVETH THE WAY OF HIS SAINTS

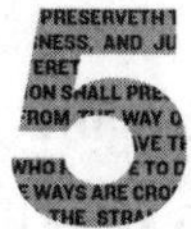

Wicked

The way of the wicked is like deep darkness;
they do not know over what they stumble.

—Proverbs 4:19

Outwardly charming, inwardly monstrous. That's a description of Ted Bundy, perhaps the most famous serial killer in American history. Though his thirty-plus murders of young women were in the 1970s, he still captures popular attention to this day. Amazon Prime did a docuseries on him in 2020 called *Falling for a Killer.* That followed the 2019 Netflix docuseries *Conversations with a Killer* and the 2019 crime drama *Extremely Wicked, Shockingly Evil and Vile.* There were, of course, plenty of books, talk shows, articles, and movies prior to that. We seem to have a fascination with evil. We are curious about what makes evil people tick and perhaps wonder how much of them is in us.

Psychologists have identified three personalities they call "the Dark Triad": narcissism, Machiavellianism, and psychopathy.[1] Narcissism combines grandiosity and a need for admiration with a lack of empathy.[2] Machiavellianism involves a mastery of manipulation, exploitation, and deceit.[3] Psychopathy is marked by impulsivity, selfishness, callousness, and a lack of remorse.[4] The Dark Triad makes one capable of extreme cruelty. It's seen in historical figures like Adolf Hitler, Joseph Stalin, and Mao Zedong. But it isn't seen only in dictators. Public figures such as Bernie Madoff, Elizabeth Holmes, and Jim Jones have been identified as exhibiting the behaviors of the Dark Triad.[5] The book of Proverbs simply calls these behaviors "wicked."

Fools Versus the Wicked

While fools stumble blindly, the wicked calculate their steps. That's the difference, and it's not inconsequential. Fools and the wicked share some of the same behaviors, but the wicked are far more nefarious. Not only are they more cunning and practiced, but their personality traits also enable them to rise to positions of power. Solomon observed, "The wicked accepts a bribe in secret to pervert the ways of justice" (Proverbs 17:23). This frustrated Solomon as he grew older. He bemoaned the success of the wicked in his final book: "In my vain life I have seen everything. There is a righteous man who perishes in his righteousness, and there is a wicked man who prolongs his life in his evildoing" (Ecclesiastes 7:15). Asaph felt the same way (Psalm 73:3), as did Jeremiah after him: "Why does the way of the wicked prosper? Why do all who are treacherous thrive?" (Jeremiah 12:1). We have all felt that sting.

Yet the Scriptures promise that the righteous will be rewarded and the wicked punished: "The fear of the LORD prolongs life, but the years of the wicked will be short" (Proverbs 10:27). This promise is repeated throughout the Old Testament (Psalms 37:13; 92:7; Proverbs 24:19–20; Isaiah 57:20–21). What should we do with our frustration over this seemingly unfulfilled promise?

Four Anchors in a Sea of Wickedness

First, feel free, fully, to *complain to God about the wickedness you see and suffer.* Job, David, and Jeremiah are among the righteous who complained to

God about the flourishing of the wicked. Let God know how you feel. Pour out your frustration and fury. Then, once you've vented your frustration, settle into your faith in God's goodness. After all, even if you don't understand or appreciate what he's doing, it's not like we have many other options to turn to. God will make it right in his time, not ours. "The LORD has made everything for its purpose, even the wicked for the day of trouble" (Proverbs 16:4).

Second, *don't take matters into your own hands.* Before Solomon penned these proverbs, his father, David, quoted an even older proverb. After passing up the chance to assassinate King Saul, David called out from a safe distance, "As the proverb of the ancients says, 'Out of the wicked comes wickedness.' But my hand shall not be against you" (1 Samuel 24:13). David modeled for us how to express our frustration while leaving vengeance to the Lord.

Third, *rejoice in what you have.* What can make suffering under the wicked even worse is that we envy them for what they have. It's bad enough that they do us wrong, but life *seems* to have rewarded them. That is seldom true. Often the wicked with wealth suffer because of it. Despite their unbridled romance, the wicked have turbulent relationships. Despite their power, they're constantly paranoid. Take the advice of Solomon's father: "Better is the little that the righteous has than the abundance of many wicked" (Psalm 37:16). The book of Psalms begins with this exhortation: "Blessed is the man who walks not in the counsel of the wicked, nor stands in the way of sinners, nor sits in the seat of scoffers" (1:1). The good life is not in your possessions but in your relationships.

Fourth, *warn the wicked.* We have an obligation, not merely as individuals but especially as the church, to be the moral compass for our culture. If not the people of God, then who will promote virtue? Who will warn of coming judgment? If we say nothing, we will be culpable along with the wicked. Ezekiel 3:18 summarizes this well: "If I say to the wicked, 'You shall surely die,' and you give him no warning, nor speak to warn the wicked from his wicked way, in order to save his life, that wicked person shall die for his iniquity, but his blood I will require at your hand."

None of us like the idea of warning the wicked. It conjures up images of contentious family conversations or abrasive street preachers shouting at strangers. While I would never disparage anyone following God's call to preach, that strategy hasn't typically had a high-yield conversion rate. So how would a normal person go about warning the wicked?

Let's start with a simple and striking observation. The word *wicked* appears in the Old Testament in some form 361 times. In the New Testament, it's used only eighteen times. God didn't have a sudden personality shift between Malachi and Matthew. The difference between the two testaments is the person of Jesus. Because of Jesus, all people have access to God. Through his sacrifice, though all are sinners and prone to wickedness, they now have access to his transformative power. Rather than rail against wickedness, we should brag about Jesus. Promoting Jesus is the most effective way of reducing wickedness in our world. By turning people to Jesus, we thwart Satan's tactics.

Wisdom in Action

When dealing with the wicked, we must balance four biblical truths: (1) "All have sinned and fall short of the glory of God" (Romans 3:23); (2) Satan "prowls around like a roaring lion, seeking someone to devour" (1 Peter 5:8); (3) "he who is in you is greater than he who is in the world" (1 John 4:4); and (4) every person is created in God's image (Genesis 1:26).

If you focus on the first two, your anthropology will be Genesis 3. If you prioritize the last two, your anthropology will be Genesis 1. Jesus clearly had an anthropology drawn from both Genesis 1 and Genesis 3, which determined how he treated people and what potential he saw in them as well as how he understood their need for rescue.

In the previous chapter you were challenged to audit how much influence you give to those outside Christ versus inside Christ. I now challenge you to revisit your audit to see whether you have sufficient influence on those around you who are in the grasp of the Evil One. The Old Testament viewed the wicked as adversaries. Jesus viewed them as victims. The power of the Spirit's wisdom can overwhelm the forces of evil in our world through love.

LINETH UNTO DEATH, AND HER PATHS UNTO THE DEAD. NONE THAT GO UNT
URN AGAIN, NEITHER TAKE THEY HOLD OF THE PATHS OF LIFE. THAT
/EST WALK IN THE WAY OF GOOD MEN, AND KEEP THE PATHS OF THE RIGH

This Week

- ☐ **Day 1:** Read this essay.
- ☐ **Day 2:** Memorize Proverbs 4:19.
- ☐ **Day 3:** Read the biography of Lot (Genesis 19:1–29) and find one thing to avoid.
- ☐ **Day 4:** Meditate on John 3:20; 2 Peter 2:4–10; 2 John 10–11.
- ☐ **Day 5:** Discuss.

Group Discussion

1. There is plenty of evil in our world. What are you seeing today that you find most troublesome?
2. Why do you think wicked people often rise to the top of their professions?
3. How do you reconcile the frustration you feel when the wicked prosper with the promises of Scripture that the wicked will ultimately face justice?
4. What obligation does the church have in being the moral compass for the world? What is your role in that?

Table Talk (in your home)

How can we represent what is right in a world full of people doing wrong?

Watercooler (at work or the gym)

What evil forces do you see at work in our world, and what do you think we should do about it?

MOUTH COMETH KNOWLEDGE AND UNDERSTANDING. HE LAYETH UP
DOM FOR THE RIGHTEOUS: HE IS A BUCKLER TO THEM THAT WALK UPRIGH
PETH THE PATHS OF JUDGMENT, AND PRESERVETH THE WAY OF HIS SAINTS

Righteous

The path of the righteous is like the light of dawn, which shines brighter and brighter until full day.

—Proverbs 4:18

It turns out that doing the right thing for people is profitable. Companies in the top 25 percent in terms of either gender or ethnic diversity on executive teams are 39 percent more likely than companies in the bottom 25 percent to financially outperform their peers.[1] Closing the racial wage gap in the United States could add an estimated $2.1 trillion to the U.S. economy annually.[2] That says nothing of the economic advantage of access to healthcare, which results in reduced costs for society. According to the Centers for Disease Control and Prevention, every dollar invested in public health programs saves $3.27 in health-related costs.[3]

Doing good for the disenfranchised is simply good business. That's what the Bible calls "righteousness." We tend to think about righteousness as what we *don't* do. We don't sleep around, get drunk, or cheat. In the Bible, however, the emphasis of righteousness is far more on what we do for the disadvantaged than what we don't do to impress our religious peers.

What Are the Benefits of Righteousness?

Righteousness as social justice makes sense of Solomon's statement "When the righteous increase, the people rejoice, but when the wicked rule, the people groan" (Proverbs 29:2). Righteousness has surprising benefits for both individuals and society. For example, it makes one resilient through difficult times (10:25). It grants favor with leaders (16:13), with God (3:33), and with family (20:7; 23:24). Righteousness even contributes to financial stability (Psalm 37:25).

In a particularly delightful expression, Solomon summarized the life of the righteous: "An evil man is ensnared in his transgression, but a righteous man sings and rejoices" (Proverbs 29:6). Pursuing wisdom is a quest not merely for personal moral improvement but for the public good.

Who Can Become Righteous?

According to the Bible, God alone is righteous: "Your righteousness, O God, reaches the high heavens" (Psalm 71:19). Humans, on the other hand, are emphatically *not* righteous: "Surely there is not a righteous man on earth who does good and never sins" (Ecclesiastes 7:20). Paul put it succinctly: "None is righteous, no, not one" (Romans 3:10). God is righteous; we are not.

That creates a conundrum. If God alone is righteous, then why are so many people in the Bible labeled as righteous?

- **Noah** was called righteous during a time of great wickedness on the earth (Genesis 6:9).
- Saul praised **David** for being more righteous than he, when David passed on the opportunity to assassinate him (1 Samuel 24:17).

- Herod knew that **John the Baptist** was a righteous man (Mark 6:20).
- Luke identified **Zechariah** and **Elizabeth** (Luke 1:6), **Simeon** (2:25), and **Joseph of Arimathea** (23:50) as righteous.
- **Abel** was twice called righteous compared with his brother (Hebrews 11:4; 1 John 3:12).

A pattern develops with this list. Those identified as righteous are righteous in comparison with the low bar set by their peers. The only way we can claim to be righteous is to compare ourselves with the people around us rather than with the God above us. Clearly, this lateral comparison will take us only so far. It will make us feel better about ourselves but can't make us more like God. If we truly desire the benefits of righteousness for ourselves and society, we must aim higher.

What Does Righteousness Look Like?

Righteousness is the practical application of the law of God for the good of the community (Deuteronomy 4:8; 16:19). It involves equal justice for rich and poor, fair weights and measures in business, care for the widow and orphan. That's why Jesus excoriated the Pharisees for appearing righteous through their religious rituals but neglecting biblical righteousness by not caring for the poor (Matthew 23:23–28).

That said, there is a moral aspect of righteousness. It isn't the Puritan ethic as much as a portrait of God. Simply put, righteousness is having the heart of God for the people of God. It's caring more about what God cares about than what we perceive would make us happy, popular, or celebrated. Righteousness is not merely *doing* right but *being* in a right relationship with God because we have adopted his values and priorities. Is it any wonder none of us measure up?

How Can We Become Righteous?

There's a fascinating description of righteousness in the Old Testament. It's a prophecy of a coming figure who would represent righteousness. The Jews called this future leader *Messiah.* This descendant of King David would rule justly on the throne of Israel: "Behold, the days are coming, declares the LORD, when I will raise up for David a righteous Branch, and he shall reign as king and deal wisely, and shall execute justice and righteousness in the land" (Jeremiah 23:5). Zechariah 9:9 predicts his coronation march into the Holy City: "Rejoice greatly, O daughter of Zion! Shout aloud, O daughter of Jerusalem! Behold, your king is coming to you; righteous and having salvation is he, humble and mounted on a donkey, on a colt, the foal of a donkey."

In a surprising turn, this righteous ruler wouldn't merely execute social justice. He would make the unrighteous righteous by being executed for their transgressions. One famous verse from Isaiah 53 says, "Out of the anguish of his soul he shall see and be satisfied; by his knowledge shall the righteous one, my servant, make many to be accounted righteous, and he shall bear their iniquities" (verse 11).

The New Testament applies these prophecies to Jesus: "Christ also suffered once for sins, the righteous for the unrighteous, that he might bring us to God, being put to death in the flesh but made alive in the spirit" (1 Peter 3:18; see also Romans 5:19; 8:1–4). Jesus is called the righteous one (Matthew 27:19; Acts 3:14; 7:52; 22:14). If we are ever to become righteous, we must find ourselves in Jesus. We can't do it on our own. Therefore, righteousness is received from Jesus before it's achieved by us.

Wisdom in Action

As James says, "Religion that is pure and undefiled before God the Father is this: to visit orphans and widows in their affliction, and to keep oneself unstained from the world" (1:27). If you want to be righteous, then do right for the least who need it the most.

Some of the most effective efforts with the lowest barrier to entry are tutoring in an after-school program, teaching ESL to refugees, visiting a nursing home, helping at a food bank, providing babysitting for foster or special needs parents, coaching a youth sports team, and participating in a community cleanup program. Take ten minutes to google several of these service opportunities in your area to see what is available and fits your interests. It's just as wise to tithe your time and talent as it is your treasure. If your goal is to be with Jesus, then showing up where he likes to hang out is your best chance of spending more time with him.

LINETH UNTO DEATH, AND HER PATHS UNTO THE DEAD. NONE THAT GO UNT
URN AGAIN, NEITHER TAKE THEY HOLD OF THE PATHS OF LIFE. THAT
/EST WALK IN THE WAY OF GOOD MEN, AND KEEP THE PATHS OF THE RIGH

This Week

- ☐ **Day 1:** Read this essay.
- ☐ **Day 2:** Memorize Proverbs 4:18.
- ☐ **Day 3:** Read the biography of Noah (Genesis 6) and find one thing to apply.
- ☐ **Day 4:** Meditate on Matthew 9:13; 23:28; 25:37–40; Galatians 3:11.
- ☐ **Day 5:** Discuss.

Group Discussion

1. How does this chapter shape your definition of righteousness?
2. How could accepting Jesus's declaration of righteousness for you empower you to do righteous acts for others?
3. What is one way you have benefited from righteousness?
4. How can pursuing social justice in business settings be a form of practicing righteousness?

Table Talk (in your home)

What could our family do to improve our community by helping the disadvantaged?

Watercooler (at work or the gym)

What could (or should) our community do to help the disadvantaged?

MOUTH COMETH KNOWLEDGE AND UNDERSTANDING. HE LAYETH UP
DOM FOR THE RIGHTEOUS: HE IS A BUCKLER TO THEM THAT WALK UPRIGH
PETH THE PATHS OF JUDGMENT, AND PRESERVETH THE WAY OF HIS SAINTS

PART 2

Words

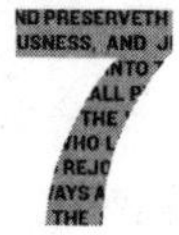

Truth

Whoever gives an honest answer kisses the lips.

—Proverbs 24:26

Jordan B. Peterson wrote a runaway bestseller, *12 Rules for Life: An Antidote to Chaos.* Rule 8 states, "Tell the truth—or, at least, don't lie." One could be tempted to reduce this to a moral cliché from a Bible class, had it not come from a world-renowned clinical psychologist. His arguments bring to bear decades of research and thousands of hours of therapy.

He made three principal arguments for telling the truth.[1] First, truth-telling is foundational for *mental health.* When people lie, they distort their perception of reality, fracturing their sense of self. Lying causes so much mental stress that trained interrogators can detect it through involuntary micro-expressions.

Second, honesty is essential for *relational integrity.* Trust is the cornerstone of any relationship, whether it's a couple falling in love or two countries negotiating a treaty. Truthfulness creates an environment of reliability and safety. In contrast, deceit erodes trust and inevitably leads to suspicion and resentment.

Third, honesty is paramount for *emotional resilience.* If you can't tell others the truth, you can't tell yourself the truth. You will bend to the will and opinions of others. Though flexibility is a good thing, pliability is demeaning and damaging, not just to your own soul, but to every relationship you value. There are simply no social organizations, public or personal, that can endure without a culture of honesty.

Truth in Court

Truth is vital in every aspect of life. In courts of law, however, it has powerful implications because that is where justice can be perverted to the greatest effect. Perhaps that's why so much of the "truth" talk in the Old Testament is set in the context of a courtroom: "Whoever speaks the truth gives honest evidence, but a false witness utters deceit" (Proverbs 12:17). Or again: "A truthful witness saves lives, but one who breathes out lies is deceitful" (14:25).

It's easy to tell the truth when nothing's at stake. But when the stakes are high, the pressure to deceive can be great. That's why we must predetermine to always tell the truth to everyone, everywhere, as Jesus adjures us: "Let what you say be simply 'Yes' or 'No'; anything more than this comes from evil" (Matthew 5:37). Truth-telling is more than a matter of doing the right thing; it's an issue of being the right kind of person. Our integrity is the most precious thing we have control over.

Personal integrity is the source of freedom and power. Solomon urged his son, "Buy truth, and do not sell it; buy wisdom, instruction, and understanding" (Proverbs 23:23), because "truthful lips endure forever, but a lying tongue is but for a moment" (12:19).

Deceit Erodes Society

Many prophets have their own accounts of how deception predicts decay in a nation (Jeremiah 5:1–3; Hosea 4:1–3; Amos 5:10–13). Isaiah mourned,

"Justice is turned back, and righteousness stands far away; for truth has stumbled in the public squares, and uprightness cannot enter" (Isaiah 59:14). Does this sound familiar?

Once upon a time, three umpires got into a debate. The first umpire said, "There's balls and there's strikes, and I calls 'em what they are." The second said, "There's balls and there's strikes, and I calls 'em like I sees 'em." The third replied, "There ain't no balls and strikes until I calls 'em balls or strikes." These three umpires represent three historical periods in their approach to truth.

The first umpire represents the *premodern* world, when people believed that God gave Truth (capital *T*). God's Truth was revealed through sacred texts, prophets, priests, and kings. The problem is that powerful people could label their own opinions as God's Truth and weaponize them to control the masses. The second umpire represents *modernism,* when science replaced religion as a reliable source of Truth. Truth (still capital *T*) wasn't revealed; it was discovered. The scientific method reigned supreme. The third umpire represents *postmodernism* with its denial of capital-*T* Truth. Truth is seen as a construct of a particular group or society. Now that Truth has been exposed as artificial and power-riddled, individuals are free to create their own. Truth is no longer out there to be discovered but inside you to be created. That's where we are.

We live in an unprecedented time in human history when fundamental truths are being reimagined. For the first time, marriage has been redefined as something other than a lifelong contract between a man and a woman. This has immense ramifications. Even the basic concept of gender has been redefined as a personal preference rather than an unyielding binary fact of X and Y chromosomes. How can we recover truth?

Redefinition of Truth in the New Testament

In the Old Testament, propositional truth was derived from the Torah—the law of God. For example, Psalm 119:160 says, "The sum of your word is truth, and every one of your righteous rules endures forever." Jesus adhered to this definition: "Sanctify them in the truth; your word is truth" (John 17:17). After his life on earth, however, truth became broader than the text. It's the living proclamation of Jesus—his life, death, and resurrection. Paul, speaking of "the hope laid up for you in heaven," put it this way: "Of this you have heard before in the word of the truth, the gospel" (Colossians 1:5). This is a significant shift in the definition of truth. Yet the next shift is more significant still.

In the gospel of John, *Truth* is generally a person, not a proposition. John didn't portray Torah as truth as in the Old Testament. He portrayed Jesus as the embodiment of truth. It begins in chapter 1: "The Word became flesh and dwelt among us, and we have seen his glory, glory as of the only Son from the Father, full of grace and truth" (verse 14).

Jesus affirmed that he is the Truth (5:33) and that knowing the Truth will set you free (8:32). He was clearest in John 14:6 when he claimed, "I am the way, and the truth, and the life." At Jesus's trial, when Pilate asked him, "So you are a king?" Jesus said, "You say that I am a king. For this purpose I was born and for this purpose I have come into the world—to bear witness to the truth. Everyone who is of the truth listens to my voice." But Pilate replied, "What is truth?" (18:37–38). Truth was standing in front of Pilate, and tragically, he missed it. It's a mistake we dare not repeat.

Wisdom in Action

One becomes a truthful person by embracing the person of Jesus as the Truth. When your identity comes from him, his truth will grow in you. His truth in you will overcome the temptation to exaggerate, omit details, or otherwise bend the truth in order to artificially prop yourself up. With Jesus in you, you can tell yourself the truth about yourself—you are a Genesis 1 person at your core, not a Genesis 3 person.

Then you can take ownership of your words. If you are ever less than truthful, commit to correcting it within twenty-four hours. Go to the person you deceived and tell the truth. When you correct your past deceptions, telling the truth in the future is much easier.

LINETH UNTO DEATH, AND HER PATHS UNTO THE DEAD. NONE THAT GO UNT
URN AGAIN, NEITHER TAKE THEY HOLD OF THE PATHS OF LIFE. THAT

This Week

- ☐ **Day 1:** Read this essay.
- ☐ **Day 2:** Memorize Proverbs 24:26.
- ☐ **Day 3:** Read the biography of Elijah (1 Kings 17) and find one thing to apply.
- ☐ **Day 4:** Meditate on Galatians 5:7; Ephesians 6:14; 2 Thessalonians 2:9–13.
- ☐ **Day 5:** Discuss.

Group Discussion

1. How have you seen dishonesty negatively affect business, relationships, politics, education, sports, or the church?
2. When have you had to pay the price for a lie? Use the following definition: "A lie is any deceit in word, act, or silence."
3. Discuss this statement: "Truth-telling is more than a matter of doing the right thing; it's an issue of being the right kind of person."
4. How could allegiance to Jesus, the Truth, remove or reduce the temptation to lie?

Table Talk (in your home)

Come up with a household principle about truth-telling that you could put on a plaque and hang on a wall.

Watercooler (at work or the gym)

On a scale of 1–10, how important do you think honesty is for this organization?

DOM FOR THE RIGHTEOUS: HE IS A BUCKLER TO THEM THAT WALK UPRIGH
PETH THE PATHS OF JUDGMENT, AND PRESERVETH THE WAY OF HIS SAINTS

Mockery

Whoever corrects a scoffer gets himself abuse, and he who reproves a wicked man incurs injury.

—Proverbs 9:7

"Sticks and stones may break my bones, but words will never hurt me." This proverb is intended to teach children resilience. But let's be honest—words hurt. After all, we have laws against defamation whether it's libel (written) or slander (spoken).

Psychologists recognize bullying as a serious threat to mental health. In response, anti-bullying campaigns have emerged, including Stomp Out Bullying, the leading U.S. organization tackling this issue. The U.S. Department of Health and Human Services now hosts a website called StopBullying.gov. Our society recognizes the danger of mockery, which Solomon warned about in Proverbs.

Everybody Does It; Everyone Receives It

We all, on occasion, make fun of others. Sometimes it's cruel; sometimes it's comical; sometimes it's justified. Why do I think so? Because even God (Proverbs 3:34) and Jesus (Matthew 23) join in from time to time. Mocking goes by a variety of names, each with its own connotations but all with negative implications: teasing, scorning, making fun of, scoffing, deriding, jeering, laughing at, taunting, reviling, cursing, and more. Whew! That's a lot. A bunch of people do it in the Bible. Equally long is the list of those who are mocked. Here's a partial list:

Slanderers	Text	Those Slandered	Text
Goliath	**1 Samuel** 17:10, 43	**Gideon**	**Judges** 8:15
Elijah	**1 Kings** 18:27	**Job**	**Job** 17:2
Rabshakeh	**2 Kings** 19:4	**David**	**Psalm** 55:12–13
Sennacherib	**2 Kings** 19:16, 22–23	**Jeremiah**	**Jeremiah** 20:7
Sanballat and Tobia	**Nehemiah** 2:19; 6:13	**Apostles**	**Acts** 2:13
Chief Priests	**Mark** 15:31	**Paul**	**Acts** 13:45; 18:6
		Martyrs	**Hebrews** 11:36
		Jesus	**Psalm** 22:6–7 **Matthew** 20:19; 27:29, 31 **1 Peter** 2:23
God	**Psalm** 2:4; 59:8	**God**	**Psalm** 74:10

This list reveals key insights: First, both saints and sinners face mockery—some deservedly, others unfairly. Therefore, being mocked says nothing of your character. Second, God is mocked by some and mocks others. Mockery, in and of itself, isn't a sign of moral failure. God and Jesus are justified when they do the jeering. Third, Jesus is mocked more than anyone else in the Bible. Perhaps I should keep that in mind when I feel like I'm unfairly targeted. I'm in the good company of Jesus (as well as other saints such as

Gideon, Job, David, Paul, and the other apostles). If they were targeted, we can hardly expect to go unscathed.

We all do it; we all receive it. Make sure you receive it for the right reasons. How? By choosing the right companions. If you associate with mockers, you will be mocked. They can't help themselves—it's just what they do. King David made an important observation: "It is not an enemy who taunts me—then I could bear it; it is not an adversary who deals insolently with me—then I could hide from him. But it is you, a man, my equal, my companion, my familiar friend" (Psalm 55:12–13). Mockery by friends cuts the deepest.

If you associate with Jesus, you will also be mocked (John 9:28; Acts 2:13). If you have the right mindset, this can be something to celebrate. As Jesus said, "Blessed are you when others revile you and persecute you and utter all kinds of evil against you falsely on my account. Rejoice and be glad, for your reward is great in heaven, for so they persecuted the prophets who were before you" (Matthew 5:11–12). Jesus will turn your mockery into victory.

When Words Wound and Wisdom Wins

Mockery has become a favorite American pastime. From stand-up comics to political pundits, from social posts to Netflix mockumentaries, from locker rooms to boardrooms. As noted above, mocking can be justified. So how can you know if you've crossed the line when you participate in mockery? The book of Proverbs offers us some helpful guidelines.

Rule 1: It's self-destructive to disrespect authority. "A wise son hears his father's instruction, but a scoffer does not listen to rebuke" (13:1). Parents, coaches, and political leaders all get mocked. That's a problem because when nothing is sacred, no one is safe. When a leader's position is disregarded, fools and chaos have free rein. It's important to honor the position our leaders hold even if we can't honor the person who holds the position.

Rule 2: Pick on someone your own size. When we use our words for blood sport against the weak and vulnerable, we make an enemy of God, who defends them. "Whoever mocks the poor insults his Maker; he who is glad at calamity will not go unpunished" (17:5). Tearing others down to build yourself up is weak, shameful, and pitiful. Scripture calls this person a "scoffer" (21:24). The honorable defend those who can't defend themselves—the odd kid at school, the immigrant or indigent in the city, the elderly or children, and the newbie at work.

What can we learn from these guidelines? Jesus railed against those who leverage their power to oppress the vulnerable: "They tie up heavy burdens, hard to bear, and lay them on people's shoulders, but they themselves are not willing to move them with their finger" (Matthew 23:4).

Similarly, God's mockery is reserved for the arrogant and wicked who oppress others: "The LORD's curse is on the house of the wicked, but he blesses the dwelling of the righteous. Toward the scorners he is scornful, but to the humble he gives favor" (Proverbs 3:33–34).

Wisdom in Action

Mockers crave attention. If you stop giving them attention, their mockery has no fuel. That's why Solomon advised, "Do not reprove a scoffer, or he will hate you; reprove a wise man, and he will love you" (Proverbs 9:8). A non-response may be the best response.

For clarity, a non-response isn't silence. Instead, it's removing yourself from their physical presence. If you stay and listen, that sends the wrong message. If you walk away, literally removing yourself from their space, your message is loud and clear. This advice opens the entire book of Psalms: "Blessed is the man who walks not in the counsel of the wicked, nor stands in the way of sinners, nor sits in the seat of scoffers" (1:1).

That works with peers. If God has put you in a position of authority, your response should be more proactive: "Drive out a scoffer, and strife will go out, and quarreling and abuse will cease" (Proverbs 22:10). This may sound harsh, but the consequences of mockery are more serious than we often realize. Proverbs 29:8 says, "Scoffers set a city aflame, but the wise turn away wrath." If you can, put out the fire.

Mockery is particularly popular online. The wise will deprive it of oxygen by walking away from peers and squelching it among subordinates.

LINETH UNTO DEATH, AND HER PATHS UNTO THE DEAD. NONE THAT GO UNT
URN AGAIN, NEITHER TAKE THEY HOLD OF THE PATHS OF LIFE. THAT
EST WALK IN THE WAY OF GOOD MEN, AND KEEP THE PATHS OF THE RIGH

This Week

- ☐ **Day 1:** Read this essay.
- ☐ **Day 2:** Memorize Proverbs 9:7.
- ☐ **Day 3:** Read the biography of Sanballat and Tobiah (Nehemiah 2) and find one thing to apply or avoid.
- ☐ **Day 4:** Meditate on 1 Corinthians 4:12; 1 Peter 2:23; 3:9.
- ☐ **Day 5:** Discuss.

Group Discussion

1. Growing up, when did you experience the pain of unwarranted teasing?
2. Proverbs 9:7–8 talks about correcting a scoffer. How do you decide when to correct someone who is bullying or mocking another person?
3. Why do you think bullying is socially unacceptable, yet online and in political discourse, mockery is accepted?
4. How can you become more resilient to criticism?

Table Talk (in your home)

How should we protect one another from hurtful comments in our home?

Watercooler (at work or the gym)

When does good-natured banter at work cross the line into mockery?

MOUTH COMETH KNOWLEDGE AND UNDERSTANDING. HE LAYETH UP
DOM FOR THE RIGHTEOUS: HE IS A BUCKLER TO THEM THAT WALK UPRIGH
PETH THE PATHS OF JUDGMENT, AND PRESERVETH THE WAY OF HIS SAINTS

Gossip

A dishonest man spreads strife, and a whisperer separates close friends.

—Proverbs 16:28

Gossip is more than idle chatter. It's a strategy for gaining status. From kindergarten playgrounds to the chambers of Congress, gossip empowers social brokers to jockey for position. This same strategic dissemination of information (or misinformation) runs through boardrooms and bedrooms as people try to secure status, privilege, and income.

In the tapestry of human interactions, few threads are as vibrant or universal as gossip. It pervades every culture at every level of society, especially through technology. We are living during the big bang of information. The internet, smartphones, and AI project our private lives to the masses. Global fame and infamy can be manufactured in a matter of hours.

This makes the book of Proverbs more relevant than ever. Solomon's wisdom helps us get a grip on gossip—how it erodes communities, fractures relationships, and deteriorates the integrity of our souls. Solomon guides us through the perilous waters of whispered words.

Gossip: The Relationship Assassin

We love gossip for the same reason we love a good story. We are interested in people—their problems, quirks, and vulnerabilities. Gossip makes us feel better about ourselves, particularly if it takes someone more powerful down a notch or two. Yet there is a paradox here. We feel powerful when we share a juicy morsel and see the look of shock, disgust, or amusement on another's face. The problem is that once we reveal the information, our power vanishes because now they know what we do. The power of gossip vanishes the moment it's shared.

Proverbs 18:8 captures gossip's addictive essence with unsettling accuracy: "The words of a whisperer are like delicious morsels; they go down into the inner parts of the body." Like the most delectable dessert, gossip is irresistibly sweet and undeniably destructive. Proverbs 16:28 warns, "A dishonest man spreads strife, and a whisperer separates close friends." This highlights a timeless truth: While gossip can inform or entertain, it damages relationships and communities.

Relationships require trust, and that is precisely what gossip destroys. Proverbs 20:19 takes it further: "Whoever goes about slandering reveals secrets; *therefore do not associate with a simple babbler.*" Solomon advised his son to steer clear of friends who gossip about others. Isn't that kind of harsh? Actually, no, because if someone gossips to your face, they will gossip behind your back. Gossips are controlled by gossip, not vice versa.

What should you do if someone gossips in front of you? If the gossip is an authority figure, walk away. A verbal challenge won't likely go well for you. Simply remove yourself from their presence. If it's a friend (or other peer), however, ask this question: "If the person you're talking about were here right now, would you say the same thing?" If they say yes, invite them to do just that before they continue. Could that cause you to lose a friend? Yes. But a friendship destroyed because of this question isn't a friendship you can afford to keep.

Solomon also described a gossip this way: "A worthless person, a wicked man, goes about with crooked speech, winks with his eyes, signals with his feet, points with his finger, with perverted heart devises evil, continually sowing discord; therefore calamity will come upon him suddenly; in a moment he will be broken beyond healing" (Proverbs 6:12–15). But gossip works only if there's an open ear. If you listen to gossip without saying something or walking away, you are participating in the problem. Your willingness to listen is fuel to the fire. "For lack of wood the fire goes out, and where there is no whisperer, quarreling ceases" (Proverbs 26:20).

Gossip Builds a Barrier Between You and God

I can remember only one time I shouted at my son. He set me off because he mistreated my daughter. He was older and quicker-witted. One day, he kept teasing her until she ran into her room crying. I walked calmly into his room to have a man-to-man with him. The more I described his behavior to him, however, the angrier I got. I found myself squeezing his cheeks and shouting, "That's my daughter." Admittedly, not my best parenting moment. But it taught me much about God. The most offensive thing you can do to God is to attack one of his kids.

That's why King David added this description to the list of those who could enter God's presence: "[He] who does not slander with his tongue and does no evil to his neighbor, nor takes up a reproach against his friend" (Psalm 15:3). His words in Psalm 101:5 are even more sobering: "Whoever slanders his neighbor secretly I will destroy. Whoever has a haughty look and an arrogant heart I will not endure."

Gossip/slander is cataloged in a list of sins throughout the New Testament. It sits alongside murder, adultery, and theft (Matthew 15:19); coveting, wickedness, deceit, sensuality, envy, and pride (Mark 7:22); hating God, insolence, haughtiness, boasting, and inventing evil (Romans 1:30); bitterness, wrath, and clamor (Ephesians 4:31); heartlessness, being unappeasable, and brutality (2 Timothy 3:3); slander, anger, and dissension (2 Corinthians 12:20; Colossians 3:8; 1 Timothy 6:4–6; 1 Peter 2:1)—just to name some of the sins. Gossip isn't as trivial as we have made it.

That's because Jesus established a new measure of morality in Matthew 5. We are judged not merely by our behavior but by our motives. Anger derives from the same motive as murder. Lust and divorce come from the same place as adultery. The reason we don't perform these more egregious sins is not that we are better people but that we fear punishment from God or judgment from others. We are just as bad as murderers and adulterers, and we are cowards to boot. Gossip has a murderous motive without the courage to carry it out.

Wisdom in Action

How do we avoid the culpability of spreading gossip by speaking it or listening to it? The answer is simple, though not easy. It's not what we refrain from but what we attend to. Jesus admonished, "Love your enemies, do good to those who hate you, bless those who curse you, pray for those who abuse you" (Luke 6:27–28). He then modeled it on the cross. Rather than cursing those who crucified him, he prayed for them.

Paul, who previously killed Christians, adopted Jesus's model himself. In a discourse describing all he and his co-laborers had suffered for the gospel, Paul said, "When we are slandered, we answer kindly" (1 Corinthians 4:13, NIV). That's a colossal transformation for the former persecutor. If he could change, so can we.

The apostle Peter had been known for his temper. He once removed an opponent's ear with a sword (John 18:10). Later in life, transformed by Christ, he said this: "In your hearts honor Christ the Lord as holy, always being prepared to make a defense to anyone who asks you for a reason for the hope that is in you; yet do it with gentleness and respect, having a good conscience, so that, when you are slandered, those who revile your good behavior in Christ may be put to shame" (1 Peter 3:15–16). If he could change, so can we.

When we talk about Jesus, our gossip will shrivel because we want our words to match our witness. The more we testify about Christ, the less we will gossip around or about those we are trying to influence for him. So if you want to avoid gossip, enlarge your witness by proclaiming the gospel.

LINETH UNTO DEATH, AND HER PATHS UNTO THE DEAD. NONE THAT GO UNT
URN AGAIN, NEITHER TAKE THEY HOLD OF THE PATHS OF LIFE. THAT
EST WALK IN THE WAY OF GOOD MEN, AND KEEP THE PATHS OF THE RIGH

This Week

- ☐ **Day 1:** Read this essay.
- ☐ **Day 2:** Memorize Proverbs 16:28.
- ☐ **Day 3:** Read the biography of Mephibosheth (2 Samuel 9 and 19) and find one thing to apply.
- ☐ **Day 4:** Meditate on 1 Corinthians 4:13; 2 Corinthians 6:3–8; 1 Peter 3:16.
- ☐ **Day 5:** Discuss.

Group Discussion

1. Proverbs 18:8 compares gossip to “delicious morsels.” Why do you think gossip is so tasty to us?
2. How can gossip improve or destroy someone’s social standing?
3. What should you do if someone gossips in front of you? How would your advice change if that person were a boss, a co-worker, a friend, or someone you are supervising?
4. What practical steps can individuals and communities take to reduce and prevent gossip?

Table Talk (in your home)

What should be our family rule if one of us is gossiping?

Watercooler (at work or the gym)

How have you seen gossip reduce the effectiveness of a team?

MOUTH COMETH KNOWLEDGE AND UNDERSTANDING. HE LAYETH UP
DOM FOR THE RIGHTEOUS: HE IS A BUCKLER TO THEM THAT WALK UPRIGH
PETH THE PATHS OF JUDGMENT, AND PRESERVETH THE WAY OF HIS SAINTS

10

Quarreling

A soft answer turns away wrath, but a harsh word stirs up anger.

—Proverbs 15:1

In 1925, a single stray dog sparked an international incident when it inadvertently emigrated from Greece. The dog, being illiterate, couldn't read the sign, so he had no idea he had violated Bulgarian sovereignty. His owner, trying to retrieve his pet, was shot by Bulgarian border guards. Given the already-high tensions between the countries, a conflict ignited.[1]

This absurd war, started by a stray dog, underscores how the smallest spark, if struck in just the right conditions, can ignite social tinder and blaze far beyond the original offense. Trivial misunderstandings can escalate into serious disputes in marriage, business, and government. We see it all around us: road rage, litigation, and social media tirades. But conflict doesn't have to characterize your personal interactions. Proverbs provides wisdom in managing conflicts before they become unmanageable.

Hotheads and Hot Water

We all have disagreements and debates. Discussions between friends, family, and business associates will inevitably involve a verbal bout from time to time. This becomes a problem only when we let disagreements escalate into disagreeable contention that lasts longer than the conversation. Quarrels have a way of outliving the original offense and bloating into a behemoth. Solomon offers this vivid metaphor: "The beginning of strife is like letting out water, so quit before the quarrel breaks out" (Proverbs 17:14). Here's what it looks like in real life:

- When friends are fighting: "Whoever meddles in a quarrel not his own is like one who takes a passing dog by the ears" (26:17).
- When siblings bicker: "A brother offended is more unyielding than a strong city, and quarreling is like the bars of a castle" (18:19).
- When a group is at odds at work, school, or church: "It is an honor for a man to keep aloof from strife, but every fool will be quarreling" (20:3).

There are times to speak your mind. However, when emotions hijack the conversation, we get mired in the quicksand of contention. It's better to let it go. This is not admitting defeat but rising above the fray, and that is wise. Solomon said, "A hot-tempered man stirs up strife, but he who is slow to anger quiets contention" (15:18). You must decide whether you want to win the argument or a friend.

The home is one of the most common places for contention, particularly between spouses. Solomon had more to say about this than any other category of quarreling. Given that he had seven hundred wives and three hundred concubines, the opportunities for marital conflict were plentiful. (For a man known for his wisdom, Solomon's bridal collection is one of the dumbest things he ever did.)

- Proverbs 21:9 (and 25:24): "It is better to live in a corner of the housetop than in a house shared with a quarrelsome wife."

- Proverbs 21:19: "It is better to live in a desert land than with a quarrelsome and fretful woman."
- Proverbs 27:15 (and 19:13): "A continual dripping on a rainy day and a quarrelsome wife are alike."

For those husbands tempted to shout "Amen," your problem may be more in the mirror than in the kitchen. Just sayin'.

Meribah and Quarreling with God

After their rescue from Egypt, the Israelites headed into the desert under Moses's leadership. They constantly grumbled against Moses, and God took it personally. Their grumbling was offensive in the extreme. Why? Because God had *always* provided for them. He provided plagues to release them from Egypt. He provided untold treasures from their captors when they fled. He parted the waters of the sea for their escape. He provided the pillars of cloud and fire to guide them. Their grumbling against their leader amounted to mutiny against God.

This all came to a head in Exodus 17:2–3: "The people quarreled with Moses and said, 'Give us water to drink.' And Moses said to them, 'Why do you quarrel with me? Why do you test the LORD?'" The people were ready to stone Moses. God provided for their needs in a humorous twist. Instead of the people striking Moses with stones because they were thirsty, Moses provided water for their thirst by striking a rock. Then he named the place Massah and Meribah, *Massah* meaning "testing" and *Meribah* meaning "quarreling."

Quarreling may seem like a minor offense, but it's not—particularly when our beef is with God. It's not that God has thin skin and can't take criticism. It's that our quarreling is evidence of shortsighted faith that denies his perpetual goodness. That's why Meribah is referenced so often (Numbers 20:13, 24; 27:14; Deuteronomy 32:51; 33:8; Psalms 81:7; 95:8; 106:32;

Ezekiel 47:19; 48:28). God will never fail in his promises or provisions, and *that* is why grumbling is so offensive to him.

You might say, "I wasn't grumbling against God; I was grumbling against my leader." That's exactly what the Israelites said about Moses. God's response was (and is) that his leaders are as much a part of his provision as manna, water, and the pillars of cloud and fire.

This isn't to say there is never a time to fight. Gideon created quite a hullabaloo when he tore down the altar of Baal (Judges 6:31–32). Elijah had a messy row with the priests of Baal (1 Kings 18:20–40). Nehemiah scrapped with the Israelites who embraced idols through intermarriage (Nehemiah 13:25). So yes, there is a time to fight. But let's be honest—most of our fights are driven more by what we want than by what is right.

James 4:1–2 gets to the root of the problem: "What causes quarrels and what causes fights among you? Is it not this, that your passions are at war within you? You desire and do not have, so you murder. You covet and cannot obtain, so you fight and quarrel. You do not have, because you do not ask." The more selfish our motives are, the less likely God will be to back our battle. That's why Isaiah 58:4 says, "Behold, you fast only to quarrel and to fight and to hit with a wicked fist. Fasting like yours this day will not make your voice to be heard on high."

Wisdom in Action

This may be a slight oversimplification, but in the Old Testament, it was right to fight for what was right. In the New Testament, the only right fight is for the rights of the oppressed. This goes to the core of who Jesus is, as Isaiah 42:2 prophesied: "He will not quarrel or cry aloud, nor will anyone hear his voice in the streets" (quoted in Matthew 12:19).

Quarreling isn't the nature of a Jesus follower. As Paul said, "If anyone is inclined to be contentious, we have no such practice, nor do the churches of God" (1 Corinthians 11:16). Yet too many churches fit Paul's description in

2 Corinthians 12:20: "I fear that perhaps when I come I may find you not as I wish, and that you may find me not as you wish—that perhaps there may be quarreling, jealousy, anger, hostility, slander, gossip, conceit, and disorder."

The best advice we can find on quarreling comes from a letter Paul wrote to young Timothy: "Have nothing to do with foolish, ignorant controversies; you know that they breed quarrels. And the Lord's servant must not be quarrelsome but kind to everyone, able to teach, patiently enduring evil" (2 Timothy 2:23–24). He gave the same advice to his other young protégé, Titus: "Avoid foolish controversies, genealogies, dissensions, and quarrels about the law, for they are unprofitable and worthless" (Titus 3:9).

This is one of the foundational requirements for church leaders: to avoid quarrels (1 Timothy 3:3). It should characterize every Christian (1 Timothy 2:8; Titus 3:2) because what is at stake is not whether we get our way but whether pre-believers find their way (Romans 14:1). Therefore, we avoid quarrels, specifically by not taking sides. When we take sides, we eliminate at least half the people we can reach for Christ or half of those who can help us reach them.

LINETH UNTO DEATH, AND HER PATHS UNTO THE DEAD. NONE THAT GO UNT
URN AGAIN, NEITHER TAKE THEY HOLD OF THE PATHS OF LIFE. THAT
(EST WALK IN THE WAY OF GOOD MEN, AND KEEP THE PATHS OF THE RIGH

This Week

- ☐ **Day 1:** Read this essay.
- ☐ **Day 2:** Memorize Proverbs 15:1.
- ☐ **Day 3:** Read the biography of Israel at Meribah (Exodus 17:1–7) and find one thing to avoid.
- ☐ **Day 4:** Meditate on Romans 14:1; 2 Timothy 2:23–24; James 4:1–2.
- ☐ **Day 5:** Discuss.

Group Discussion

1. Proverbs 15:1 says, "A soft answer turns away wrath, but a harsh word stirs up anger." When has this been true for you?
2. Why do you think family quarrels are often more intense than other disputes?
3. Proverbs 26:17 warns against meddling in quarrels not your own. How can we distinguish between helpful intervention and unhealthy meddling?
4. What are strategies to prevent disagreements from escalating into more serious quarrels?

Table Talk (in your home)

When we have a disagreement in this house, what responses are out of bounds?

Watercooler (at work or the gym)

If you have a beef with someone, are you more likely to confront them, avoid them, or slander them?

MOUTH COMETH KNOWLEDGE AND UNDERSTANDING. HE LAYETH UP
DOM FOR THE RIGHTEOUS: HE IS A BUCKLER TO THEM THAT WALK UPRIGH
PETH THE PATHS OF JUDGMENT, AND PRESERVETH THE WAY OF HIS SAINTS

11

Flattery

A lying tongue hates its victims, and a flattering mouth works ruin.

—Proverbs 26:28

Compliments are addictive, literally. That sounds crazy, but it's God's design. When you receive a compliment, your brain releases two highly addictive chemicals: dopamine and oxytocin. Dopamine is a feel-good chemical that opens us up to new experiences. Oxytocin creates a connection between people. Both are triggered by praise. Positively, that's why compliments are powerful in creating community, but negatively, it's why flattery makes us vulnerable to swindlers, manipulators, and con artists. What God created for good can be twisted for evil.

To make matters worse, human beings have what psychologists call "confirmation bias": Our brains latch on to information that confirms our existing beliefs. This makes us more likely to trust those who flatter us, even with ample evidence that their intentions are nefarious. We must discern between community-forming compliments and manipulative flattery.

Flattery in the Public Square

Because flattery works, flatterers work it. It feels good when people affirm you, even when you know they don't mean it. I learned this at nineteen. It was the first time a prostitute propositioned me. On my way back to college in Missouri, my car had been totaled in Missoula, Montana. After paying for the bus ticket to Joplin, I had no money left for food. For three days, I fasted (not by choice). Exhausted and hangry, I changed buses in Kansas City. As I passed a young lady in a stairwell, she said, "You are really cute." Well, how could anyone deny that?

This was the only kind word I had heard all week. It triggered some dopamine, which led to a brief conversation down a single flight of stairs, which culminated in a question. She asked me, "Do you want to have sex?" I was a nineteen-year-old virgin, so the answer was obviously yes but still no! There was no way I was having sex with a stranger (or anyone else, for that matter). Yet her flattery made me curious, and I heard myself ask, "Where?" We were in a bus station! She invited me into a bathroom stall. I declined.

As I walked away, I wondered why I had asked where she proposed our misadventure take place. My answer to her offer was a hard pass. Yet I still left the door cracked. Why? Perhaps it was just curiosity. Or perhaps flattery is more effective than we imagine.

Centuries before modern psychology understood flattery's influence, Solomon warned his son about flattery "from the forbidden woman, from the adulteress with her smooth words" (Proverbs 2:16). Four more times, he warned of seductive flattery with words like these: "The lips of a forbidden woman drip honey, and her speech is smoother than oil" (5:3; see also 6:24; 7:5, 21).

Sexual seduction is but one form of flattery. We find flattery in every social circle. Some people may envy your position at work, power in business, prowess in sports, or possessions at home. Consequently, they coddle you with compliments to get close enough to use you for their own advantage. Many want good *from* you, not good *for* you. They are not your friends. "Whoever hates disguises himself with his lips and harbors deceit in his heart; when he speaks graciously, believe him not, for there are seven abominations in his heart; though his hatred be covered with deception, his wickedness will be exposed in the assembly" (26:24–26).

As a public figure, I have seen this firsthand. Some who praise you most to your face are the quickest to stab you in the back. Be warned: "A man who flatters his neighbor spreads a net for his feet" (29:5). There is, however, something worse than being duped by a flatterer. It's being deceived by the person in the mirror.

Flattery in the Mirror

"The crucible is for silver, and the furnace is for gold, and a man is tested by his praise" (Proverbs 27:21). Criticism can sting, but praise can cripple. It can cripple your discernment and stunt your improvement. Praise, like dessert, is delightful in moderation, but too much leaves you bloated and lethargic. Many public figures are in a sugar coma from admiring sycophants.

Sometimes we flatter ourselves to justify sin we are about to commit or to soothe our battered conscience afterward. King David's warning is worth remembering: "Transgression speaks to the wicked deep in his heart; there is no fear of God before his eyes. For he flatters himself in his own eyes that his iniquity cannot be found out and hated. The words of his mouth are trouble and deceit; he has ceased to act wisely and do good" (Psalm 36:1–3).

Your true friends are those who tell you what you need to hear, not what you want to hear. That's how I got my first accountability partner. I had spoken at a conference and received criticism from an older woman in the crowd. I shared what she had said with Richard, one of the conference directors. He was a friend. So I expected him to bash the woman for having the audacity to challenge me. He didn't. Instead, he said, "Mark, if she's right, then change. If she's wrong, then let it go." But . . . but . . . he was right. He was virtually the only truth-teller I had in my life at the time. I asked if we could meet regularly for accountability. We met monthly for the next three years until he died unexpectedly. He was one of the greatest gifts of my life. "Whoever rebukes a man will afterward find more favor than he who flatters with his tongue" (Proverbs 28:23).

Without truth-tellers, we believe our own lies and are susceptible to the lies of others. In Isaiah 30:10, God's people said to the prophets, "Do not prophesy to us what is right; speak to us smooth things, prophesy illusions." This is one of the warnings of the last days: "The time is coming when people will not endure sound teaching, but having itching ears they will accumulate for themselves teachers to suit their own passions" (2 Timothy 4:3). Flattery is effective from the top to the bottom of society and from the beginning to the end of time.

Flattery with God

Because flattery is so effective with people, people often try it with God (to ill effect). Asaph bemoaned this fact in Psalm 78:35–36: "They remembered that God was their rock, the Most High God their redeemer. But they flattered him with their mouths; they lied to him with their tongues." Think about that. We even try to flatter God to get what we want. He isn't fooled. He says himself, "This people draw near with their mouth and honor me with their lips, while their hearts are far from me, and their fear of me is a commandment taught by men" (Isaiah 29:13).

What's shocking is that flatterers are often found in church leadership. Paul warns us about them: "Such persons do not serve our Lord Christ, but their own appetites, and by smooth talk and flattery they deceive the hearts of the naive" (Romans 16:18). So does Peter: "In their greed they will exploit you with false words. Their condemnation from long ago is not idle, and their destruction is not asleep" (2 Peter 2:3). If both Paul and Peter warned about flatterers in church leadership, perhaps we should pay attention.

Wisdom in Action

How can we protect ourselves from flattery if God wired us to respond to praise? We don't have control over whether we will respond to praise. We do have control, however, over whose praise we prioritize. This is worth repeating: You can determine who has influence over you by deciding whose praise you will prioritize. Make a mental note of the three people whose opinions matter to you spiritually. Do the same for those who influence your dress, entertainment, education, and news feed. Pay attention to who you pay attention to.

If you don't want to be like them, stop "liking" them. The more you listen to their chatter, the more it will matter. The influence others have on you is in proportion to the time and attention you give to them. You can't control whether others will influence you. However, you have full control over the volume.

LINETH UNTO DEATH, AND HER PATHS UNTO THE DEAD. NONE THAT GO UNT
URN AGAIN, NEITHER TAKE THEY HOLD OF THE PATHS OF LIFE. THAT
EST WALK IN THE WAY OF GOOD MEN, AND KEEP THE PATHS OF THE RIGH

This Week

☐ **Day 1:** Read this essay.

☐ **Day 2:** Memorize Proverbs 26:28.

☐ **Day 3:** Read the biography of Hezekiah (Isaiah 39) and find one thing to apply or avoid.

☐ **Day 4:** Meditate on Romans 16:18; 1 Thessalonians 2:5; 2 Timothy 4:3.

☐ **Day 5:** Discuss.

Group Discussion

1. When was a time you were overtaken by flattery?
2. What are the key differences between genuine compliments and flattery? How can we discern between the two?
3. How have you seen flattery used to manipulate people in various social circles—friendships, work, church?
4. What steps can we take to guard ourselves against the dangers of flattery?

Table Talk (in your home)

What is the greatest compliment someone in this family could give you?

Watercooler (at work or the gym)

Do you think some people give compliments to get something in return?

MOUTH COMETH KNOWLEDGE AND UNDERSTANDING. HE LAYETH UP
DOM FOR THE RIGHTEOUS: HE IS A BUCKLER TO THEM THAT WALK UPRIGH
PETH THE PATHS OF JUDGMENT, AND PRESERVETH THE WAY OF HIS SAINTS

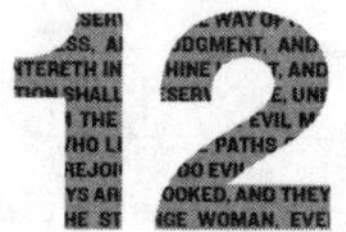

Boasting

Do not boast about tomorrow, for you do not know what a day may bring. Let another praise you, and not your own mouth; a stranger, and not your own lips.

—Proverbs 27:1–2

Everyone does it. No one likes it. So why does everyone do it? Irene Scopelliti is a professor and researcher who has studied the psychology of boasting. In her TEDx Talk, she revealed some stunning findings. When a person is bragging, they sense a negative reaction from approximately 25 percent of those hearing their self-promotion. Seventy-five percent of those listening, however, have a negative reaction. Braggarts feel better about themselves while bragging, which keeps them from seeing how they are really being perceived.[1]

Why does bragging blind us to others' negative perceptions of us? Researchers scanned people's brains and found out that when subjects talked about themselves, the same areas of the brain lit up as when people eat food or have sex.[2] In other words, we like talking about ourselves . . . *a lot.*

In another study by Scopelliti and her colleagues, some participants were instructed to write their bio in a way that made them more likable. When they did, it had the opposite effect of making them less likable.[3] It's human nature to want to put your best foot forward, to present yourself in a positive light. Generally, this works well when you promote your skills. It can get you a job or a promotion. With relationships, however, it has quite the opposite effect. Solomon gave sage advice three thousand years ago: If you want to be liked, avoid bragging like the plague.

Boasting Is Worse Than We Think

Boasting seems like a minor moral flaw. We all do it from time to time. Given our need for recognition, it's almost impossible to avoid. Yet the Old Testament consistently connects boasting with other evils, like greed. According to Proverbs, one of the most common brags is how we cheat others: "'Bad, bad,' says the buyer, but when he goes away, then he boasts" (20:14). It's no accident that when we get a particularly good deal, we call it a "steal."

For some reason, we feel better about ourselves when we gain financially at others' expense. But boasting about financial gain is a form of ungrateful atheism because it emphasizes our ability, not God's gracious provision. How much of your wealth are you responsible for? Even if you worked hard to achieve it, does it not come from the Lord? Does a farmer create the crop he harvests? Does an entrepreneur create the opportunities he leverages? Did you choose the time and place you were born, the parents you had, or the education you received? Our response to wealth should be gratitude and generosity, not boasting or pride. Jesus concluded a parable about a financial braggart with this warning: "God said to him, 'Fool! This night your soul is required of you, and the things you have prepared, whose will they be?' So is the one who lays up treasure for himself and is not rich toward God" (Luke 12:20–21).

Another common boast the Bible talks about is one's mental, physical, or social strength. Yet like wealth, our strength is far more to God's credit than our own. Like wealth, it can disappear far more quickly than it can be built. Even the wicked king Ahab rebuked his enemy Ben-hadad of Syria: "Let not him who straps on his armor boast himself as he who takes it off"

(1 Kings 20:11). Before he could blink, Ben-hadad's troops were routed by the hand of God. Likewise, David enshrined Saul's hubris in the lyrics of Psalm 52:1: "Why do you boast of evil, O mighty man? The steadfast love of God endures all the day." Both wealth and power come from the Lord. He bestows and removes according to his will and often in response to our humility or pride. This is why David could say, "The boastful shall not stand before your eyes; you hate all evildoers" (5:5). You caught that, right? According to God, boasting isn't petty; it's evil.

This is why we should humbly submit our plans to our Creator. Let's appraise our days, our wealth, and our strength with humility and gratitude to God. We don't know what tomorrow will hold or what we will hold tomorrow. As James suggested, our greatest strategies should account for God's lordship: "Yet you do not know what tomorrow will bring. What is your life? For you are a mist that appears for a little time and then vanishes" (James 4:14).

God warns us: "Let not the wise man boast in his wisdom, let not the mighty man boast in his might, let not the rich man boast in his riches, but let him who boasts boast in this, that he understands and knows me, that I am the LORD who practices steadfast love, justice, and righteousness in the earth" (Jeremiah 9:23–24). Paul quoted this passage to remind us of the gift we have in Christ Jesus (1 Corinthians 1:31; see also 2 Corinthians 10:17). He chose us to receive the greatest gift of time and eternity. This warrants humble devotion, not arrogant boasting.

How Believers Should Boast

Christians should boast. We're told to. But our boasting is different from the world's. Rather than bragging about our talents or assets, we boast in the Lord and about our weaknesses. The longest passage in the Bible on boasting is Paul's diatribe in 2 Corinthians 10–12. It's a delightful piece of cynical rhetoric. Paul summarized all three chapters in a single pithy sentence: "If I must boast, I will boast of the things that show my weakness" (11:30). How can this be?

Since all our talents and assets are gifts from God, it makes sense to give him credit. When we have a natural ability that we submit to God, we call it a "spiritual gift." If we have wealth or education, freedom or family, health or security, these are gifts of God in the lottery of time, geography, and genetics. All are gifts to be stewarded, not achievements to flaunt. "What do you have that you did not receive? If then you received it, why do you boast as if you did not receive it?" (1 Corinthians 4:7).

And we should boast about our weaknesses because God uses them to shame the arrogant: "God chose what is foolish in the world to shame the wise; God chose what is weak in the world to shame the strong; God chose what is low and despised in the world, even things that are not, to bring to nothing things that are, so that no human being might boast in the presence of God" (1 Corinthians 1:27–29).

When we admit our weaknesses, we highlight God's strengths. When we are empty, God's power fills us. When we are poor, his riches provide. Our abasement accomplishes his glory, and we get caught in the updraft of his exaltation. Or as James 1:9 says succinctly, "Let the lowly brother boast in his exaltation."

Wisdom in Action

Gratitude and transparency are the antidote to bragging. Gratitude gives credit to God for your strengths. Try keeping a gratitude list by your bed, and every night, before going to sleep, add one item. This is kryptonite to boasting.

Transparency, on the other hand, births strength from the struggles you experience. Rather than hiding your weaknesses, start sharing them. Not only will this increase your likability (and by a lot), but it will also help you embrace suffering as an advantage. Deprivation, opposition, oppression, and other trials are fuel for endurance, strength, and character. This is why Paul said, "We rejoice [literally *boast*] in our sufferings, knowing that suffering produces endurance" (Romans 5:3).

LINETH UNTO DEATH, AND HER PATHS UNTO THE DEAD. NONE THAT GO UNT
URN AGAIN, NEITHER TAKE THEY HOLD OF THE PATHS OF LIFE. THAT
EST WALK IN THE WAY OF GOOD MEN, AND KEEP THE PATHS OF THE RIGH

This Week

- ☐ **Day 1:** Read this essay.
- ☐ **Day 2:** Memorize Proverbs 27:1–2.
- ☐ **Day 3:** Read the biography of Nebuchadnezzar (Daniel 4) and find one thing to apply or avoid.
- ☐ **Day 4:** Meditate on 1 Corinthians 1:29, 31; 3:21; 4:7.
- ☐ **Day 5:** Discuss.

Group Discussion

1. What is an example of a "humble brag"—something someone brags about in a roundabout way?
2. Why do you think it feels good to boast? And why is boasting so off-putting to those listening?
3. How can we shift from boasting about our achievements to expressing gratitude for God's blessings?
4. What are some practical ways to boast about our weaknesses, as Paul suggested in 2 Corinthians 11:30?

Table Talk (in your home)

Why do you think people are put off when someone brags?

Watercooler (at work or the gym)

Do you think the company culture encourages or discourages bragging?

MOUTH COMETH KNOWLEDGE AND UNDERSTANDING. HE LAYETH UP
DOM FOR THE RIGHTEOUS: HE IS A BUCKLER TO THEM THAT WALK UPRIGH
PETH THE PATHS OF JUDGMENT, AND PRESERVETH THE WAY OF HIS SAINTS

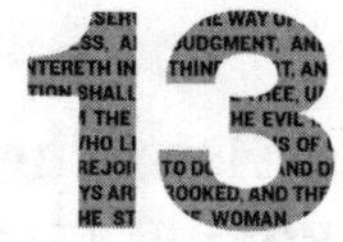

Reproof

> If you turn at my reproof, behold, I will pour out my spirit to you; I will make my words known to you.
>
> —Proverbs 1:23

This past week I had a difficult conversation with a staff member who had just been fired. She's in her early twenties and has so much going for her. She's good-hearted and kind, intelligent and likable. Normally, she would be a great asset to our church. However, she had one fatal flaw that led to her dismissal. She was unteachable. Rather than humbly listening (even if she disagreed), she took the opportunity to "teach" me. She dismissed my forty years of ministry experience and postured as my superior. Twentysomethings often have much to teach their elders, but that's not something a young person should ever want to say out loud to an elder. My reproof fell on deaf ears.

Solomon was right: "A rebuke goes deeper into a man of understanding than a hundred blows into a fool" (Proverbs 17:10). My heart grieves for her because she lost more than her job. She lost a chance to grow in wisdom and love. Solomon warned his own errant son about this: "My son, do not despise the Lord's discipline or be weary of his reproof, for the Lord reproves him whom he loves, as a father the son in whom he delights" (3:11–12).

The Harder It Is to Hear, the More Carefully We Should Listen

Solomon portrayed wisdom as a winsome woman calling to us: "If you turn at my reproof, behold, I will pour out my spirit to you; I will make my words known to you" (Proverbs 1:23). Lady Wisdom promises to pour out her spirit on us if we respond to her reproof. Seen through the lens of the New Testament, this wisdom is none other than the Holy Spirit, poured out by Jesus when we repent (Acts 2:38–39).

Responding well to reproof illuminates the path of life (Proverbs 6:23; 10:17). It brings honor (13:18), prudence (15:5), knowledge (19:25), and wisdom (29:15). We all know this is true, but that doesn't make it any easier to hear hard truths. Nonetheless, teachable people tend to surpass their peers.

Proverbs 15:32 warns, "Whoever ignores instruction despises himself, but he who listens to reproof gains *intelligence.*" This word for "intelligence" isn't cognitive knowledge. It's usually translated as "heart." Heeding rebuke develops the right heart in us.

Rejecting rebuke puts up barriers and creates animosity toward the person who's trying to help us: "Whoever corrects a scoffer gets himself abuse, and he who reproves a wicked man incurs injury. Do not reprove a scoffer, or he will hate you; reprove a wise man, and he will love you" (Proverbs 9:7–8).

Fools spurn the person trying to help them. We have a modern proverb: "Don't bite the hand that feeds you." Anyone who risks rejection to help us improve should receive our praise, not our incisors. For "better is open rebuke than hidden love" (Proverbs 27:5). Or as Solomon said in his sunset years, "It is better for a man to hear the rebuke of the wise than to hear the song of fools" (Ecclesiastes 7:5). Solomon's father, David, sang a song about this: "Let a righteous man strike me—it is a kindness; let him rebuke me—it is oil for my head; let my head not refuse it" (Psalm 141:5).

This is so serious that Lady Wisdom reserves what is perhaps her harshest rebuke for the fool who refuses to listen: "Because I have called and you refused to listen, have stretched out my hand and no one has heeded, because you have ignored all my counsel and would have none of my reproof, I also will laugh at your calamity; I will mock when terror strikes you" (Proverbs 1:24–26). To put it more bluntly, "He who hates reproof is stupid" (12:1).

The Harder It Is to Say, the More We Need to Say It

Few excel at having hard conversations. We know Solomon was right when he wrote that fools often reject the one who rebukes them. Solomon also said it's worth the risk: "Whoever rebukes a man will afterward find more favor than he who flatters with his tongue" (Proverbs 28:23). Rebuke is even compared to riches: "Like a gold ring or an ornament of gold is a wise reprover to a listening ear" (25:12).

Jesus commands us to rebuke an erring brother (Luke 17:3). Paul followed suit with his protégé Timothy: "As for those who persist in sin, rebuke them in the presence of all, so that the rest may stand in fear" (1 Timothy 5:20). This is an essential mandate for anyone who teaches Scripture (2 Timothy 3:16; 4:2; Titus 1:9, 13; 2:15). One can't correctly teach the Bible without including rebuke.

There is no love without rebuke. The problem is, many of us love to be liked. Yet you can't truly love someone if you won't rebuke them. In fact, Jesus rebuked more than anyone else in the Bible. If you want to be like him, rebuke isn't optional. What is most telling is *who* Jesus rebuked. The disciples were his primary target (Mark 16:14; Luke 9:55). For sure, he criticized the Pharisees, Sadducees, and teachers of the law. But the word *rebuke* is reserved for Jesus's closest followers. He reflects his Father in heaven, who tends to reserve his rebuke for those he put in positions of power (2 Samuel

7:13–14; Psalms 6:1; 38:1; 105:14; Zechariah 3:2). This sets a precedent for whom we should rebuke. Don't rebuke strangers. Reserve your rebuke for those you've invested in.

Here are some helpful guidelines for rebuke that will vastly increase the probability of a positive response:

1. You must earn the right to rebuke through significant investment. Don't rebuke people you haven't invested in nor those you're unwilling to invest in.
2. Telegraph the conversation. Through a text, call, or passing mention, say, "There is something I need to say to you." That simple comment will keep you from putting off this important conversation and help them emotionally prepare for it.
3. Start the conversation by saying, "This will be difficult for me to say and hard for you to hear." You might even apologize up front for fumbling through a difficult conversation and end with "I care more about you than us. So, I'm willing to risk our relationship so you can hear this truth."
4. Be as brief as possible. Focus on their behavior, not their intentions, and avoid *always* and *never* since neither is likely true.

We often put off a rebuke because we wonder if it's worth the risk. However, ask yourself, "If they repeated this behavior a thousand times, would I say something?" If you say nothing, they probably will repeat that behavior a thousand times. Your rebuke is not simply for past behavior but for future habits.

Wisdom in Action

The hardest part of a difficult conversation is letting it go after it's over. The only immediate way you should follow up is by sending a text within the hour, thanking them for listening and assuring them of your care. Don't chase after them to clarify. Don't add commentary or examples. Don't apologize for hurting their feelings. And don't judge their response in the first seventy-two hours. Rebuke is so rare that some people don't know how to take it. Moreover, some take longer than others to adjust to what they have heard or to wrestle it to the ground. My daughter was strong-willed (and still is). She seldom responded well to rebuke on the first day. She always responded well after three days. Give this person you love time and space to respond well. Their response isn't your responsibility; the hard truth is.

LINETH UNTO DEATH, AND HER PATHS UNTO THE DEAD. NONE THAT GO UNT
URN AGAIN, NEITHER TAKE THEY HOLD OF THE PATHS OF LIFE. THAT

This Week

- ☐ **Day 1:** Read this essay.
- ☐ **Day 2:** Memorize Proverbs 1:23.
- ☐ **Day 3:** Read the biography of Peter (John 21) and find one thing to apply or avoid.
- ☐ **Day 4:** Meditate on 1 Timothy 5:20; Hebrews 12:5–6; Revelation 3:19.
- ☐ **Day 5:** Discuss.

Group Discussion

1. How would you rate yourself on both giving and receiving constructive criticism on a scale of 1–10?
2. How do you tend to respond to reproof: immediately, after an hour, after two or three days? What mental or emotional process do you go through?
3. How can we discern between loving reproof and a critical spirit?
4. Using the guidelines above, what is the most important change you need to make the next time you offer a rebuke?

Table Talk (in your home)

We are going to speak straight in this house. What ground rules should we set to minimize hurt feelings when we do? [These can be rules particular to individuals to fit their personalities.]

Watercooler (at work or the gym)

Do you think you're good at giving and receiving constructive criticism?

DOM FOR THE RIGHTEOUS: HE IS A BUCKLER TO THEM THAT WALK UPRIGH
PETH THE PATHS OF JUDGMENT, AND PRESERVETH THE WAY OF HIS SAINTS

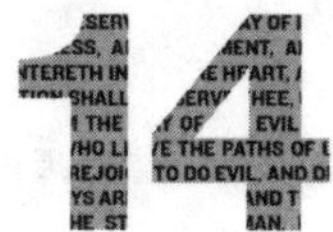

Encouragement

Gracious words are like a honeycomb, sweetness to the soul and health to the body.

—Proverbs 16:24

About a decade ago, I experienced a dark night of the soul. In the shadow of my own self-pity, I felt unappreciated at work (which tells you more about me than about the people I worked with). I'm kind of embarrassed to admit this, but I started writing notes of encouragement to people at work *so they would like me more.* You can criticize me, but it worked. It will work for you too. Perhaps you will have nobler motives than I, but here's a bit of wisdom for you: Positive action with imperfect motives is nobler than no action.

Back to the notes. What stunned me was how many people replied, "How did you know I needed that at this specific time?" I'm not that insightful. Most people desperately need encouragement most of the time. This small gesture of encouragement had a disproportionate upside for the meager effort it required. I've been writing notes ever since. Ten notes per week takes about thirty minutes. I can't think of anything else I do in a half hour every week that has more of an impact. In case you're wondering, my motives are far better these days (though still imperfect).

Words Create Worlds

God spoke this world into existence. That's how the Bible begins. God said, "Let there be light" (Genesis 1:3), and *boom!* There was light, then water, land, plants, solar systems, and animals. From the subatomic to the galactic, God's words created worlds. So do yours. Your words are more than symbols or emotions, more than logic or propositions. They become works of art such as plays, novels, and poems. They make pursuits as varied as business, education, and coaching possible. They broker the most important realities of romance, ethics, and faith.

Words are far more powerful than we imagine. Consider this: God the Son, before he was Jesus, existed with God the Father as the Logos (John 1:1–3). That is the Greek word for "word." Colossians 1:16 declares, "By him all things were created, in heaven and on earth, visible and invisible, whether thrones or dominions or rulers or authorities—all things were created through him and for him."

This means that when God spoke the world into existence in Genesis 1, it was Jesus, the Logos, who enacted his orders. Is it possible that our words have a similar effect? I'm not saying that we order Jesus around or that he jumps at our command as he did for his Father. But if we pray in faith, our requests are given a yes according to his will. Is it such a stretch that when we speak, the Spirit moves into action to empower our words and accomplish God's will in the world?

Even apart from prayer, our words have spiritual power to create or destroy, to build up or tear down. Language is a spiritual power God gave only to humans (and angels). Our daily conversations may not feel spiritual to us, because we use words so routinely. Words are so routine, in fact, that we rarely stop to wonder at what they create. Our words are responsible not only for business, literature, sermons, songs, and romance but also for the comfort and identity of those we love most. Their ubiquity doesn't diminish their power. Language has the power to heal, direct, correct, reveal, and save. And words cost you nothing.

Proverbs speaks of *encouragement* as being endowed with spiritual power. Consider the good a good word can do. It can bring health to the body: "Gracious words are like a honeycomb, sweetness to the soul and health to the body" (16:24). A good word can bring joy to a troubled soul: "Anxiety in a man's heart weighs him down, but a good word makes him glad" (12:25). With this kind of power, we should carefully consider how to leverage language to God's glory.

How to Use Words to Create Worlds

Encouragement is a skill that can be learned. It comes more naturally to some than others. You may be a person who doles out compliments like a little girl gives giggles. Or perhaps you hold your acclamations like classified documents. Regardless, all of us can be trained to implement encouragement to greater effect. Here's a starting kit for encouragement.

Time it right. "To make an apt answer is a joy to a man, and a word in season, how good it is!" (Proverbs 15:23). Some times are more strategic than others. You've probably been coached to criticize in private and praise in public. This is most important with your boss, spouse, and kids. There are seasons when people require extra love or patience—puberty, grief, or sickness, for example. If a friend gets divorced, is fired, or loses a child, the right word at this time will go further and last longer. When a family member gets diagnosed, has an accident, or moves away, a timely word of encouragement is "like cold water to a thirsty soul" (Proverbs 25:25). Timing matters.

Make it specific. Malcolm Gladwell did a fascinating podcast on which genre of music is sadder—country or rock. He found that country was sadder by far. Why? Because it's more specific. Rock stars come from all over the globe; country singers hail primarily from the South. Some come from other places, of course, but the geographic similarities of the majority make their lyrics far more specific.[1] When you can write a whole song around a red Solo cup, that's tangible!

Greater specificity makes songs sadder. It also makes encouragement brighter. Rather than vague phrases such as "I appreciate you more than you know," name a specific quality you've observed: "You are insightful / a team builder / self-aware / sensitive / organized / detailed / etc." Then express how it makes you feel or what effect it has on others. These specific descriptors add power to your encouragement.

Recognize your role. Virtually all the encouragement in the Old Testament is top down. It comes from an older leader encouraging a younger leader (Deuteronomy 1:38; 3:28) or the king encouraging his people (David, 2 Samuel 11:25; Hezekiah, 2 Chronicles 30:22; Josiah, 2 Chronicles 35:2). This doesn't mean that we can't encourage people around us or above us. What it does suggest, however, is that encouragement given to those under our authority will have a deeper and longer-lasting impact. This truth is easy for people to overlook when they encourage someone they are hoping to get something out of. Encouragement that moves downward tends to be more altruistic than encouragement we push upward to bosses, coaches, teachers, or parents.

Wisdom in Action

In the book of Acts, we meet a man named Joseph, whose nickname was Barnabas, "son of encouragement." He is associated with five of the ten verses in Acts that speak about encouragement.

We learn from Barnabas that people sometimes need more than encouraging words. They need an advocate—someone to stand up for them. He stood up for Saul of Tarsus by introducing him to the apostles when everyone else avoided him (9:26–27). You can't really blame them. Saul had overseen the execution of Christian leaders, leaving widows and orphans in his wake. The church must have been livid with Barnabas for standing by Paul.

Barnabas did more than stand by Paul; he included him in his ministry in Antioch and took him on his first evangelistic tour (11:22–26; 13:1–14:28). Later, he clashed with Paul in order to stand up for John Mark, whom Paul had rejected (15:36–41). Barnabas wouldn't back down from defending one beaten down. Being an encourager isn't for the faint of heart. You may need to stand by those who can't stand up for themselves. Often our words become actions, accelerating the creation of a new world.

LINETH UNTO DEATH, AND HER PATHS UNTO THE DEAD. NONE THAT GO UNT
URN AGAIN, NEITHER TAKE THEY HOLD OF THE PATHS OF LIFE. THAT
EST WALK IN THE WAY OF GOOD MEN, AND KEEP THE PATHS OF THE RIGHT

This Week

- ☐ **Day 1:** Read this essay.
- ☐ **Day 2:** Memorize Proverbs 16:24.
- ☐ **Day 3:** Read the biography of Barnabas (Acts 4:32–37; 9:26–31; 11:19–30; 12:25–13:3; 15:36–41) and find one thing to apply.
- ☐ **Day 4:** Meditate on 2 Corinthians 1:3–4; Philippians 2:1–2; 1 Thessalonians 5:11.
- ☐ **Day 5:** Discuss.

Group Discussion

1. When has timely encouragement had a significant impact on you?
2. If specificity is important for impact, what are some specific words that would most encourage you?
3. What is one practical way you could stand up for one person who can't stand up for themselves?
4. How can your small group encourage one another consistently?

Table Talk (in your home)

In one week, we will go out for ice cream if every person here today can write one encouraging thing about every other person at the table by then. Here's an erasable marker to write on a window. No one is allowed to write anything until tomorrow.

Watercooler (at work or the gym)

Has someone encouraged you recently in a way that really stuck with you?

MOUTH COMETH KNOWLEDGE AND UNDERSTANDING. HE LAYETH UP
DOM FOR THE RIGHTEOUS: HE IS A BUCKLER TO THEM THAT WALK UPRIGH
PETH THE PATHS OF JUDGMENT, AND PRESERVETH THE WAY OF HIS SAINTS

PART 3

Relationships

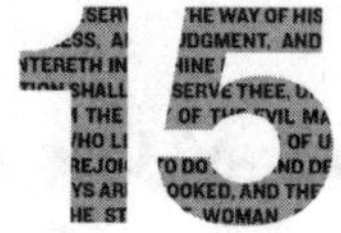

Parents

Hear, my son, your father's instruction, and forsake not your mother's teaching.

—Proverbs 1:8

I was born in 1963, a time when intact families were, by far, the majority. Only 9 percent of kids lived in single-parent homes. By the time my parents divorced in 1975, that number had risen to 17 percent. Today it has climbed to 25 percent. That means one in four kids are from single-parent homes.[1]

Between 2009 and 2021, major depressive episodes in adolescence rose from 8.1 percent to 20.1 percent.[2] Opioid overdoses rose from 21,089 in 2010 to 79,358 in 2023.[3] Medical referrals for gender dysphoria has exploded. For example, in the UK, child and adolescent referrals for gender dysphoria were less than 200 in 2010 but reached 5,000 in 2022.[4] Obviously, there are complicated social factors at play, but one thing is clear: The nuclear family is in trouble. This isn't merely an issue of defending traditional values. The family always has been (and always will be) the foundational institution of society. We can express frustration with political leaders, complain about corrupt systems, and argue for equity all we want. But if we don't deal with the breakdown of the family, there will be no hope for society. We must get this one right.

It's a Matter of Life and Death

An old parental proverb says, "I brought you into this world, and I can take you out of it." This obvious exaggeration is the opposite of what Proverbs states. Discipline doesn't take a child out of this world but preserves their life in it. Solomon's version is in Proverbs 4:10: "Hear, my son, and accept my words, that the years of your life may be many." The same idea is embedded in the Ten Commandments: "Honor your father and your mother, that your days may be long in the land that the LORD your God is giving you" (Exodus 20:12; Deuteronomy 5:16; see also Ephesians 6:1–4). In other words, it's a big deal. The long-term benefits of discipline are immense, ensuring a healthy and fulfilling life for a child.

The simple advice of parents to make your bed, brush your teeth, and eat your vegetables turns out to be invaluable advice for longevity. Parents tell you to get your rest, go outside to play, do your homework, and finish your chores. These are the keystone habits for healthy adults. We aren't training children to be good little boys and girls. We are training them to be great men and women.

Our saying "Spare the rod and spoil the child" comes directly from Proverbs. Solomon's original wording is far more urgent: "Whoever spares the rod hates his son, but he who loves him is diligent to discipline him" (13:24). And this: "Do not withhold discipline from a child; if you strike him with a rod, he will not die. If you strike him with the rod, you will save his soul from Sheol" (23:13–14).

Some are uncomfortable with spanking. That's okay. There are other effective ways to discipline. The important thing is not the method of discipline but the boundaries we provide for children. Boundaries help them regulate behavior and emotions. Perhaps most importantly, discipline trains children to delay gratification, which is one of the keys to developing adult grit. Solomon summarized this whole concept in one of his most frequently cited proverbs: "Train up a child in the way he should go; even when he is old he will not depart from it" (22:6).

Discipline is, in fact, evidence of a parent's love. That's why God disciplines us: "It is for discipline that you have to endure. God is treating you as sons. For what son is there whom his father does not discipline?" (Hebrews 12:7). Discipline is more than mere love for a child; it's kindness to the community.

Disobedient children are such a danger to society that the Old Testament ordered them to be executed. That's hard to even hear in our current culture (and one can only assume it was reserved for truly patricidal narcissists). Nonetheless, the command is given multiple times, like in Exodus 21:17: "Whoever curses his father or his mother shall be put to death" (see also Exodus 21:15; Leviticus 20:9; Deuteronomy 21:18–21; Proverbs 20:20). While we would never advocate such a public policy today, neither should we ignore the grave danger of disrespecting parents. It has a direct and detrimental effect on society.

Fathering like the Father

When my wife got pregnant, it was a crisis for me. I didn't know how to be a great dad, and it scared me to death. I didn't think I had it in me, because I didn't know what God had instilled in me. One night shortly after my son, Joshua, was born, my wife went out and his little life was my sole responsibility. I remember laying him on the bed as the moonlight streamed across his face. I was overwhelmed (and I don't use that word lightly) with the love I felt for this human being. It began to erupt from the depths of my soul, and I heard myself say, "I love you." That one utterance seemed minuscule in this avalanche of affection. I said it again . . . and again and again. It just kept rolling off my tongue dozens of times. I knew he couldn't comprehend what I was saying, but it didn't matter. I was saying it involuntarily as it burst forth from my soul. In that moment, I understood in a new way a fraction of the affection the Father in heaven has for me.

This love in me flowed directly from the Father in heaven. I could take no credit for it, but it helped me understand Proverbs 10:1: "A wise son makes a glad father, but a foolish son is a sorrow to his mother." Psalm 127:3–5 adds this: "Behold, children are a heritage from the LORD, the fruit of the womb a reward. Like arrows in the hand of a warrior are the children of one's youth. Blessed is the man who fills his quiver with them! He shall not be put to shame when he speaks with his enemies in the gate."

Our parental instincts flow directly from our Father in heaven. Though God as Father is clearly a theme advanced by Jesus, we do get glimpses of it throughout the Old Testament. For example, when telling David he would have a regal heir perpetually on his throne, God said, "I will be to him a father, and he shall be to me a son. When he commits iniquity, I will discipline him with the rod of men, with the stripes of the sons of men" (2 Samuel 7:14). This very passage is cited in 2 Corinthians 6:18 but with a twist. It isn't a reference to a Jewish king. It's a description of regular Christians. The promise to David is fulfilled in the church. We are royal sons and daughters of the King of kings. Take a breath and let that sink in.

Wisdom in Action

Parenting is the noblest vocation on the planet. It helps parents understand the heart of God, and it prepares children to respond to God's heart. That's partly why the biblical command to obey your parents is the first with a promise: "that it may go well with you and that you may live long in the land" (Ephesians 6:3). It's not merely that obedience to parents is good. Obedience to parents is practice for submitting to God.

The breakdown of the nuclear family is a social tragedy, but it's even worse spiritually because the healthy parent-child relationship trains us to have a right relationship with God. Parents learn to love sacrificially, and children learn to trust implicitly. Both are core characteristics of a Christ follower.

That's why families need to appreciate and practice the sacred duty of turning their home into a temple in which God has ample room to work. Your living room and kitchen table are every bit as holy as any cathedral, for it's in this sacred space that God's greatest work is accomplished. It's here that devotion is demonstrated and faith is fostered.

LINETH UNTO DEATH, AND HER PATHS UNTO THE DEAD. NONE THAT GO UNT
URN AGAIN, NEITHER TAKE THEY HOLD OF THE PATHS OF LIFE. THAT
YEST WALK IN THE WAY OF GOOD MEN, AND KEEP THE PATHS OF THE RIGH

This Week

- ☐ **Day 1:** Read this essay.
- ☐ **Day 2:** Memorize Proverbs 1:8.
- ☐ **Day 3:** Read the biography of Hophni and Phinehas (1 Samuel 2:12–36) and find one thing to avoid.
- ☐ **Day 4:** Meditate on Matthew 10:37; 15:4; Hebrews 12:7–11.
- ☐ **Day 5:** Discuss.

Group Discussion

1. How did your parents discipline you? What techniques did you or would you change with your kids?
2. What are practical ways we can emulate God's discipline in our parenting?
3. What positive impact did your parents have on your life that you hope to pass along to your kids?
4. What are practical ways to instill respect and honor for parents in children, especially in a culture that often promotes independence and self-reliance?

Table Talk (in your home)

What discipline practices in our home could we improve, remove, or replace?

Watercooler (at work or the gym)

What's one piece of advice from your parents that's had a significant impact on you?

MOUTH COMETH KNOWLEDGE AND UNDERSTANDING. HE LAYETH UP
DOM FOR THE RIGHTEOUS: HE IS A BUCKLER TO THEM THAT WALK UPRIGH
PETH THE PATHS OF JUDGMENT, AND PRESERVETH THE WAY OF HIS SAINTS

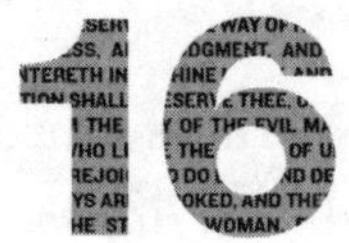

Siblings

A friend loves at all times, and a brother is born for adversity.

—Proverbs 17:17

There is a special bond between siblings and a unique kind of friction. Last night, my grandson Duke spent the night. He is the thermostat of their family. If he is in a bad mood, he will go from person to person, deliberately sending them into hysteria. We were chuckling about this when I asked, "Duke, who is the easiest to irritate?" Without taking a breath, he said, "Jackson," his older brother. Then his younger sister, Lennon, followed by the youngest, Dean. My follow-up question was, "Do you know what sets each one of them off?" Oh yes, he had a strategy for each. Final question: "Why do you enjoy this so much?" He claimed he didn't know, but when I asked, "Does it make you feel powerful?" his sly grin whispered, *Yessss.*

Sibling Rivalry

No one fights like siblings, but God help anyone who gets between them. This is reflected in our key verse: "A friend loves at all times, and a brother is born for adversity" (Proverbs 17:17). Brothers and sisters do *not* "love at all times" (at least in their actions). There are explosive moments on the regular, but they will defend one another to the death.

Given the previous chapter on parenting and the importance of the nuclear family, it's shocking that Scripture has so many negative things to say about siblings. Aside from our key verse, every other proverb about siblings has a bite to it, like this one: "A brother offended is more unyielding than a strong city, and quarreling is like the bars of a castle" (18:19). There are ample illustrations of this throughout Scripture.

It begins with the very first brothers of the Bible, Cain and Abel. Because of sibling rivalry, Cain killed his brother, even after God warned him about his rage. After the murder, God confronted Cain with a question: "Where is Abel your brother?" His famous reply has become a battle cry for parents: "Am I my brother's keeper?" (Genesis 4:9). Yes, you are. Siblings must look out for one another.

The most famous sibling rivalry in Scripture is between Jacob and Esau. It spans a dozen chapters, from Genesis 25 to 36. These twins were adversaries from birth: "Afterward his brother came out with his hand holding Esau's heel, so his name was called Jacob" (25:26). The name Jacob means "he takes by the heel" or "he cheats," which Esau reminded him of when Jacob swindled him out of his birthright and blessing (27:36). Esau had every intention of murdering his brother as Cain had done (27:41).

Joseph, in another well-known example of sibling rivalry, would have been killed by his jealous brothers had it not been for the good sense of Reuben and Judah (Genesis 37:21–27). This narrative covers more than a dozen chapters from Genesis 37 to 50. Could it be that God is trying to tell us something about siblings in the first book of the Bible? A significant portion of it has to do with bad sibling relationships: Cain and Abel, Jacob and Esau, and Joseph and his brothers.

The theme doesn't end in Genesis. David's brother Eliab mocked him on the battlefield before he killed Goliath (1 Samuel 17:28). David's son Absalom killed his older brother Amnon for raping his sister (2 Samuel

13:23–38). David's son Adonijah tried to take the throne before Solomon could be coronated (1 Kings 1:5). That's a lot of bad blood between brothers.

Throughout the Bible, there are only three sets of siblings who are positive examples: Mary, Martha, and Lazarus; James and John; and Peter and Andrew. All of them were close associates of Jesus. Could it be that their tie to Jesus made their own sibling relationships a model of what God had intended all along?

Blood Is *Not* Thicker Than Water

Even Jesus recognized that brothers would be divided over him: "Brother will deliver brother over to death, and the father his child, and children will rise against parents and have them put to death" (Matthew 10:21). After all, his own brothers were his adversaries until after the Resurrection (John 7:1–8). The tension between them manifested early in his ministry. They thought him crazy: "When his family heard it, they went out to seize him, for they were saying, 'He is out of his mind' " (Mark 3:21). The word Mark used for "seize" is the same word he used to describe the soldiers arresting Jesus in Gethsemane (14:46). Clearly, Jesus's siblings had issues with his ministry and were ready to curtail him forcefully.

The problem for Jesus's siblings was that the crowds were so thick they couldn't get into the house where Jesus was teaching. They sent a message to him that they were outside. Normally, that would be an automatic backstage pass. Jesus's response insulted them deeply and established a new definition of *family* for Christians: " 'Who are my mother and my brothers?' And looking about at those who sat around him, he said, 'Here are my mother and my brothers! For whoever does the will of God, he is my brother and sister and mother' " (3:33–35).

This is unquestionably one of the most offensive things Jesus ever said. Denying the primacy of blood ties in Jewish culture was anathema. What

Jesus suggested, however, was not the degradation of family ties but the exaltation of spiritual ties.

When our primary commitment is to our Father in heaven, then his children on earth take precedence over our own bloodlines. This commitment comes with a promise: "Everyone who has left houses or brothers or sisters or father or mother or children or lands, for my name's sake, will receive a hundredfold and will inherit eternal life" (Matthew 19:29).

I can testify to the truth of Jesus's promise. My family is divided exactly as Jesus predicted: "two against three" (Luke 12:52). My father and I both believe; my mother and brothers do not. At eighteen, I moved halfway across the country to pursue my calling to ministry. Our family relationships have been thin and strained ever since. It saddens me that my faith has caused a disconnect and sometimes significant tension. Yet I can testify to the promise of God in that I have thousands of Christian brothers and sisters who are closer to me than my kin. There are to be no orphans in the kingdom of God.

Proverbs contains a promise that points to Jesus: "A man of many companions may come to ruin, but there is a friend who sticks closer than a brother" (18:24). Jesus is that friend. He doesn't fight with you; he fights for you.

Wisdom in Action

Though a Christian's priority is the family of God, taking care of our biological family is a spiritual mandate. Paul couldn't have been clearer: "If anyone does not provide for his relatives, and especially for members of his household, he has denied the faith and is worse than an unbeliever" (1 Timothy 5:8). Even while he was hanging on the cross, Jesus commissioned one of his disciples to look after his mother (John 19:26–27).

Jesus also cared for his biological (half) brother James by appearing to him after the Resurrection. James became a believer and a key leader of the

Jerusalem church. Both James and Jude wound up writing a book that became part of the Bible. Jesus modeled how important it is to care for your biological family.

If we are to represent him well, we must do the same. This includes at least the following: encouraging siblings' healthy pursuits, sharing the gospel, including them in family events, and working with them to protect aging parents. Your relationships with your siblings will be some of the most challenging in your life. Your best hope is when you share the hope of Jesus.

LINETH UNTO DEATH, AND HER PATHS UNTO THE DEAD. NONE THAT GO UNT
URN AGAIN, NEITHER TAKE THEY HOLD OF THE PATHS OF LIFE. THAT
/EST WALK IN THE WAY OF GOOD MEN, AND KEEP THE PATHS OF THE RIGH

This Week

- ☐ **Day 1:** Read this essay.
- ☐ **Day 2:** Memorize Proverbs 17:17.
- ☐ **Day 3:** Read the biography of Jacob and Esau (Genesis 27) and find one thing to apply or avoid.
- ☐ **Day 4:** Meditate on Matthew 12:50; 1 Timothy 5:8; 1 John 3:12.
- ☐ **Day 5:** Discuss.

Group Discussion

1. How have you experienced sibling rivalry?
2. How has your spiritual family (church community) provided support and companionship in ways your biological family wasn't able to? Share specific examples.
3. What wisdom could you share with the group on managing difficult family members, particularly those who don't believe in Jesus?
4. What does it mean to you that Jesus is closer than a brother?

Table Talk (in your home)

What are some strategies we can use to promote harmony among siblings?

Watercooler (at work or the gym)

How do you deal with tensions with siblings?

MOUTH COMETH KNOWLEDGE AND UNDERSTANDING. HE LAYETH UP
DOM FOR THE RIGHTEOUS: HE IS A BUCKLER TO THEM THAT WALK UPRIGH
PETH THE PATHS OF JUDGMENT, AND PRESERVETH THE WAY OF HIS SAINTS

17

Spouses

He who finds a wife finds a good thing and obtains favor from the LORD.

—PROVERBS 18:22

According to the latest statistics, 45 percent of U.S. adults are married.[1] That's a huge drop from 72 percent in 1960.[2] For the first time in U.S. history, more adults are single than married. Clearly, marriage is struggling. We saw in the last decade the redefinition of marriage to include same-sex partners. Regardless of one's stance on same-sex partners, this redefinition represents a stunning shift since no culture at any time in history has defined marriage as anything other than the lifelong commitment of a heterosexual couple. If the family is the bedrock of society, we had better tread carefully on such sacred soil.

Same-sex coupling, co-habitation, and divorce are significant challenges for traditional family values. Currently, approximately 41 percent of first marriages end in divorce. Subsequent marriages fare far worse. Some estimate 67 percent of second marriages and 73 percent of third marriages also end in divorce.[3]

The consequences of divorce extend to children and society. In a 1990s study, children from divorced families are twice as likely to repeat a grade and five times as likely to be suspended or expelled.[4] This says nothing of the economic impact of divorce. On average, divorced individuals experience a 77 percent decrease in wealth.[5] Divorce is costly because of legal fees, division of assets, and alimony. Then there is the cost of setting up and maintaining a new household (utilities, rent, furnishings) and the toll of time and travel for child visitation, to say nothing of the spiritual costs. We desperately need God's wisdom when it comes to relationships.

For Better, For Worse

While marriage is a good thing, it can also be turbulent. Solomon, with his seven hundred wives and three hundred concubines, spoke from experience. Perhaps that's why he has such a negative description of the adulteress in chapters 5 and 7. King Lemuel's mother, however, has much higher praise for a godly wife in Proverbs 31. These chapters contrast two very different types of women, and each deserves a careful look.

The Wonderful Wife

- "He who finds a wife finds a good thing and obtains favor from the LORD" (18:22).
- "Let your fountain be blessed, and rejoice in the wife of your youth, a lovely deer, a graceful doe" (5:18–19).
- "An excellent wife who can find? She is far more precious than jewels. The heart of her husband trusts in her, and he will have no lack of gain. She does him good, and not harm, all the days of her life" (31:10–12).

The Bad Bride

- "A wife's quarreling is a continual dripping of rain" (19:13; see also 27:15–16).

- “It is better to live in a corner of the housetop than in a house shared with a quarrelsome wife” (21:9; 25:24).
- “It is better to live in a desert land than with a quarrelsome and fretful woman” (21:19).

Solomon was a man talking to his son in a society where women were considered more as property than persons. We should recognize, therefore, that men are at least as culpable for bad marriages as women.

God was more positive about wives than Solomon. Even before God created one, he said, “It is not good that the man should be alone; I will make him a helper fit for him” (Genesis 2:18). A few short verses later, we read, “Therefore a man shall leave his father and his mother and hold fast to his wife, and they shall become one flesh” (verse 24). Jesus himself cited this very passage as the model for marriage (Mark 10:7), as did Paul twice (1 Corinthians 6:16; Ephesians 5:31).

No one who has been married for more than three days would deny its difficulty. Yet few married for more than a decade would deny its beauty. My wife and I recently celebrated our fortieth anniversary by taking our adult children to Ireland. It was magnificent. The food, the scenery, and the music were all grand. Yet it was the conversations and the connections that were most significant. And then there are the grandchildren. . . . My cup overflows!

What we’ve discovered after decades of marriage is this: At some point, you can’t remember life without your spouse. It’s then that you begin to remember forward—becoming familiar with things that haven’t yet happened. I already imagine, as if it’s a memory, sitting in our courtyard next to my bride, with walkers next to us, having a mundane conversation we’ve had ten thousand times before and finding as much joy in it as on our honeymoon. It’s not the words of the conversation but the comfort, trust, and gratitude that are as evident in the silence as in the words.

Marriage in the New Testament

Rodney Stark, in *The Rise of Christianity,* discussed Christian marriage as one of the causes for the stunning growth of the early church.[6] The way Christian husbands treated their wives was so different. They weren't property like their Jewish counterparts (which was better still than the treatment of women in their surrounding cultures). Several factors contributed to this transformation of marriage.

First, Christian wives were sisters in Christ. Women now had access to God (through Jesus), independently of their fathers or husbands. This liberation elevated them as co-heirs in Christ. Second, all Christians were called to serve sacrificially. Because humility was highlighted as a virtue, husbands of humility were honored in the church. Third, the Christian community shifted their meetings from synagogues (or forums for Romans) to private homes where women had a voice.

The discussion of marriage in Proverbs is male oriented. In the New Testament, however, all the household codes are bilateral, giving equal voice to men's obligations as husbands and fathers (Ephesians 5:21–6:9; Colossians 3:18–4:1; Titus 2:1–10; 1 Peter 2:18–3:7).

Why this equal emphasis on men and women in the New Testament versus the Old Testament? Because marriage is a spiritual metaphor for Christ and his church. This is overt in Ephesians 5:32–33: "This mystery is profound, and I am saying that it refers to Christ and the church. However, let each one of you love his wife as himself, and let the wife see that she respects her husband." Our marriages model for the world the kind of relationship Jesus wants to have with the church. In this sense, every marriage is a sermon either promoting or denying Jesus. That makes our marriages more important than we've imagined.

As surprising as that sounds, it's nothing new. God called Hosea to marry a faithless woman as a living metaphor for what Israel was doing to him (Hosea 1:2). Likewise, Ezekiel 16 uses the extended (and horrid) metaphor of Israel being a faithless bride to Yahweh. God didn't just see Israel as a child to be cared for; he saw her as a bride to partner with. The church is the bride of Christ. His love for us is as robust and binding as a marriage contract. Marriages have the divine privilege and responsibility of modeling Christ's love on earth.

Wisdom in Action

Marriage isn't merely for your personal pleasure. It's more than the security of your family. It goes beyond the foundation of society. It's all those things, but mostly, marriage models Christ and his church. It's an image of the most profound sacrifice on earth and the highest love in the heavens.

Marriage is hard, but it's worth fighting for. *Yours* is worth fighting for. There are mountains of books and throngs of counselors that could be helpful to the success of your marriage. Attending church weekly, praying together daily, and expressing gratitude will safeguard your relationship. Nonetheless, the most helpful marriage advice was given by a single man who said, "Whatever you wish that others would do to you, do also to them" (Matthew 7:12). If you follow this one simple rule, you can protect your marriage and proclaim Christ through it.

LINETH UNTO DEATH, AND HER PATHS UNTO THE DEAD. NONE THAT GO UNT
URN AGAIN, NEITHER TAKE THEY HOLD OF THE PATHS OF LIFE. THAT
EST WALK IN THE WAY OF GOOD MEN, AND KEEP THE PATHS OF THE RIGH

This Week

- ☐ **Day 1:** Read this essay.
- ☐ **Day 2:** Memorize Proverbs 18:22.
- ☐ **Day 3:** Read the biography of Sarah (Genesis 17:15–18:21) and find one thing to apply or avoid.
- ☐ **Day 4:** Meditate on Colossians 3:18–19; Hebrews 13:4; 1 Peter 3:5–6.
- ☐ **Day 5:** Discuss.

Group Discussion

1. What was your model of marriage like growing up?
2. What's the best marriage advice anyone has ever given to you?
3. What's something you wish someone would have told you before you got married?
4. Ephesians 5:32–33 compares marriage to the relationship between Christ and the church. What practical steps can couples take to reflect this spiritual metaphor in their daily lives?

Table Talk (in your home)

What are some things you admire about the marriage in this home? What things do you wish were different?

Watercooler (at work or the gym)

What do you think are the key ingredients to a successful and lasting marriage?

MOUTH COMETH KNOWLEDGE AND UNDERSTANDING. HE LAYETH UP
DOM FOR THE RIGHTEOUS: HE IS A BUCKLER TO THEM THAT WALK UPRIGH
PETH THE PATHS OF JUDGMENT, AND PRESERVETH THE WAY OF HIS SAINTS

18

Friends

Iron sharpens iron, and one man sharpens another.

—Proverbs 27:17

How many Facebook friends do you have? According to research by Dr. Robin Dunbar, we are capable of about 150 social relationships.[1] Friendships, of course, are a smaller circle than all our social relationships. So, whatever those connections are on Facebook (or your go-to brand of social media), they aren't friendships. We all know that.

A person typically has around three to five close friendships, but that number has been in decline in recent decades, especially for men.[2] A 2021 American Perspectives Survey found that 49 percent of Americans have three or fewer close friends and 12 percent have no close friends at all.[3]

As social media leaves us feeling more isolated, the value of true friendship is even greater. Studies consistently show the physical and mental benefits of supportive friendships.[4] According to God's design, friendships aren't optional. Our culture and technology make deep relationships significantly more challenging to develop and maintain. Perhaps we need a bit of wisdom.

Friendships to Foster

A famous modern proverb says, "Show me your friends, and I'll show you your future." It's an undeniable rule that we gravitate to the interests and attitudes of our closest friends. Not all friends are good friends. Here are the friendships we should foster.

Friends who give godly counsel. "Oil and perfume make the heart glad, and the sweetness of a friend comes from his earnest counsel" (Proverbs 27:9). That's why Larrie is my best friend. During a particularly precarious season for me professionally, his wise counsel was life giving. He warned me of land mines I was about to step on. He helped me put my feelings into perspective. He called me out and built me up. A friend like that I will always keep close.

Friends who make you better. "Iron sharpens iron, and one man sharpens another" (Proverbs 27:17). Doug was that man for me in my first ministry in San Antonio. He was older and wiser and took the time to buy me lunch and sharpen me in ministry. We laughed a lot. Sometimes we wept. We prayed for each other, but he mostly poured into me. Over the years, we have done mission work, written books, and mentored college students. I'm a better scholar, pastor, and husband because of my friend Doug.

Friends who sacrifice for you. The most famous friendship in the Bible was between David and Jonathan (1 Samuel 18:1). Jonathan was heir to the throne. Yet he willingly gave that up for David. When Saul, Jonathan's father, wanted to kill David, Jonathan spoke up and stood up for him (19:1–7). Jonathan's self-sacrifice was a key reason David rose to power and prominence. Perhaps it's no coincidence that every leadership mistake David made was after the death of his best friend, Jonathan. It's also no coincidence that Jesus defined friendship as sacrifice: "Greater love has no one than this, that someone lay down his life for his friends" (John 15:13).

I met Stuart in the sixth grade. He was a new kid in our Sacramento school and had just moved from Mississippi. He came with a funny accent the girls found adorable, so naturally, I didn't like him. I couldn't understand why he liked me. Later, he told me why. When he and I got top scores on a math test (I barely beat him), our teacher gave us the choice to be either the crossing guard or the teacher's assistant—two roles coveted by every sixth grader. I learned Stuart wanted to be her assistant, so I took the crossing guard position. I just figured he needed a win as a new kid. We became friends because, in a small way, I acted like Jesus one day when he was a stranger.

Friendships to Avoid

We are easily attracted to people for the wrong reasons. Proverbs identifies two friendships that are particularly dangerous.

My enemy's enemy. People sometimes say, "The enemy of my enemy is my friend." This proverb is a fast track to trouble. Sure, it feels good to get the goods on someone you dislike. But anyone who gossips about your enemy is just as likely to gossip about you. Those who align with you against another will be the first to align against you with another. Don't be gullible: "A dishonest man spreads strife, and a whisperer separates close friends" (Proverbs 16:28).

King David was as good a friend as anyone could hope to have (with the unfortunate exception of Uriah). Yet he had friends abandon him when it benefited them. He wrote a mournful ode about this: "It is not an enemy who taunts me—then I could bear it; it is not an adversary who deals insolently with me—then I could hide from him. But it is you, a man, my equal, my companion, my familiar friend" (Psalm 55:12–13).

David wasn't the only one. The great prophet Jeremiah felt the pain of betrayal by former friends: "I hear many whispering. Terror is on every side! 'Denounce him! Let us denounce him!' say all my close friends, watching for my fall. 'Perhaps he will be deceived; then we can overcome him and take our revenge on him' " (Jeremiah 20:10). No pain cuts as deep as the betrayal of a friend. They know just where to place the knife. That's why your choice of friends is the most important choice you will ever make, other than faith in Jesus Christ.

The wealthy. This isn't to say that wealthy people can't have good friends or be good friends. But when financial gain is the foundation of a friendship, neither party fares well. If you bribe someone for friendship, you become a slave to serve them. "Many seek the favor of a generous man, and everyone is a friend to a man who gives gifts" (Proverbs 19:6). This always comes with a cost, and that cost is often competition. The wealthy have plenty of people at their beck and call. You will find yourself easily replaced by a more powerful person. Whatever is purchased can be discarded. That's as true with friendships as with trinkets. "Wealth brings many new friends, but a poor man is deserted by his friend" (19:4). Solomon had plenty of money, so take his advice: "It is better to be of a lowly spirit with the poor than to divide the spoil with the proud" (16:19).

Job knew this all too well. When his wealth suddenly vanished, the three friends who showed up turned on him. They were brutal in their attacks and relentless in their baseless accusations. Typically, we think of Job as a lesson on suffering, and while it does speak to this, no biblical book speaks more about friendship (see 6:14, 27; 16:20; 17:5; 19:14, 19, 21).

There's a fascinating line in Job about why God rescued him: "The LORD restored the fortunes of Job, *when he had prayed for his friends.* And the LORD gave Job twice as much as he had before" (42:10). Did you catch that? God restored Job's fortunes "*when he had prayed for his friends.*" I'm not saying that was the only cause of Job's restoration. However, there's something telling in this text. Our willingness to pray for the good of our faithless friends puts us in a place to receive God's blessing and friendship.

Wisdom in Action

Who you befriend (this includes your spouse) has more bearing on your life's direction than any other decision. You might ask, "What about my decision to follow God?" That is also a friendship decision. We aren't merely worshipping God or serving him. We are *befriending* him. Abraham was called "a friend of God" (James 2:23; see also 2 Chronicles 20:7; Isaiah 41:8).

It was Jesus, however, who made a way for us to be friends of God. The night before he died, Jesus told his disciples, "You are my friends if you do what I command you. No longer do I call you servants, for the servant does not know what his master is doing; but I have called you friends, for all that I have heard from my Father I have made known to you" (John 15:14–15). Therefore, our friendships on earth should foster our most important friendship with God. If you choose the right friends on earth, they will point to your best Friend in heaven.

LINETH UNTO DEATH, AND HER PATHS UNTO THE DEAD. NONE THAT GO UNT
URN AGAIN, NEITHER TAKE THEY HOLD OF THE PATHS OF LIFE. THAT
EST WALK IN THE WAY OF GOOD MEN, AND KEEP THE PATHS OF THE RIGH

This Week

- ☐ **Day 1:** Read this essay.
- ☐ **Day 2:** Memorize Proverbs 27:17.
- ☐ **Day 3:** Read the biography of Jonathan (1 Samuel 20) and find one thing to apply.
- ☐ **Day 4:** Meditate on Mark 5:19; Luke 7:34; John 15:13.
- ☐ **Day 5:** Discuss.

Group Discussion

1. Who was your best friend growing up, and what made that relationship so special?
2. What criteria do you use to determine if a friendship is beneficial or detrimental?
3. Have you ever had to distance yourself from a friend because the relationship was unhealthy? How did you handle it, and what did you learn from the experience?
4. How can we cultivate a deeper friendship with God in our daily lives?

Table Talk (in your home)

What qualities should we look for in friends, and how can we model these qualities ourselves?

Watercooler (at work or the gym)

What qualities do you look for in a friend?

MOUTH COMETH KNOWLEDGE AND UNDERSTANDING. HE LAYETH UP
DOM FOR THE RIGHTEOUS: HE IS A BUCKLER TO THEM THAT WALK UPRIGH
PETH THE PATHS OF JUDGMENT, AND PRESERVETH THE WAY OF HIS SAINTS

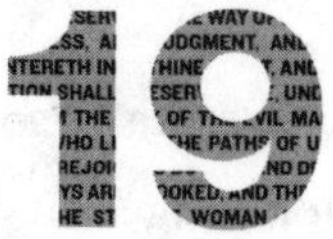

Influencers

Whoever walks with the wise becomes wise, but the companion of fools will suffer harm.

—Proverbs 13:20

If you got onto an elevator and everyone was facing the back wall rather than the door, would you conform to everyone else's odd behavior, or would you face forward like a normal person? This experiment was performed on an episode of *Candid Camera* in 1962.[1] It confirmed psychologist Solomon Asch's earlier research that approximately 75 percent of us will conform to a group even if their declarations are demonstrably false.[2] We're much more vulnerable than we'd like to admit regarding outside influences. In the previous chapter, we talked about the power of good friends. Now we turn to the other side of that coin—the power of negative peer pressure.

Red Flags for Influence

We can't choose *whether* our community will influence us—it will. God hardwired us this way. We can, however, choose who we allow into our circle of influence. Somewhere in the pre-teen years, parents' influence gives way to peers'. For a season, friends loom large on our values and habits. This is good and healthy as young adults learn to make independent decisions. It's necessary, but it can also be dangerous. Parents determine the habits and beliefs of their children up to about age ten. Between ten and sixteen, their friends determine their habits, though parents can still control which friends they spend time with. After kids learn to drive, however, only your previous parenting will prevail on their values. That's why teaching teens to choose their friends wisely is the single most important responsibility of parents during that season.

Solomon knew this. Right after his prologue in Proverbs, he wrote to his son about peer pressure: "My son, if sinners entice you, do not consent" (1:10). Scripture points out several red flags for friendships.

Red Flag 1: Anger. "Make no friendship with a man given to anger, nor go with a wrathful man, lest you learn his ways and entangle yourself in a snare" (22:24–25). Young people are often drawn to the brash and bold. It feels exciting to run with the bulls and bully the weak. Be warned. Boys who can't control their temper often lack a father to control them. Often girls who bully have been bullied.

In Pilanesberg National Park, more than fifty rhinos were killed, but their horns weren't taken. So, this wasn't the work of poachers. The culprits were found upon investigation: a gang of adolescent male elephants. They were killing for sport. These youngsters had been transported to the park to build up the elephant population but had never had a male role model.

The park decided to introduce six big bulls from Kruger National Park. Their presence had an immediate effect. They sparred with the younger males, establishing dominance. The rhino killings stopped immediately.[3] Likewise, young men need father figures to help manage their anger and aggression.

Red Flag 2: Deceit. King David said, "I do not sit with men of falsehood, nor do I consort with hypocrites. I hate the assembly of evildoers, and I will not sit with the wicked" (Psalm 26:4–5). Honesty is the foundation of every human relationship. Where there is deception, there can be no intimacy between lovers, no trust in business, no teamwork in sports, and no alliance between nations. Deception is the camouflage for addiction, the weapon of political corruption, and the tool of swindlers, charlatans, and thieves. "The deceiver" is the nickname of the Antichrist (2 John 7) and the devil (Revelation 12:9). You can't afford a deceptive friend.

As we turn to the New Testament, we find two more categories of people to avoid. What is surprising is that they are both from within the church.

Red Flag 3: Pride. Paul warned the Corinthians, "Your boasting is not good. Do you not know that a little leaven leavens the whole lump?" (1 Corinthians 5:6). The metaphor about leaven was also used by Jesus in the same context of pride: "Watch and beware of the leaven of the Pharisees and Sadducees" (Matthew 16:6). The Jewish religious leaders opposed Jesus because of his popularity. Their desire for power and prominence blinded them. Likewise, the leaders of the Corinthian church opposed Paul because of his influence in the community. A person of pride is easy to identify. They demean others behind their backs and build themselves up to your face. Beware. They aren't your friend; you are their puppet. It may feel good to be in the orbit of the proud and popular, but there is far more to lose than gain from their association.

Red Flag 4: Laziness. The New Testament adds one more category of those we should avoid: "Keep away from any brother who is walking in idleness and not in accord with the tradition that you received from us" (2 Thessalonians 3:6). Don't get sucked into their insignificant vortex. Unless you want your world to shrink to their size, avoid a lazy friend.

Bad Company Ruins Good Morals

First Corinthians 15:33 quotes a proverb: "Bad company ruins good morals." That's not from Solomon. It's a citation from the Greek playwright Menander (*Thais*), who died several hundred years before 1 Corinthians was written (c. 292 B.C.). This is *not* a new idea or even a Christian one. My father observed the same thing. He was a probation officer for most of his career. He noted that all his convicts who changed their friendship circle successfully stayed out of prison. All who didn't went back to prison.

This is difficult to hear, but you may need new friends. I understand your objection: "Didn't Jesus tell us to be salt and light?" Yes, he did (Matthew 5:13–16)! You absolutely should influence those around you. However, your five closest friends will have as great an impact on you as you do on them.

This is also why "missionary dating" is a bad idea. The person you give your heart to has the most influence in your life. God created you to conform to the person with whom you have a romantic attachment. That's why we are told, "Do not be unequally yoked with unbelievers. For what partnership has righteousness with lawlessness? Or what fellowship has light with darkness?" (2 Corinthians 6:14). Even kings are vulnerable to their brides. Ahab was arguably the worst king of the Old Testament. His evil is credited to the influence of his wife: "There was none who sold himself to do what was evil in the sight of the LORD like Ahab, whom Jezebel his wife incited" (1 Kings 21:25).

This was also true of Solomon, the most successful king of Israel: "When Solomon was old his wives turned away his heart after other gods, and his heart was not wholly true to the LORD his God, as was the heart of David his father" (1 Kings 11:4). Of all the people who could negatively influence you, the one you give your heart to is at the top of the list. Who you marry matters.

Wisdom in Action

How can we be salty without being squishy? Social science research has confirmed that people convert to any religious group when the weight of influence in the group is greater than that outside it.[4] So, the math should be simple enough. If you are the average of your five closest friends, make sure at least three are believers. Hang with those whose values and habits align with yours.

LINETH UNTO DEATH, AND HER PATHS UNTO THE DEAD. NONE THAT GO UNT
URN AGAIN, NEITHER TAKE THEY HOLD OF THE PATHS OF LIFE. THAT
/EST WALK IN THE WAY OF GOOD MEN, AND KEEP THE PATHS OF THE RIGH

This Week

- ☐ **Day 1:** Read this essay.
- ☐ **Day 2:** Memorize Proverbs 13:20.
- ☐ **Day 3:** Read the biography of Amnon (2 Samuel 13:1–22) and find one thing to avoid.
- ☐ **Day 4:** Meditate on Matthew 5:13–16; Romans 12:2; 1 Corinthians 15:33.
- ☐ **Day 5:** Discuss.

Group Discussion

1. How have you seen negative influences shape your life, whether currently or in a past season?
2. How do you balance positively influencing others and protecting yourself from negative influences?
3. Which of the four red flags for friendships resonates with you the most? What other red flags have you had to look out for?
4. Is there anyone in your circle you need to influence more? Is there anyone you need to allow less influence over you?

Table Talk (in your home)

Which friend has the most influence on your behavior and attitude?

Watercooler (at work or the gym)

What red flag would make you cautious about befriending someone?

MOUTH COMETH KNOWLEDGE AND UNDERSTANDING. HE LAYETH UP
DOM FOR THE RIGHTEOUS: HE IS A BUCKLER TO THEM THAT WALK UPRIGH
PETH THE PATHS OF JUDGMENT, AND PRESERVETH THE WAY OF HIS SAINTS

20

Neighbors

Do not plan evil against your neighbor, who dwells trustingly beside you.

—Proverbs 3:29

If you have a neighbor, then you have likely had some awkward encounters. It could be a barking dog, a teenager learning to drive, loud late-night parties, gaudy Christmas decorations, or unkept lawns. Let's play a game. I'll share with you a real-life encounter. You guess who was at fault—me or a neighbor.

1. We have block walls separating our backyards. Since our neighborhood is on a hill, the uphill neighbor could overwater without knowing it, causing the lower bricks of the block wall to rot out. That is an expensive repair.
2. If you park your car in the driveway, and your bedroom is in the back of the house, it's entirely possible that your car alarm could go off in the middle of the night, waking up your neighbors while you never hear it.
3. After a particularly violent windstorm, a full-grown oak tree made a visit to a neighbor's kitchen, creating a gaping hole in the

roof. It's then that we learned that a fallen tree belongs to the property owner where it fell, not where it grew. Who knew?

Answers: (1) My neighbor overwatered; (2) my wife's car alarm was broken and kept going off; (3) my giant oak tree fell through my neighbor's kitchen.

The Bible has abundant advice about being a good neighbor. This is my favorite: "Whoever blesses his neighbor with a loud voice, rising early in the morning, will be counted as cursing" (Proverbs 27:14). We will focus on the two most prominent attributes of being a good neighbor.

Respect Your Neighbor's Property

Have you ever borrowed a tool from a neighbor and it broke while you were using it? It's embarrassing and problematic. Maybe you misused the tool unintentionally, and it's your fault, or maybe you didn't, and he loaned you a piece of junk. Either way, it's awkward. If you pay for the tool, you lose the money you were trying to save and you both feel uncomfortable. If you don't pay for it, you feel guilty and your neighbor may resent you. Did you know the Bible addresses this issue? Exodus 22:14–15: "If a man borrows anything of his neighbor, and it is injured or dies, the owner not being with it, he shall make full restitution. If the owner was with it, he shall not make restitution; if it was hired, it came for its hiring fee." That's very specific.

Exodus 22 addresses various disagreements between neighbors. What happens if your animal grazes in another's field (verse 5) or a brush fire you started to clear thorns winds up destroying your neighbor's crop (verse 6)? Who is responsible if your neighbor gives you something for safekeeping and it's stolen from your house (verses 7–8) or if there is a dispute over who owns something you both say is yours (verse 9)? If an animal you're watching for a neighbor dies, who pays for it (verses 10–13)? The complexity of living with neighbors is nothing new.

Solomon's best advice is to deal with the issue sooner rather than later. The sooner you hash it out, the less likely it will escalate. Solomon said, "My son, if you have put up security for your neighbor, have given your pledge for a stranger, if you are snared in the words of your mouth, caught in the words of your mouth, then do this, my son, and save yourself, for you have come into the hand of your neighbor: go, hasten, and plead urgently with your neighbor" (Proverbs 6:1–3). Be hasty and humble when resolving an issue.

Jesus repeated Solomon's advice in the Sermon on the Mount: "Come to terms quickly with your accuser while you are going with him to court, lest your accuser hand you over to the judge, and the judge to the guard, and you be put in prison" (Matthew 5:25). You may think you have a legitimate claim. Everyone who goes to court is convinced they are right. But there are always two sides to the story, and at least 50 percent are wrong. Your case may blow up in your face. "What your eyes have seen do not hastily bring into court, for what will you do in the end, when your neighbor puts you to shame? Argue your case with your neighbor himself, and do not reveal another's secret" (Proverbs 25:7–9). Dealing generously with your neighbor's property is important because more than money is at stake. Your integrity is more valuable than your bank account.

Protect Your Neighbor's Reputation

Solomon's second most important piece of advice: Don't lie about your neighbor. What you whisper in your backyard has a way of reaching their front door. "Be not a witness against your neighbor without cause, and do not deceive with your lips" (Proverbs 24:28). This is one of the Ten Commandments: "You shall not bear false witness against your neighbor" (Exodus 20:16).

God promised to punish those who violate this rule: "Whoever slanders his neighbor secretly I will destroy" (Psalm 101:5). Why is this such a big deal? Because communities are built on trust. When trust is broken, societies shatter.

Most slander is rooted in financial gain. That's why the rules against slander are not merely to promote personal morality but to protect the poor. It's critical for neighbors to care for the most vulnerable in their communities. Leviticus 19:13 addresses this directly: "You shall not oppress your neighbor or rob him. The wages of a hired worker shall not remain with you all night until the morning." Solomon recognized the sad reality that the poor are easy to disregard: "The poor is disliked even by his neighbor, but the rich has many friends. Whoever despises his neighbor is a sinner, but blessed is he who is generous to the poor" (Proverbs 14:20–21). For the good of the community and the pleasure of God, be the first to look out for those most overlooked.

Whether our neighbor is well off or struggling, our responsibility comes down to one simple rule: "You shall love your neighbor as yourself" (Leviticus 19:18). This principle from the Old Testament is repeated multiple times in the New Testament, starting with Jesus. He summarized all the law in two commands: Love God and love your neighbor (Matthew 22:37–40; see also 19:19). The apostle Paul followed suit: "Love does no wrong to a neighbor; therefore love is the fulfilling of the law" (Romans 13:10; see also Galatians 5:14). James called it "the royal law": "If you really fulfill the royal law according to the Scripture, 'You shall love your neighbor as yourself,' you are doing well" (James 2:8).

Wisdom in Action

Loving your neighbor is a big deal, but it's not always easy, and Jesus didn't make it any easier. In fact, he made it much harder. First, in the Sermon on the Mount, Jesus extended the command to include our enemies: "You have heard that it was said, 'You shall love your neighbor and hate your enemy.' But I say to you, Love your enemies and pray for those who persecute you"

(Matthew 5:43–44). When he spoke these words, Roman soldiers occupied Jewish lands. If Jesus said to love *them,* then a rude, inconvenient neighbor isn't beyond the pale.

Second, Jesus redefined *neighbor* in his famous parable of the good Samaritan (Luke 10:25–37). Your neighbor is not merely someone who lives near you but anyone in physical proximity to you. Wherever you go, if you can reach out your hand and touch someone, regardless of where they reside, they are your neighbor. They may not look like you, but if they are near you, they are your neighbor and deserve your love.

LINETH UNTO DEATH, AND HER PATHS UNTO THE DEAD. NONE THAT GO UNT
URN AGAIN, NEITHER TAKE THEY HOLD OF THE PATHS OF LIFE. THAT
EST WALK IN THE WAY OF GOOD MEN, AND KEEP THE PATHS OF THE RIGH

This Week

- ☐ **Day 1:** Read this essay.
- ☐ **Day 2:** Memorize Proverbs 3:29.
- ☐ **Day 3:** Read about the good Samaritan (Luke 10:25–37) and find one thing to apply or avoid.
- ☐ **Day 4:** Meditate on Romans 13:9; Galatians 5:14; James 2:8.
- ☐ **Day 5:** Discuss.

Group Discussion

1. Have you ever had a problem with a neighbor? How did you handle it, and what did you learn from it?
2. What advice would you give a friend about settling issues with a neighbor?
3. What could you do this week to love a difficult person as you love yourself?
4. How can you contribute to building and maintaining trust among your neighbors, to make your community safer and more enjoyable?

Table Talk (in your home)

Who is your favorite and least favorite neighbor? Why?

Watercooler (at work or the gym)

What community programs serving the disadvantaged would you promote?

MOUTH COMETH KNOWLEDGE AND UNDERSTANDING. HE LAYETH UP
DOM FOR THE RIGHTEOUS: HE IS A BUCKLER TO THEM THAT WALK UPRIGH
PETH THE PATHS OF JUDGMENT, AND PRESERVETH THE WAY OF HIS SAINTS

21

Enemies

When a man's ways please the LORD, he makes even his enemies to be at peace with him.

—PROVERBS 16:7

On July 16, 2012, Baptist Press published an interview that included a statement defending the traditional biblical values for family.[1] There is nothing surprising about that. Yet it created a firestorm because the statement came from Dan Cathy, then the president and COO of Chick-fil-A. The fast-food chain faced immediate backlash from the LGBTQ community through a boycott and protests.

Dan Cathy, a committed Christian, chose an unexpected path. Instead of retreating into the safety of like-minded supporters or responding defensively, he reached out to Shane Windmeyer, the founder of Campus Pride and a leading advocate for LGBTQ rights. This move was not a strategic public relations effort but a sincere attempt to understand and engage with those who opposed his views.

Their initial conversations were tense, colored by years of hurt and misunderstanding. Over time, however, a profound transformation occurred as they continued to talk. Cathy listened to Windmeyer's experiences and concerns, gaining a deeper understanding of the challenges faced by the LGBTQ community. Windmeyer, in turn, learned about Cathy's values and the motivations behind his faith.

This unlikely friendship culminated in a public expression when Cathy invited Windmeyer to be his guest at a Chick-fil-A Bowl game. Though neither changed their views, they did build a bridge.[2] Their journey from enmity to empathy models how a man of peace can turn enemies into associates.

How to Turn Enemies into Allies

Proverbs 16:7 seems a bit out of reach and perhaps out of touch. Can we realistically expect our enemies to become friends? Yes, we can. Both Solomon and Jesus believed that you could love your enemies, and both gave specific action steps to turn them into allies.

First, keep your enemy's best interests in mind. "Do not rejoice when your enemy falls, and let not your heart be glad when he stumbles, lest the LORD see it and be displeased, and turn away his anger from him" (Proverbs 24:17–18). Similarly, Jesus said, "Love your enemies and pray for those who persecute you" (Matthew 5:44). Most reconciliation fails because we want to change others' minds. We are trying to leverage peace for our own prosperity. Reconciliation begins with a generous heart toward others. It's way easier to reach reconciliation when your enemy is convinced that you see their needs.

Second, meet the needs of those who oppose you. "If your enemy is hungry, give him bread to eat, and if he is thirsty, give him water to drink, for you will heap burning coals on his head, and the LORD will reward you" (Proverbs 25:21–22). Paul used this proverb in Romans 12:20 to punctuate his prohibition on revenge: "Repay no one evil for evil, but give thought to do what is honorable in the sight of all. If possible, so far as it depends on you, live peaceably with all. Beloved, never avenge yourselves, but leave it to the wrath of God, for it is written, 'Vengeance is mine, I will repay, says the Lord' " (verses 17–19).

This is countercultural yet highly effective. What does it mean to heap burning coals on your enemy's head? Scholars aren't exactly sure. If you ask me, it most likely refers to the guilt your enemy will feel when you unexpectedly act kindly. When Jesus prohibited revenge (Matthew 5:38–41), he offered these three examples: (1) If someone slaps you on the right cheek, offer him the other. (2) If anyone sues you to take your tunic (your inner garment), let him have your cloak (your outer garment) as well. (3) If someone forces you to go one mile, go the second mile willingly. In each example, the extravagant and unexpected response publicly shames your enemy, forcing them to reveal their true malicious motives.

The command to care for an enemy goes back to the law of Moses (Exodus 23:4), but Jesus took it further: "Love your enemies, and do good, and lend, expecting nothing in return, and your reward will be great, and you will be sons of the Most High, for he is kind to the ungrateful and the evil" (Luke 6:35). Being a peacemaker requires more than conciliatory words. It requires sacrificial actions contrary to every impulse of the offended party.

How to Identify Enemies Among Your Associates

When we think of enemies, we often imagine nameless terrorists or foreign invaders. Most enemies are much closer. Strangers can threaten our possessions. Acquaintances can irritate us. Friends and family, however, can demolish our self-esteem and perpetuate a string of hurtful situations. That's why Solomon warned, "Faithful are the wounds of a friend; profuse are the kisses of an enemy" (Proverbs 27:6). Your most dangerous enemy is close enough to kiss you. The more you open your heart to someone, the deeper they can wound you.

One way to identify your closest enemies is through their profuse praise.

True friends speak hard truths. Enemies do the opposite: "Whoever hates disguises himself with his lips and harbors deceit in his heart; when he speaks graciously, believe him not, for there are seven abominations in his heart" (26:24–25).

This hardly means that every kind word is a hidden dagger. It does mean that we shouldn't trust praise, even from people closest to us. This was the case with David and Saul. After David killed Goliath (1 Samuel 17), Saul wouldn't let him return home. He lavished attention on him. He had him eat at his table. But in this same context, it says, "Saul was even more afraid of David. So Saul was David's enemy continually" (18:29). Proximity and praise are the lair of many enemies. Jesus predicted, "A person's enemies will be those of his own household" (Matthew 10:36).

If we stitch together these first two sections, we see two things. First, our greatest enemies may be closest to us and lavish us with the most praise. Second, the best strategy for dealing with an enemy is not cruelty but kindness. This makes sense considering a third observation. When Saul attacked David, 1 Samuel 18:10 notes, "a harmful spirit from God rushed upon Saul, and he raved within his house while David was playing the lyre, as he did day by day." Was Saul an enemy? For sure. But he didn't act independently. An evil spirit drove him. This makes sense of 1 Peter 5:8: "Be sober-minded; be watchful. Your adversary the devil prowls around like a roaring lion, seeking someone to devour."

Jesus recognized that his enemies were POWs of Satan. That's why he could pray, even while hanging on the cross, that they would be reconciled to God (Luke 23:34). That's the heart of the Father: "If while we were enemies we were reconciled to God by the death of his Son, much more, now that we are reconciled, shall we be saved by his life" (Romans 5:10). This doesn't mean they will never be punished. Jesus's patience with enemies will end, as will their opportunity to repent. He will return in full battle regalia, determined to defeat his enemies fully and finally (Revelation 19:11–21). He promised this, citing Psalm 110:1: "The Lord said to my Lord, 'Sit at my right hand, until I put your enemies under your feet'" (Matthew 22:44). This promise is repeated in Acts 2:34–35; 1 Corinthians 15:25–26; and Hebrews 1:13; 10:13. You can count on it.

Wisdom in Action

If you believe in Jesus's justice, you can release the right to take revenge. Jesus's coming justice frees us from our own need for vengeance. That should be a huge relief because we are incapable of justly dispensing punishment. We lack the power to punish the worst offenders as they deserve. We can't always see their motives and desires. We lack the self-control needed for righteous retribution.

Therefore, we should leave vengeance to God, resting in his watchful care. As King David proclaimed, "You prepare a table before me in the presence of my enemies; you anoint my head with oil; my cup overflows" (Psalm 23:5). The promise to Abraham still applies to us as his spiritual offspring: "Your offspring shall possess the gate of his enemies" (Genesis 22:17). When we show mercy to our enemies as the Bible teaches, we will experience the victory God promised. Now isn't the time for revenge; it's the time for reconciliation. Do this for God and see what he does for you.

LINETH UNTO DEATH, AND HER PATHS UNTO THE DEAD. NONE THAT GO UNT
URN AGAIN, NEITHER TAKE THEY HOLD OF THE PATHS OF LIFE. THAT

This Week

- ☐ **Day 1:** Read this essay.
- ☐ **Day 2:** Memorize Proverbs 16:7.
- ☐ **Day 3:** Read the biography of David (1 Samuel 24) and find one thing to apply or avoid.
- ☐ **Day 4:** Meditate on Luke 6:35; 10:19; Romans 12:20.
- ☐ **Day 5:** Discuss.

Group Discussion

1. Describe a time you reconciled with someone who initially opposed you. What were the keys that unlocked reconciliation?
2. In what practical ways can you demonstrate love and kindness to someone who has wronged you or holds opposing views?
3. How can we distinguish between genuine friends and those with ill intentions? Share strategies for navigating these complex relationships.
4. How can praying for your enemies change your perspective on and attitude toward them?

Table Talk (in your home)

Who is someone you need to pray for that you might not want to?

Watercooler (at work or the gym)

Do you think it's a good idea to be kind to someone who wrongs you? Why or why not?

DOM FOR THE RIGHTEOUS: HE IS A BUCKLER TO THEM THAT WALK UPRIGH
PETH THE PATHS OF JUDGMENT, AND PRESERVETH THE WAY OF HIS SAINTS

22

God

The rich and the poor meet together; the LORD is the Maker of them all.

—PROVERBS 22:2

Research has shown that people who attend church live longer—seven years longer![1] If you do that math, that is 61,344 hours. If you spent two hours in church every week for seventy years, that's a total investment of 7,280 hours. Every hour you spend in church adds 8.4 hours to your life. Obviously, that's not exactly scientific, but it's not nothing! That's not all. Study after study shows the powerful benefits of faith. Here are three specific examples:

1. After addiction rehabilitation, faith improves one's chances of keeping clean by nearly 30 percent.[2]
2. Faith is also linked to better mental health, lower rates of depression, and faster recovery from depression.[3]
3. Parents who take their kids to church tend to have stronger bonds leading to a host of improved parenting practices.[4]

Why Should We Have a Relationship with God?

The answer may seem obvious for those who have a vibrant faith. For a pre-Christian, however, it's not so apparent. Atheists can live their whole lives without God and get along quite well. So, let me ask again, "Why should we have a relationship with God?"

The answer from Proverbs is that knowing God better will make your life better: "The name of the LORD is a strong tower; the righteous man runs into it and is safe" (18:10). This promise is repeated in different words throughout the Bible (2 Samuel 22:33; Psalms 18:2; 61:3; Proverbs 10:29; Joel 3:16).

God is our refuge because he guides our steps. Proverbs 3:5–6 says, "Trust in the LORD with all your heart, and do not lean on your own understanding. In all your ways acknowledge him, and he will make straight your paths." Does that mean that every believer is better off than every atheist? Obviously not. However, as demonstrated in the introduction of this essay, there is strong data to suggest believers *are* generally better off.

There's not only a benefit to knowing the Lord but also a danger in ignoring him. God isn't distant or uninterested in our actions. Proverbs 15:3 says, "The eyes of the LORD are in every place, keeping watch on the evil and the good." He will judge all humankind at the end of time. Even now, he is weighing our actions and intentions. Twice we read this proverb in nearly identical words: "Every way of a man is right in his own eyes, but the LORD weighs the heart" (21:2; see also 16:2).

He doesn't just weigh our hearts; he pronounces judgment: "The crucible is for silver, and the furnace is for gold, and the LORD tests hearts" (17:3). How does he test our hearts to determine their purity? This is stunning: "The crucible is for silver, and the furnace is for gold, and a man is tested by his praise" (27:21). What we do with praise is one of the quickest ways to reveal what's truly in our hearts.

How Can We Have a Relationship with God?

God loves all his children equally: "The poor man and the oppressor meet together; the LORD gives light to the eyes of both" (Proverbs 29:13). All are welcome, and the path is the same for everyone. At the risk of oversimplification, here are three steps to foster a relationship with God.

1. **Fear the Lord.** Some seventy times we are told to fear the Lord (only three are in the New Testament).[5] We've already covered the fear of the Lord in chapter 2, so here I'll simply reiterate that the fear of the Lord is where wisdom begins.

2. **Read Scripture.** Several times the fear of the Lord is directly connected to the public reading of Scripture (Deuteronomy 17:19; 31:12–13; Psalm 19:9). This practice wasn't confined to the temple or synagogue. It was one of the primary duties of the head of every household:

> These words that I command you today shall be on your heart. You shall teach them diligently to your children, and shall talk of them when you sit in your house, and when you walk by the way, and when you lie down, and when you rise. You shall bind them as a sign on your hand, and they shall be as frontlets between your eyes. You shall write them on the doorposts of your house and on your gates. (Deuteronomy 6:6–9)

If you're a family leader, you're called to be wisdom's doorkeeper, guiding your household in God's truth, whether through a shared Bible reading plan, times of prayer, or intentional discipleship conversations. You may have no clue how to do that. Here's a secret—none of us do. There is no one right way, and no single practice will fit every season. My best advice is to fumble forward. The only wrong thing to do is nothing.

3. **Obey.** The only individual to be identified as a friend of God in the

Bible was Abraham, and he was called God's friend three times (2 Chronicles 20:7; Isaiah 41:8; James 2:23). Curiously, it never says *why* Abraham was God's friend.

If we fast-forward to Jesus, however, it becomes clear. The night before he died, Jesus finally called his disciples friends: "Greater love has no one than this, that someone lay down his life for his friends. You are my friends if you do what I command you. No longer do I call you servants, for the servant does not know what his master is doing; but I have called you friends, for all that I have heard from my Father I have made known to you" (John 15:13–15).

Obedience to God is the foundation of friendship with him. Abraham, albeit imperfectly, obeyed God's most difficult commands. When God called him to leave his family and country, he did (Genesis 12:1–5). When God called him to sacrifice his only son, he obeyed (22:1–18). Abraham prefigured the incarnation of Jesus by leaving those he loved and going to a distant place. Abraham represented God the Father in his willingness to sacrifice his only son. Obedience isn't a matter of senseless submission. It's a means of becoming like God as his ambassador and representative on earth. No wonder this is the foundation for friendship with God.

Wisdom in Action

It may seem like friendship with God is impossibly difficult. It's not. We all have equal access to God because he created us in his image and views us as precious children. He's not looking at your past with disappointment; he's looking at your future with hope. He invites you into an intimate friendship with him. It can start now. Find a Bible reading plan. Read one chapter a day. Find one verse that challenges you. Ask one question: "Lord, how can I honor you today by obeying this verse?" This is the path to friendship with God.

LL KEEP THEE: TO DELIVER THEE FROM THE WAY OF THE EVIL MAN, FRO
N THAT SPEAKETH FROWARD THINGS; WHO LEAVE THE PATHS OF UPRIGH
VALK IN THE WAYS OF DARKNESS; WHO REJOICE TO DO EVIL, AND DELIGHT

This Week

- ☐ **Day 1:** Read this essay.
- ☐ **Day 2:** Memorize Proverbs 22:2.
- ☐ **Day 3:** Read the biography of Abraham (Genesis 18:1–33, with 2 Chronicles 20:7; James 2:23) and find one thing to apply or avoid.
- ☐ **Day 4:** Meditate on Matthew 5:45; John 3:13; 14:21.
- ☐ **Day 5:** Discuss.

Group Discussion

1. How would you categorize your friendship with God? Besties, inner circle, colleagues, acquaintances, or Facebook friends?
2. How has your faith produced physical or mental health benefits in your life?
3. How was God's Word taught in your family of origin?
4. What can you do to cultivate a deeper friendship with God?

Table Talk (in your home)

What are some helpful ways we could read Scripture together in our home?

Watercooler (at work or the gym)

Do you think spiritual practices are important to mental or physical health? Why or why not?

UNTO DEATH, AND HER PATHS UNTO THE DEAD. NONE THAT GO UNTO HER
GAIN, NEITHER TAKE THEY HOLD OF THE PATHS OF LIFE. THAT THOU
ALK IN THE WAY OF GOOD MEN, AND KEEP THE PATHS OF THE RIGHTEOUS

23

Leadership

When the righteous increase, the people rejoice, but when the wicked rule, the people groan.

—Proverbs 29:2

James Kouzes and Barry Posner have researched leadership expectations since the 1980s, relating their findings in their seminal work, *The Leadership Challenge.*[1] They surveyed thousands of people, asking what traits they looked for in leaders. Followers want leaders to be honest, competent, inspiring, and forward-looking. It turns out that leaders look for the same top two traits in followers—honesty and competence.

What followers expect leaders to be	What leaders expect followers to be
Honest	**Honest**
Competent	**Competent**
Inspiring	**Trustworthy**
Forward-looking	**Consistent**

Young managers are affirmed for their honesty and competence, so they strive to be inspiring and forward-looking. They assume they will be rewarded for being good leaders but are punished for being bad managers by stepping out of their lane to lead. Something similar was experienced by General Douglas MacArthur.

General MacArthur was a world-class leader. In March 1942, MacArthur became supreme commander of the Southwest Pacific Area. Because of his distinguished leadership during World War II, he personally accepted the surrender of Japan on September 2, 1945. So why did President Truman fire such a hero on April 11, 1951? It wasn't because he was a poor leader. It was because he was a poor follower.

What Makes a Wise Leader?

The government's role is quite simple: provide security and enforce justice. National leaders are responsible for keeping citizens safe, and when that safety is violated, they are responsible for dispensing justice equitably and swiftly. This is an important responsibility of all leaders—corporate leaders, religious leaders, and heads of households. Solomon was aware of the primary role of rulers: "By justice a king builds up the land, but he who exacts gifts tears it down" (Proverbs 29:4).

When leaders are righteous, the people prosper: "When the righteous increase, the people rejoice, but when the wicked rule, the people groan" (Proverbs 29:2). However, when they are wicked, suffering is inevitable: "Like a roaring lion or a charging bear is a wicked ruler over a poor people. A ruler who lacks understanding is a cruel oppressor, but he who hates unjust gain will prolong his days" (28:15–16). The character of a leader makes all the difference. That's why Solomon said, "It is not fitting for a fool to live in luxury, much less for a slave to rule over princes" (19:10).

If you desire to be a leader, that is a noble goal. It's more than a personal privilege. It's a powerful role of discerning God's will and leading into a future only he knows. Solomon described it like a celestial game of hide-and-seek: "It is the glory of God to conceal things, but the glory of kings is to search things out" (25:2). It's honorable to heighten your leadership potential, and Proverbs tells you how. While there are innumerable potential practices, Proverbs highlights three that will expedite your journey:

1. **Diligence:** "The hand of the diligent will rule, while the slothful will be put to forced labor" (12:24). Outwork everyone around you. Arrive before everyone else and turn out the lights when you leave.
2. **Advisers:** "Without counsel plans fail, but with many advisers they succeed" (15:22). Seek out mentors for each aspect of your life. Ask questions at every opportunity. Wisdom is always around you before it's in you.
3. **Sobriety:** "It is not for kings, O Lemuel, it is not for kings to drink wine, or for rulers to take strong drink" (31:4). While this refers to drunkenness, it's an expansive principle about priorities. Are you disciplined in your habits? Are your priorities consequential? Are you living for the urgent or for the important? (There's a difference.) Netflix, video games, and social media are distractions for leaders.

What Makes a Wise Follower?

Pray for your leaders, as God commanded (1 Timothy 2:1–2), for God can move them like pawns on a chessboard for the good of his people: "The king's heart is a stream of water in the hand of the LORD; he turns it wherever he will" (Proverbs 21:1). Beyond prayer, study your leaders to know what they want and how they might respond. After all, "a king's wrath is like the growling of a lion, but his favor is like dew on the grass" (19:12; see also 16:14–15; 20:2). Since every leader is also a follower, this exercise will inevitably increase your leadership potential. Here's Solomon's advice on improving your leadership by being a better follower:

1. **Honesty:** "Righteous lips are the delight of a king, and he loves him who speaks what is right" (16:13). Our natural inclination is to tell leaders what they want to hear. Granted, many narcissistic leaders feed on lip service. However, strong leaders need someone to speak hard truths. If you do this privately and with humility, it tends to pay off.
2. **Competence:** "A servant who deals wisely has the king's favor, but his wrath falls on one who acts shamefully" (14:35). How can you deal wisely? First, do your job so well that your leader doesn't have to think about you. Second, never bring a problem to your leader without at least one reasonable solution. Third, consistently ask your leader, "What can I take off your plate?" Not only does this show you have their interests in mind, but it also shows your willingness to rise in responsibility.
3. **Loyalty:** "Steadfast love and faithfulness preserve the king, and by steadfast love his throne is upheld" (20:28). The higher a leader rises, the more loyalty trumps competence. That's because the higher a leader rises, the more people want from them. If you want something *for* them, not *from* them, you will find favor. How do you accomplish this? First, promote your leader's agenda, not your own. You can give input, but don't lobby for your position. If it's good, the leader will adopt it in time. Second, never speak ill of your leader behind their back. Factions are worse than poor leadership: "When a land transgresses, it has many rulers, but with a man of understanding and knowledge, its stability will long continue" (28:2).
4. **Humility:** "Do not put yourself forward in the king's presence or stand in the place of the great, for it is better to be told, 'Come up here,' than to be put lower in the presence of a noble" (25:6–7). Don't promote yourself. Leaders see through that, as do their colleagues, and all will disrespect you for it. Patience,

time, and humility are your most formidable allies. This is exactly what Jesus taught in Luke 14:7–11 when he rebuked guests at a dinner for taking the seats of honor.

Wisdom in Action

The most formative leadership lesson in the Gospels (and, I would argue, in all human history) is when Jesus coached his apostles to become great through service and sacrifice (Mark 10:32–45). It's stunning that no one before Jesus taught servant leadership. Not only did he teach it; he also modeled it by going to the cross.

This lesson goes back to a pivotal point in Jewish history when Solomon's son Rehoboam (to whom the book of Proverbs was written) took over the throne. The people came to him and pleaded with him to lighten their tax burden. Solomon's great kingdom had come at an oppressive price. Rehoboam's testosterone-laden young advisers counseled him to be ruthless. Tell the people, they said, "My father disciplined you with whips, but I will discipline you with scorpions" (1 Kings 12:11). Rehoboam's older advisers gave the opposite counsel: "If you will be a servant to this people today and serve them, and speak good words to them when you answer them, then they will be your servants forever" (verse 7).

Rehoboam took the foolish counsel of his peers, destroying the unity of the twelve tribes. Jesus, as Messiah, was tasked with reunifying God's chosen people. He took the twelve back to the proverbial fork in the leadership road and took a path that none had taken before him—servant leadership. By this, he didn't just change our eternal zip code; he transformed leadership for future generations worldwide.

The only way to follow in Jesus's steps is to adopt his leadership ideology: There is one supreme ruler—God the Father. All other rulers are delegates of his divine authority. As Solomon himself said, "Many seek the face of a ruler, but it is from the LORD that a man gets justice" (Proverbs 29:26).

LL KEEP THEE: TO DELIVER THEE FROM THE WAY OF THE EVIL MAN, FRO
N THAT SPEAKETH FROWARD THINGS; WHO LEAVE THE PATHS OF UPRIGH
WALK IN THE WAYS OF DARKNESS; WHO REJOICE TO DO EVIL, AND DELIGHT

This Week

- ☐ **Day 1:** Read this essay.
- ☐ **Day 2:** Memorize Proverbs 29:2.
- ☐ **Day 3:** Read the biography of Rehoboam (1 Kings 12:1–15) and find one thing to apply or avoid.
- ☐ **Day 4:** Meditate on Mark 10:32–45; Romans 13:1–7; 1 Peter 2:13–17.
- ☐ **Day 5:** Discuss.

Group Discussion

1. Who is the greatest leader you have personally worked with?
2. Which of these practices (diligence, advisers, sobriety) would most benefit you as a leader, and why?
3. Which of these practices (honesty, competence, loyalty, humility) would most benefit you as a follower, and why?
4. How does the concept of servant leadership, as modeled by Jesus, challenge our culture's view of leadership?

Table Talk (in your home)

Share what leadership qualities you admire in the people around this table.

Watercooler (at work or the gym)

What qualities do you think are most important in a leader?

UNTO DEATH, AND HER PATHS UNTO THE DEAD. NONE THAT GO UNTO HER
AIN, NEITHER TAKE THEY HOLD OF THE PATHS OF LIFE. THAT THOU
LK IN THE WAY OF GOOD MEN, AND KEEP THE PATHS OF THE RIGHTEOUS

PART 4

Behavior

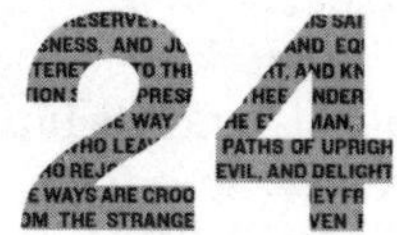

Adultery

Can a man carry fire next to his chest and his clothes not be burned? Or can one walk on hot coals and his feet not be scorched?

—Proverbs 6:27–28

It was a moment of unusual vulnerability as I rode with Skip through the hill country just north of San Antonio. He was a seasoned pastor in his thirties. I was a rookie pastor in my mid-twenties. There were very few people I would feel comfortable asking this question. Skip was a straight shooter and a down-to-earth pastor. I had been having invasive thoughts about what it would be like to have an affair. I had no plans or any person in mind. It was just the wandering imagination of a young man with two small children underfoot.

I white-knuckled the nerve to ask, “Have you ever thought about having an affair?” Skip responded nonchalantly, “Of course. I'm a man.” As my jaw met my chest, he continued, “I've thought about it carefully. There is no woman, no matter how appealing, who is worth the life I've built with my wife. No woman, no matter how appealing, is worth the relationship with my children. No woman, no matter how appealing, is worth my ministry, my integrity, or my reputation.”

I'll never forget that conversation. It reminds me a lot of what Solomon said to his son: “He who commits adultery lacks sense; he who does it destroys himself. He will get wounds and dishonor, and his disgrace will not be wiped away" (Proverbs 6:32–33).

What Are the Causes of Adultery?

The most common trigger for adultery is feeling unappreciated by your spouse. When an outsider offers the emotional support missing in the home, we become vulnerable to adultery. I have a friend who used to be a pastor. Because of his childhood trauma, he was a black hole for affirmation. His wife, through no fault of her own, couldn't keep up with his emotional needs. After multiple affairs, a painful divorce, therapy, and medical treatment for depression, he admitted to me that he had been a predator. I asked him how he knew if a woman in the church was open to an affair. His response left me breathless: "I would walk into a room and look for a beautiful woman whose husband was ignoring her. She would be vulnerable if I gave her attention." According to this former pastor/predator, the best way to protect your wife from men like him is to pay attention to your spouse's emotional needs.

The second most common factor in affairs is the allure of excitement. Solomon was right: "Stolen water is sweet, and bread eaten in secret is pleasant" (Proverbs 9:17). Did you know that the most common season for affairs is around the seven-year mark of marriage and that marriages of thirty or more years are also especially vulnerable (for men)?[1] In both seasons, we see friends' social feeds and their apparently exciting lives. Our imaginations run wild with images of exotic romance without bills, halitosis, dirty diapers, or complaints.

No woman caring for toddlers at 6 A.M. is as alluring as a single woman dolled up for a date. Even Solomon, with his harem of hundreds, warned of being bewitched by unfamiliar beauty: "Do not desire her beauty in your heart, and do not let her capture you with her eyelashes" (6:25). A wild woman might make fine arm candy at a company party: "She is loud and wayward; her feet do not stay at home; now in the street, now in the market, and at every corner she lies in wait. She seizes him and kisses him" (7:11–13). Yet this is hardly the woman you want to grow old with. My friend Skip gave sound advice. Count the cost carefully, for you will pay for an affair for decades.

What Are the Costs of Adultery?

My pastor friend, fired after multiple affairs, described the aftermath as a series of price tags. Some of them he had known were potential costs—his marriage and ministry. What stunned him was the wide range of unsuspected costs—his children and grandchildren, holidays, financial loss, medical treatment, abandonment by friends, an unfulfilled calling, a second failed marriage, loneliness, premature aging, and more.

Solomon warned his son about "a forbidden woman": "Keep your way far from her, and do not go near the door of her house, lest you give your honor to others and your years to the merciless, lest strangers take their fill of your strength, and your labors go to the house of a foreigner" (Proverbs 5:3, 8–10).

The wise king continued, "The price of a prostitute is only a loaf of bread, but a married woman hunts down a precious life" (6:26). It's true—a prostitute is far less expensive than an affair. To be clear, Solomon isn't advising you to pay for sex. After all, "a prostitute is a deep pit; an adulteress is a narrow well. She lies in wait like a robber and increases the traitors among mankind" (23:27–28). He is merely pointing out the high cost of an affair.

Jesus went further, comparing divorce and adultery because both destroy God's foundational institution on earth—marriage: "I say to you that everyone who divorces his wife, except on the ground of sexual immorality, makes her commit adultery, and whoever marries a divorced woman commits adultery" (Matthew 5:32). Jesus wasn't calling divorcées adulterers.

Rather, he was saying divorce is metaphorically *like* adultery. Both make a woman the object of scandal. Both bring shame and economic strain on a woman, particularly as the primary caretaker of her children. Both lead to loneliness and vulnerability.

The cost of adultery isn't merely personal. It threatens the family, which is the bedrock of society. Adultery has the deepest possible ramifications for society, which is why God warns against it in the Ten Commandments (Exodus 20:14).

What Cures Adultery?

If you are trying to rebuild a marriage after adultery, three Bible stories offer hope. The most famous is the story of David and Bathsheba. After King David got caught, he wrote an entire poem detailing his journey of repentance (Psalm 51). Make his song your refrain to get you through this season.

There are two other pertinent stories. Tamar's tale is all kinds of messed up. Genesis 38 details the damage, but the gist of it is this: Tamar pretended to be a prostitute to seduce her father-in-law, Judah. She was "forced" to do this to produce an heir since her first two husbands (Judah's sons) died and Judah refused to give her his third son. The other story is about a Canaanite woman named Rahab (Joshua 2; 6). She was a prostitute who wisely hid the Israelite spies when they came to Jericho.

Each story would make an interesting Netflix docudrama. However, the Old Testament scripts aren't nearly as powerful as the passing mention of these women in the New Testament. All three find their place in Jesus's genealogy (Matthew 1:3–6). If these women played a role in divine history, you can too.

One final story. As Jesus was teaching in the temple, the Jewish leaders threw a woman at his feet who had been caught in adultery (John 8:2–11). It was clearly a setup to trap Jesus, not the woman. Against all expectations, he was going to allow a stoning, *but* the sinless one had to cast the first stone. Since the eyewitnesses were part of the plot, they couldn't cast the first stone without implicating themselves. Stones peppered the floor of the temple as they dropped their case against the woman. Jesus released her without condemnation. He will also release you, as he has paid the price for your sin. He will tell you what he told her: "Go, and from now on sin no more" (verse 11).

Wisdom in Action

Whether you are single or married, sexual fidelity has significance beyond your bedroom. If family is the foundation of society, then sexual boundaries benefit entire communities. Sex is the only force on earth that can create life. It has equal power to destroy it. While culture attempts to equate your identity with your sexual proclivities, God does not. You are *not* your gender, your sexual expression, or your sexual history. You are a child of God, created in his image. Sexual self-control or even abstinence is worth the benefit to society, even if it's personally challenging. The secret to sexual self-control is finding your worth and purpose in your Creator and finding *agapē* love in the community rather than *eros* love in seclusion.

LINETH UNTO DEATH, AND HER PATHS UNTO THE DEAD. NONE THAT GO UNT
URN AGAIN, NEITHER TAKE THEY HOLD OF THE PATHS OF LIFE. THAT
(EST WALK IN THE WAY OF GOOD MEN, AND KEEP THE PATHS OF THE RIGH

This Week

- ☐ **Day 1:** Read this essay.
- ☐ **Day 2:** Memorize Proverbs 6:27–28.
- ☐ **Day 3:** Read the biography of the woman caught in adultery (John 8:2–11) and find one thing to apply or avoid.
- ☐ **Day 4:** Meditate on Matthew 5:27–28; 1 Corinthians 6:18–20; James 4:4.
- ☐ **Day 5:** Discuss.

Group Discussion

1. What is your primary language for showing and receiving love: acts of service, words of affirmation, receiving gifts, physical touch, or quality time?[2]
2. Why do you think the most common trigger for adultery is feeling unappreciated by a spouse?
3. Reflect on Jesus's response to the woman caught in adultery (John 8:2–11). How does this story highlight the balance between justice and grace when dealing with sin?
4. What steps can we take to affair-proof our marriages and relationships?

Table Talk (in your home)

How can we support one another to ensure we all feel appreciated and valued?

Watercooler (at work or the gym)

What do you think is the biggest potential cost of an affair?

MOUTH COMETH KNOWLEDGE AND UNDERSTANDING. HE LAYETH UP
DOM FOR THE RIGHTEOUS: HE IS A BUCKLER TO THEM THAT WALK UPRIGH
PETH THE PATHS OF JUDGMENT, AND PRESERVETH THE WAY OF HIS SAINTS

25

Drinking

Wine is a mocker, strong drink a brawler, and whoever is led astray by it is not wise.

—Proverbs 20:1

Alcohol is a clever little chemical. It absorbs quickly into the bloodstream, making a beeline to the brain. There it latches on to your GABA-A receptors, slowing your brain functions. On the upside, this leads to relaxation and lower anxiety. The downside, however, is that alcohol impairs your physical functions, which is why drunks stagger and slur their speech. It also impairs pain receptors (an advantage in a barroom brawl) and decision-making (which can lead to a barroom brawl).

Alcohol releases dopamine and serotonin, making you feel braver, more attractive, and more clever than you actually are. Here's where it gets truly problematic: The more you drink, the more likely you are to drink. And the longer you drink, the more your mood shifts from euphoria to depression and aggression. This explains why 40 to 60 percent of domestic violence cases involve substance abuse,[1] as well as up to 80 percent of child maltreatment cases.[2] Alcohol is a factor in 28 percent of aggravated assaults,[3] 32 percent of murders,[4] and more than 75 percent of rapes.[5]

What's the Big Deal with Drinking?

Solomon's description of a drunkard rings true to what we've seen in the movies or in our own backyard:

> Who has woe? Who has sorrow? Who has strife? Who has complaining? Who has wounds without cause? Who has redness of eyes? Those who tarry long over wine; those who go to try mixed wine. Do not look at wine when it is red, when it sparkles in the cup and goes down smoothly. In the end it bites like a serpent and stings like an adder. Your eyes will see strange things, and your heart utter perverse things. You will be like one who lies down in the midst of the sea, like one who lies on the top of a mast. "They struck me," you will say, "but I was not hurt; they beat me, but I did not feel it. When shall I awake? I must have another drink." (Proverbs 23:29–35)

The rest of the biblical descriptions of drunkenness are equally familiar:

Description	Biblical Text
Merriment	Isaiah 56:12; Jeremiah 51:39; Ezekiel 23:42
Foolishness and Mockery	Psalm 69:12; 1 Corinthians 6:10
Overindulgence	Luke 21:34
Garbled Speech	1 Samuel 1:13–15
Fighting	Matthew 24:49; Romans 13:13
Dizziness	Isaiah 24:20
Stumbling	Job 12:25; Psalm 107:27; Isaiah 19:14; 24:20; 28:7; 29:9
Vomiting	Isaiah 19:14; 28:8; Jeremiah 48:26
Oversleeping	Jeremiah 51:39; Joel 1:5; 1 Corinthians 15:34

Alcohol can also be a gateway to other self-destructive behaviors such as gluttony: "Be not among drunkards or among gluttonous eaters of meat, for the drunkard and the glutton will come to poverty, and slumber will clothe them with rags" (Proverbs 23:20–21).

The New Testament is even more explicit, categorizing drunkenness with sexual immorality, fighting, greed, swindling, thievery, mockery, and envy (Romans 13:13; 1 Corinthians 6:10; Galatians 5:21; 1 Timothy 3:3; 1 Peter 4:3). That's quite a litany. In fact, Paul advises us not to associate with such people (1 Corinthians 5:11), who won't "inherit the kingdom of God" (1 Corinthians 6:10; Galatians 5:21).

Alcohol, Kings, and the King of Kings

Drunkenness leads to dereliction of duty. That's why King Lemuel's mother advised her son to avoid it: "It is not for kings, O Lemuel, it is not for kings to drink wine, or for rulers to take strong drink, lest they drink and forget what has been decreed and pervert the rights of all the afflicted" (Proverbs 31:4–5).

Solomon followed her advice (for the most part), as he recorded this saying in his final book: "Happy are you, O land, when your king is the son of the nobility, and your princes feast at the proper time, for strength, and not for drunkenness!" (Ecclesiastes 10:17). Shortly after Solomon, two kings faced disaster, partially because of drunkenness—Elah, the king of Israel, was murdered (1 Kings 16:8–10), and Ben-hadad, the king of Syria, narrowly escaped during a devastating military defeat (20:16–21).

In the New Testament, sobriety is a requirement for church leaders. Paul laid out the requirements for both Timothy and Titus, who followed in his footsteps as pastors at Ephesus and Crete, respectively. A leader must be "sober-minded," "self-controlled," and "not a drunkard" (1 Timothy 3:1–7; Titus 1:5–9).

Should alcohol be prohibited at all times? Not necessarily. For more than two decades, I served as a professor at a Christian college where, in those days, professors signed an agreement to be alcohol abstinent. I loved that role, that place, and those people, though I didn't fully agree with the policy. After all, Timothy was told to drink a little wine for his stomach ailment since water in the ancient world was frequently unsafe to drink (1 Timothy 5:23). It was also suggested as a sedative: "Give strong drink to the one who is perishing, and wine to those in bitter distress; let them drink and forget their poverty and remember their misery no more" (Proverbs 31:6–7).

Then there is Jesus. His first miracle was turning water into wine at a wedding (John 2:1–11)—and not just a little bit of wine. It was somewhere between 120 and 180 gallons of wine. . . . That's a blessing you can swim in! And we're not talking about the cheap stuff; this was premium Mogen David. This was the first of the seven signs of Jesus in John's gospel, a metaphor for following Jesus and a promise of the coming marriage supper of the Lamb.

Jesus was so popular at parties that he was labeled "a glutton and a drunkard" (Matthew 11:19). I will never understand how a man so morally virtuous was so welcome among sinners. Without compromising his values and without demeaning or judging others, he called drunkards, prostitutes, and tax collectors to a higher vision of themselves. He raised their morality without lowering their self-esteem.

A wedding is an invitation to celebrate. That's a metaphor for the Christian life. And wine is a metaphor for the joy of the Holy Spirit. This becomes clearer in Ephesians 5:18: "Do not get drunk with wine, for that is debauchery, but be filled with the Spirit." The manifestation of the Holy Spirit was mistaken for drunkenness on the Day of Pentecost as the apostles spoke in the dialects of their audience (Acts 2:1–15).

To be filled with the Spirit also leads to celebration through singing. Ephesians 5 goes on to say that we should be "addressing one another in psalms and hymns and spiritual songs, singing and making melody to the Lord with your heart, giving thanks always and for everything to God the Father in the name of our Lord Jesus Christ, submitting to one another out of reverence for Christ" (verses 19–21). The Holy Spirit is our best libation and more than an ample substitute for intoxication.

Wisdom in Action

Drunkenness is always wrong; drinking isn't necessarily. Paul rebuked the Corinthians for getting drunk at the Lord's Supper without reprimanding them for drinking wine: "In eating, each one goes ahead with his own meal. One goes hungry, another gets drunk. What! Do you not have houses to eat and drink in?" (1 Corinthians 11:21–22).

Some will argue that drinking defiles your body, which is God's temple. However, the passages that mention the body as the temple of God have more relevance to the church body than your individual physical body (1 Corinthians 3:16; 6:15–19; see also 2 Corinthians 6:14–18; Ephesians 2:19–21; 4:4). Does that make drinking permissible for you? Perhaps that's the wrong question. Paul suggested that some things are permissible but not profitable (1 Corinthians 10:23). And by "profitable," he means not only for you but also for others around you. This is especially true if you're a leader. We hold ourselves to higher standards. If you want to be wise, here's the question you should ask yourself about drinking: "What would set a standard of healthy behavior for those following my example?"

LINETH UNTO DEATH, AND HER PATHS UNTO THE DEAD. NONE THAT GO UN
URN AGAIN, NEITHER TAKE THEY HOLD OF THE PATHS OF LIFE. THAT
EST WALK IN THE WAY OF GOOD MEN, AND KEEP THE PATHS OF THE RIGH

This Week

- ☐ **Day 1:** Read this essay.
- ☐ **Day 2:** Memorize Proverbs 20:1.
- ☐ **Day 3:** Read the biographies of Noah and Lot (Genesis 9:18–29; 19:29–38) and find one thing to apply or avoid.
- ☐ **Day 4:** Meditate on Matthew 11:19; Romans 13:13; Ephesians 5:18.
- ☐ **Day 5:** Discuss.

Group Discussion

1. In what ways, if any, has your family suffered because of alcohol abuse?
2. How do you reconcile instances in the Bible where alcohol is used for positive purposes, such as in 1 Timothy 5:23 and John 2:1–11, with warnings against drunkenness?
3. How did Jesus attract drunkards, prostitutes, and tax collectors without compromising his values? How can we adopt his approach in our interactions with those struggling with addiction or other moral issues?
4. In Ephesians 5:18–21, how does the exhortation to be filled with the Spirit instead of getting drunk with wine offer a positive alternative to substance abuse? What practical steps can we take to live this out?

Table Talk (in your home)

What rules should we have as a household concerning alcohol?

Watercooler (at work or the gym)

How do you determine if someone has had too much to drink?

MOUTH COMETH KNOWLEDGE AND UNDERSTANDING. HE LAYETH UP
DOM FOR THE RIGHTEOUS: HE IS A BUCKLER TO THEM THAT WALK UPRIGH
PETH THE PATHS OF JUDGMENT, AND PRESERVETH THE WAY OF HIS SAINTS

26

Scheming

Deceit is in the heart of those who devise evil, but those who plan peace have joy.

—Proverbs 12:20

How stressed would you be if you were a zebra on the Serengeti in constant danger of a lion attack? Here's a fascinating fact: When a lion attacks, the zebra's body is flooded with adrenaline and cortisol in response to the intense stress. It runs for its life, but not for long. Though lions can accelerate faster than zebras, zebras have far more stamina, so if the zebra has a head start of at least five seconds, it can outrun the lion. The danger is gone as quickly as it came. The zebra's stress levels return to normal almost immediately, and it can resume its tranquil grazing.[1]

Humans don't do that. We are seldom in mortal danger, yet even potential threats can activate our stress response. A chronic stress response can lead to adrenaline and cortisol overload, resulting in anxiety disorders and other related health issues.[2]

That's why scheming is so detrimental. Schemers create a danger of exploitation, betrayal, and manipulation, which keeps our minds on high alert, perpetuating a cycle of anxiety. Unlike the zebra's, our limbic system works overtime, producing stress hormones even though there's no immediate threat.

Why Scheming Inevitably Backfires

I asked my wife if she'd ever schemed. She is genuinely the kindest and most innocent person I know. Imagine my shock when she didn't hesitate: "Oh yeah." I'm never surprised at my own penchant for manipulation, but learning that the woman I live with, the person with whom I'm most vulnerable, has this same penchant was unsettling. I had to ask for an example. She had one at the ready. Recently she'd surreptitiously hired a technician to put a protective coating on my car as a surprise gift. That's very nice but hardly scheming in the biblical sense of the word. The Bible describes scheming as trying to orchestrate future outcomes for personal gain. It goes by several names—conniving, conspiring, contriving, hustling, plotting—and may involve tricks, ruses, and manipulation.

Thinking about and planning for future events is a human trait, but it also reflects God's image in us. It's the character of God to create futures, and that's deeply embedded in all of us. Whether our planning is philanthropic or nefarious depends entirely on our motive.

If our motive is to make life better for ourselves at the cost of someone else, that's *scheming.* If our motive is to make life better for someone else at the cost of ourselves, that's *sacrifice.* If our motive is a win-win, that's *business.* Business, sacrifice, and scheming are part of the human experience. We will all do at least one of these throughout our lives, but likely all three.

Business *creates,* which is God's nature. Sacrifice *rescues and re-creates,* which is Jesus's nature. Scheming *manipulates,* which is Satan's nature. We all attempt to shape the future as an expression of God's character in us. Our motive will determine whether we reflect God, Jesus, or the devil.

The gravitational pull toward scheming comes from the desire to play God over others rather than participate with God in the ongoing act of creation (through business, art, education, science, etc.). We would rather control than create. This desire is rooted in pride, a sin as old as Eden. When humans attempt to displace God, they wind up acting more like animals than humans. Scheming seldom works out as planned, for several reasons.

First, scheming destroys your vertical relationship with God because you reject him as Lord. Second, it destroys your horizontal relationships, eroding trust with those around you. If your scheme works, you are hated. If it fails, you are punished. Either way, you dehumanize yourself in your attempt to become God. Third, scheming damages your relationship with yourself because you spend your energy manipulating the future rather than fully experiencing the present.

Proverbs 1:11–18 describes the folly of scheming in detail, concluding with this warning: "These men lie in wait for their own blood; they set an ambush for their own lives." Verse 31 follows: "They shall eat the fruit of their way, and have their fill of their own devices." Proverbs is clear—scheming backfires.

How to Recognize a Schemer

It takes discernment to detect a schemer. Proverbs helpfully provides a profile of one: "A worthless person, a wicked man, goes about with crooked speech, winks with his eyes, signals with his feet, points with his finger, with perverted heart devises evil, continually sowing discord; therefore calamity will come upon him suddenly; in a moment he will be broken beyond healing" (6:12–15). This is a good summary of what to look for. Watch out for someone whose body language reveals a hidden agenda. In Solomon's day it looked like crooked speech, winking, signaling with their feet, pointing, or pursing their lips (16:27, 30). Pay attention to a person's posture. It can sometimes expose their position.

David saw the signs with Saul: "David knew that Saul was plotting harm against him" (1 Samuel 23:9). Nehemiah saw the signs with Sanballat, Tobiah, and their allies: "They all plotted together to come and fight against

Jerusalem and to cause confusion in it" (Nehemiah 4:8). Then there is Jeremiah: "They said, 'Come, let us make plots against Jeremiah, for the law shall not perish from the priest, nor counsel from the wise, nor the word from the prophet. Come, let us strike him with the tongue, and let us not pay attention to any of his words' " (Jeremiah 18:18).

What makes Jeremiah so interesting is how much he looked like Jesus when the schemers planned their attack against him: "I was like a gentle lamb led to the slaughter. I did not know it was against me they devised schemes, saying, 'Let us destroy the tree with its fruit, let us cut him off from the land of the living, that his name be remembered no more' " (11:19). Is it any wonder that when Jesus asked his disciples who people thought he was, they replied, "Some say John the Baptist, others say Elijah, and others Jeremiah or one of the prophets" (Matthew 16:14)? All of them faced lethal schemers.

David, Nehemiah, and Jeremiah all prefigure Jesus. Yet Jesus was the victim of a far worse plot under Caiaphas: "The chief priests and the elders of the people gathered in the palace of the high priest, whose name was Caiaphas, and plotted together in order to arrest Jesus by stealth and kill him" (Matthew 26:3–4).

For those of us who follow Jesus, should we not expect to walk his path? The closer we are to Jesus, the more likely we will experience what he did. That was true for the apostle Paul, who constantly faced plots, precisely for preaching the gospel (Acts 9:23–24; 20:3, 19; 23:30). And like Jesus, we should be acutely aware that the schemes aren't merely of human origin. Satan is a schemer and a catalyst for human manipulation. That's why we are told to "put on the whole armor of God, that you may be able to stand against the schemes of the devil" (Ephesians 6:11).

Wisdom in Action

If you want to deal shrewdly with schemers, start by admitting you are one. Part of our spiritual DNA is the innate drive to shape the future. Part of our fallen DNA is the desire to control the future—even at the expense of others. Once you admit that, you can begin to question your motives. Are you trying to create a future with others that is a win-win? God does that, and it's the nature of doing business. Or are you trying to manipulate someone else for your own advantage? Satan does that, and so do schemers. Or are you trying to sacrifice for the good of someone else, like Jesus? Our motives are generally mixed. They will never be perfect, but they can be better if we honestly question them. Then we can shift the percentage in the right direction.

Only when you've questioned your own intentions will you be adept at questioning the motives of others. What is their agenda? Everyone has one. What do they have to gain? What do you have to lose? This isn't cynical; it's sensible so long as you avoid becoming jaded or paranoid. Training yourself to identify those motives will make you wise. Discerning the ways others try to manipulate the future enables you to influence a better outcome.

LINETH UNTO DEATH, AND HER PATHS UNTO THE DEAD. NONE THAT GO UNT
URN AGAIN, NEITHER TAKE THEY HOLD OF THE PATHS OF LIFE. THAT

This Week

- ☐ **Day 1:** Read this essay.
- ☐ **Day 2:** Memorize Proverbs 12:20.
- ☐ **Day 3:** Read the biography of Paul (Acts 20:17–38) and find one thing to apply.
- ☐ **Day 4:** Meditate on Matthew 22:15; Acts 4:25; Ephesians 6:11.
- ☐ **Day 5:** Discuss.

Group Discussion

1. When have you hatched a scheme to play a joke on someone?
2. How can we monitor our motives?
3. How can you recognize when someone is scheming against you?
4. What are some healthy responses when someone is scheming against you?

Table Talk (in your home)

How can we use the armor of God (Ephesians 6:11) to protect ourselves from the schemes of the devil and others? What practical steps can we take to put on this armor daily?

Watercooler (at work or the gym)

What signs might indicate someone is scheming at home or at work?

DOM FOR THE RIGHTEOUS: HE IS A BUCKLER TO THEM THAT WALK UPRIGH
PETH THE PATHS OF JUDGMENT, AND PRESERVETH THE WAY OF HIS SAINTS

27

Anger

Whoever is slow to anger has great understanding,
but he who has a hasty temper exalts folly.

—Proverbs 14:29

Anger management is a hot topic. Because of its major impact on physical health, Mayo Clinic, arguably the leading medical institution in the world, has weighed in. They offer ten tips for anger management.[1] It's striking how many of them can be directly supported by Scripture.

1. Think before you speak (James 1:19)
2. Once you're calm, express your concerns (Proverbs 15:1)
3. Get some exercise (1 Timothy 4:8)
4. Take a time-out (Psalm 37:7–8)
5. Identify possible solutions (Proverbs 15:22)
6. Stick with "I" statements
7. Don't hold a grudge (Ephesians 4:26)
8. Use humor to release tension (Proverbs 15:13)
9. Practice relaxation skills
10. Know when to seek help (Proverbs 19:20)

Only two of the ten don't derive directly from Scripture. The Bible was thousands of years ahead of Mayo Clinic.

God Has a Long Nose

The Hebrew phrase "slow to anger" is literally "a long nose." What in the world does that mean? When we get angry, two things happen physiologically: blood rushes to our faces and our nostrils flare. Both are telltale signs of anger. So, to say God has a long nose means it takes a while before his nostrils flare.

That's how God described *himself* to Moses in Exodus 34:6: "The LORD, the LORD, a God merciful and gracious, slow to anger, and abounding in steadfast love and faithfulness." God highlighted four features of his character: merciful, gracious, slow to anger, and loving. These four pillars of God's personality are recited six times throughout the Old Testament (Nehemiah 9:17; Psalms 86:15; 103:8; 145:8; Joel 2:13; Jonah 4:2).

Two things are peculiar about this. First, God is the only one the Bible describes as slow to anger. Though Proverbs urges us to be slow to anger four times (14:29; 15:18; 16:32; 19:11), no one else is said to have achieved it.

Using slightly different wording, the aged Solomon gave one last exhortation to be slow to anger: "Be not quick in your spirit to become angry, for anger lodges in the heart of fools" (Ecclesiastes 7:9). The only other place the phrase is used is in James 1:19–20: "Know this, my beloved brothers: let every person be quick to hear, slow to speak, slow to anger; for the anger of man does not produce the righteousness of God."

Second, even though God is slow to anger, he still gets mad, and he gets mad a lot! He was displeased with Moses when he balked at being God's spokesperson (Exodus 4:14). He was so infuriated with Israel in the desert that Moses had to talk him out of annihilating the nation (Exodus 32:11–12). In Numbers 11:1, God set fire to the outskirts of their encampment. He struck down Uzzah for touching the ark of the covenant (2 Samuel 6:7).

Then there is this terrifying text where God incited David to count the troops as a pretext for punishing Israel for her sins (2 Samuel 24:1). Even Solomon was subject to God's wrath after his wives seduced him into idolatry (1 Kings 11:9). If God got mad so often in the Old Testament, isn't that the opposite of Jesus in the New Testament?

Actually, no. Psalm 2:12 predicted an angry Messiah: "Kiss the Son, lest he be angry, and you perish in the way, for his wrath is quickly kindled. Blessed are all who take refuge in him." Jesus expressed anger against the synagogue rulers who prioritized their traditions over the suffering of a crippled man (Mark 3:5). Jesus flipped the tables of the vendors in the temple because they had set up shop in the court of the Gentiles (John 2:14–16). In Revelation 6, unbelievers run to the mountain crevasses and call on the boulders, "Fall on us and hide us from the face of him who is seated on the throne, and from *the wrath of the Lamb*" (verse 16). Both the Father and the Son model unprecedented love and ferocious wrath.

How can God be slow to anger yet so full of fury? Have you ever met someone who was slow to anger but blew up once you pushed them past the breaking point? You could push and push and push, and then *boom!* Look out! God's patience is immensely gracious, but it isn't eternal. Though never reactive or unjustified, God's anger rises like a flood (Numbers 14:18).

This is as true in the New Testament as in the Old. Romans 1:18 says, "The wrath of God is revealed from heaven against all ungodliness and unrighteousness of men, who by their unrighteousness suppress the truth." It's especially true for the worst sin of all, when people reject God's one and only Son after he died to save them. We rightly revel in the truth of John 3:16—that God loves the world. Are we as keen to acknowledge John 3:36? It says, "Whoever does not obey the Son shall not see life, but the wrath of God remains on him." Here's a bit of good news on the heels of God's wrath: "His anger is but for a moment, and his favor is for a lifetime. Weeping may tarry for the night, but joy comes with the morning" (Psalm 30:5).

Is There Righteous Indignation?

Ephesians 4:26 commands us to "Be angry"; however, it's joined to a second command: "Do not sin," or, more literally, "Stop sinning." Paul continued with two more imperatives: "Do not let the sun go down on your anger, and give no opportunity to the devil" (verses 26–27). Here are all four commands in order:

1. Be angry.
2. Stop sinning.
3. Stop allowing the sun to set on your anger.
4. Stop giving an opportunity to the devil.

This passage does *not* advocate righteous indignation. Rather, it suggests altering our response to the inevitable emotion of anger. Fact-check me on this. In the Bible, only God has righteous indignation. Sustained anger erodes our motives and opens the door for demonic influence. If we hold on to anger longer than sunset, we open the door for the devil to gain a foothold. That's why James 1:20 states, "The anger of man does not produce the righteousness of God." Humans don't have the capacity to harbor anger righteously. We must release it to God, who will enact righteous retribution on our behalf.

Ephesians 4:26 quotes from Psalm 4:4: "Be angry, and do not sin; ponder in your own hearts on your beds, and be silent." David modeled this when he had to flee from his own son Absalom, who marched an army into Jerusalem, chased David into the desert, and raped David's concubines on the roof of his palace (Psalm 3; 2 Samuel 15–16). David had every right to be furious and to seek revenge, but he didn't. He submitted his anger to God. This warrior-king is our model for releasing anger into God's hands.

Wisdom in Action

Proverbs is full of warnings against harboring anger, such as Proverbs 19:19, "A man of great wrath will pay the penalty, for if you deliver him, you will only have to do it again." The quicker you can rid yourself of anger, the better off you will be. Let's stop kidding ourselves that our anger is righteous. God's anger is righteous; ours is not. Release it before the sun sets!

Not only should you release your own anger, but you should also limit your exposure to others' anger, which tends to be contagious. Solomon warns us: "Make no friendship with a man given to anger, nor go with a wrathful man" (22:24). You have the right to set boundaries in all your relationships, particularly those that tend to be toxic. Share your boundaries with your friends and family and then remove yourself from their presence when they cross the boundaries you've established. It might make them angry, but their anger will no longer rub off on you. Your response to their anger, or anyone's anger, should follow this simple rule: "A soft answer turns away wrath, but a harsh word stirs up anger" (15:1). If you master this single idea, you can master anger management.

LINETH UNTO DEATH, AND HER PATHS UNTO THE DEAD. NONE THAT GO UNT
URN AGAIN, NEITHER TAKE THEY HOLD OF THE PATHS OF LIFE. THAT
VEST WALK IN THE WAY OF GOOD MEN, AND KEEP THE PATHS OF THE RIGHT

This Week

- ☐ **Day 1:** Read this essay.
- ☐ **Day 2:** Memorize Proverbs 14:29.
- ☐ **Day 3:** Read the biography of Cain (Genesis 4) and find one thing to avoid.
- ☐ **Day 4:** Meditate on Matthew 5:22; Ephesians 4:26; Hebrews 11:4.
- ☐ **Day 5:** Discuss.

Group Discussion

1. Would you describe yourself as a pouter or a shouter? How long can you hold a grudge?
2. Which of Mayo Clinic's ten suggestions for anger management do you find most helpful?
3. Why do you think humans are incapable of righteous anger?
4. Proverbs 15:1 says, "A soft answer turns away wrath." How would you advise your kids or co-workers to apply this principle in their daily interactions, especially in conflict situations?

Table Talk (in your home)

What rule(s) should we establish as a family for expressing our anger in appropriate ways?

Watercooler (at work or the gym)

What advice would you give about managing anger at work?

MOUTH COMETH KNOWLEDGE AND UNDERSTANDING. HE LAYETH UP
DOM FOR THE RIGHTEOUS: HE IS A BUCKLER TO THEM THAT WALK UPRIGHT
PETH THE PATHS OF JUDGMENT, AND PRESERVETH THE WAY OF HIS SAINTS

28

Revenge

Do not say, "I will repay evil"; wait for the LORD,
and he will deliver you.

—PROVERBS 20:22

On the border between West Virginia and Kentucky brewed the most infamous family feud in U.S. history. Supposedly, it started over a pig. In 1878, Randolph McCoy accused Floyd Hatfield of stealing his hog. Those in the know, however, suggest the family feud was ignited during the Civil War in 1863, when Asa Harmon McCoy, a Union soldier, was murdered by a Confederate sympathizer. The assassin was thought to be part of the Hatfield clan.

Tensions had been simmering for a while, and the pilfered pig gave the families a pretext to go hog wild. Upon McCoy's accusation, Hatfield was taken to court. The case was presided over by a Hatfield relative, and when Floyd Hatfield was acquitted, the McCoys were furious.

The perceived injustice erupted into a cycle of violence, culminating in the New Year's Day massacre of 1888, where Randolph McCoy's son and daughter were killed and his wife was badly injured.[1] The feud between the Hatfields and the McCoys is a classic illustration of the futility of vengeance. Their story underscores the wisdom found in Proverbs, which warns of the dangers of revenge.

Anger's Child: Revenge

Indeed, he's a God of love—incredible, vast, inestimable love. But he's also a God of vengeance. God's love and God's vengeance are cut from the same cloth. The depth of your love determines the breadth of your vengeance. Here's the problem for humans: Our vengeance is typically driven by our love for ourselves. We think, *You hurt me. I will hurt you worse.* God's vengeance is driven by his love for his children. God says, "You hurt my children, and you will discover how much I love them!"

Does that mean God will punish one of his children for hurting another child? Absolutely! Parents get this. This is why God's vengeance has appropriate limits—he loves both children. Our vengeance, in contrast, is driven by self-importance, and for most of us, there's no limit to that. So, God put a legal limit to our vengeance: "Life for life, eye for eye, tooth for tooth, hand for hand, foot for foot" (Deuteronomy 19:21).

Without this limit, a simple slight could escalate to extreme revenge. Solomon warned his son, "Do not say, 'I will do to him as he has done to me; I will pay the man back for what he has done' " (Proverbs 24:29). What we consider payback inevitably comes with considerable interest. As Proverbs 6:34 observes, "Jealousy makes a man furious, and he will not spare when he takes revenge."

In the last chapter, we read Cain's biography. He couldn't get ahold of his anger, so his anger got ahold of him. He murdered his brother. Cain's descendant Lamech took matters even further: "Adah and Zillah, hear my voice; you wives of Lamech, listen to what I say: I have killed a man for wounding me, a young man for striking me. If Cain's revenge is sevenfold, then Lamech's is seventy-sevenfold" (Genesis 4:23–24).

God Is Better at Vengeance Than We Are

The most compelling reason to release vengeance to God is that he has the resources to carry it out. Often those who hurt us have more power than we do. Revenge is beyond our capacity. So, we meditate on a future revenge that rarely occurs. We live with imaginary retaliation, seething against an enemy that is ignorant of our planned assault. In the process, our souls absorb the poison of vengeance. It seeps into other relationships in ways we don't even realize. Our families and friends, however, hear it in the tone of our voice, see it in the lines of our eyes, and feel it in the deterioration of our health.

That's why it's imperative to release our right to take revenge. Scripture is clear: God will right the wrong on our behalf and do so with appropriate boundaries and timing. Deuteronomy 32:35 says, "Vengeance is mine, and recompense, for the time when their foot shall slip; for the day of their calamity is at hand, and their doom comes swiftly." This promise of God's vengeance is peppered through the pages of the Bible (Deuteronomy 32:41, 43; Psalm 99:8; Isaiah 34:8; 35:4; 61:2; Ezekiel 25:14, 17; Nahum 1:2; Romans 12:17–20; 1 Thessalonians 4:6; Revelation 6:10; 19:2). That's a *lot.* God *will* right all the wrongs done to you. He will heal the pain of your soul and restore what was taken from you.

Revenge is the attempt to take from someone else what we perceive they took from us. If we are successful—and sometimes we are—it leaves two people with wounds in their hearts. God desires to heal us and punish the perpetrator while drawing them to himself. Our motive in revenge is hurt; God's motive is restoration. Let me ask you a simple question: Do you believe God has your best interests in mind? If yes, release the right to take revenge. But this still leaves a massive question: How should we respond to enemies? The answer may surprise you.

How to Kill with Kindness

Solomon's most famous advice for dealing with an enemy is Proverbs 25:21–22: "If your enemy is hungry, give him bread to eat, and if he is thirsty, give him water to drink, for you will heap burning coals on his head, and the LORD will reward you." This passage was quoted by the apostle Paul in the context of leaving vengeance to God:

> Beloved, never avenge yourselves, but leave it to the wrath of God, for it is written, "Vengeance is mine, I will repay, says the Lord" [Deuteronomy 32:35]. To the contrary, "if your enemy is hungry, feed him; if he is thirsty, give him something to drink; for by so doing you will heap burning coals on his head" [Proverbs 25:21–22]. Do not be overcome by evil, but overcome evil with good. (Romans 12:19–21)

Jesus rewrote the law of vengeance: "You have heard that it was said, 'An eye for an eye and a tooth for a tooth.' But I say to you, Do not resist the one who is evil. But if anyone slaps you on the right cheek, turn to him the other also" (Matthew 5:38–39). This new law is not "eye for eye" but "good for evil." Both Paul and Peter reiterated Jesus's new command. Paul said, "See that no one repays anyone evil for evil, but always seek to do good to one another and to everyone" (1 Thessalonians 5:15). Peter said, "Do not repay evil for evil or reviling for reviling, but on the contrary, bless, for to this you were called, that you may obtain a blessing" (1 Peter 3:9).

This is a difficult teaching. Repaying good for evil goes against the grain of our psyche. It challenges our deep desire for justice. At times, it feels immoral. But here's the thing: God won't merely bring about judgment in the end; he has already begun the process by taking the punishment for sin on the cross—not only our sins, but those of our enemies also. Jesus's own death was the definitive declaration against the sins of humanity, ours included. The most appropriate response to God's grace is to extend that grace to our enemies.

Wisdom in Action

We are commanded to love our neighbor as ourselves. Jesus identified this as the second greatest commandment after loving God (Matthew 22:37–39). Surely, you're familiar with that command, but did you know its Old Testament context is about releasing the right to take revenge? "You shall not take vengeance or bear a grudge against the sons of your own people, but you shall love your neighbor as yourself: I am the LORD" (Leviticus 19:18).

So, how do you release the right to take revenge? Answer two questions. First, "What did they take from me?" You won't be able to release it until you can clearly articulate what they took (your innocence, your trust, the dream of a family, etc.). Second, "What do they owe me?" You will likely discover that they can't repay what they owe you even if they wanted to. Holding revenge will only scar your soul since they can't give you what only God can. On the other hand, there is immense freedom in releasing the albatross of revenge. It's time to find that freedom.

LINETH UNTO DEATH, AND HER PATHS UNTO THE DEAD. NONE THAT GO UNT
URN AGAIN, NEITHER TAKE THEY HOLD OF THE PATHS OF LIFE. THAT
EST WALK IN THE WAY OF GOOD MEN, AND KEEP THE PATHS OF THE RIGH

This Week

- ☐ **Day 1:** Read this essay.
- ☐ **Day 2:** Memorize Proverbs 20:22.
- ☐ **Day 3:** Read the biography of Joab (2 Samuel 3:20–39) and find one thing to apply or avoid.
- ☐ **Day 4:** Meditate on Matthew 5:38–39; Romans 12:17–20; 13:3–4.
- ☐ **Day 5:** Discuss.

Group Discussion

1. Who was your biggest rival growing up?
2. Why do you think our desire for revenge does more damage than the person who hurt us in the first place?
3. When have you had success in killing with kindness?
4. How does Jesus's sacrifice release us from the need to seek revenge?

Table Talk (in your home)

Do you have any grudges you need to release? If so, what are they?

Watercooler (at work or the gym)

Why do you think it's so hard for people to let go of grudges?

MOUTH COMETH KNOWLEDGE AND UNDERSTANDING. HE LAYETH UP
DOM FOR THE RIGHTEOUS: HE IS A BUCKLER TO THEM THAT WALK UPRIGH
PETH THE PATHS OF JUDGMENT, AND PRESERVETH THE WAY OF HIS SAINTS

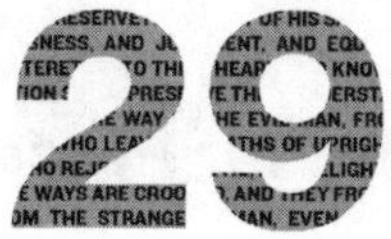

Prudence

I, wisdom, dwell with prudence, and I find knowledge and discretion.

—Proverbs 8:12

Sometimes I purposely create awkward situations for my personal entertainment. I have plenty of examples, most of which are too embarrassing to share. Here's one, however, that illustrates my propensity for foolishness. In my senior year of high school, I was student body president, respected by faculty and students. I didn't just want respect; I wanted admiration for being a wild card. One wing of classrooms had very heavy doors that were difficult to open. A friend and I smeared Vaseline on the oversize doorknobs, making them impossible to turn.

Little did I know the school board was touring campus that day. Our teachers were embarrassed, livid, and looking for the culprits. I kept my secret. My friend did not. The principal called me in, saying, "Rumor has it that you're responsible for this, but I can't believe that's true." Imagine my embarrassment when I had to confess that it *was* true. The ancient philosopher Cicero described me well in his proverb: "Rashness attends youth, as prudence does old age."[1]

Praise for Prudence

Prudence isn't a common word, and those who use it sound like prudes. Ancient philosophers like Cicero, however, considered it one of the greatest of all virtues, along with moderation, courage, and justice. Solomon included it in the prologue of Proverbs: "to give prudence to the simple" (1:4). Perhaps we could give prudence a fresh hearing.

Prudence isn't caution or moralism. It's a perceptive view of the future, leading to astute restraint in the present. In the words of Saint Thomas Aquinas, "Prudence is *right reason applied to action*."[2] It requires two things: discernment and discipline. Discernment is seeing both motives and consequences, and discipline is doing the right thing in the right way at the right time.

Prudence is one of the main metrics we use to judge people: "A man is commended according to his good sense, but one of twisted mind is despised" (Proverbs 12:8). This is why Jesus's advice is so important: "Be wise as serpents and innocent as doves" (Matthew 10:16). Christians have prioritized being innocent as doves. Yet it seems that we have neglected to be shrewd as serpents. Shrewd somehow feels shady or worldly. It is not. Shrewd discernment is Christlike, and it's no longer optional for Christians in a world increasingly opposed to God.

So how does one develop this critical life skill?

How to Develop Prudence

The Bible is full of people notable for their prudence: Joseph (Genesis 41), Jethro (Exodus 18:19–23), David (1 Samuel 16:18), Abigail (1 Samuel 25:32–33), the Shunammite (2 Kings 4:9–10), Ezra (Ezra 8:21–33), Nehemiah (Nehemiah 2:11–15), Job (Job 21:27), Daniel (Daniel 1–2). Their stories offer insight into how to develop prudence. Let me summarize my top gleanings from their biographies. If you do these simple things, you will quickly elevate your prudence.

Restrain Your Words. One of the most common mistakes of youth is the belief that you will be heard in proportion to the speed and volume of your words. The opposite is true. The longer you wait to speak and the fewer words you say, the more likely you are to influence those around you positively. Proverbs 17:28 says, "Even a fool who keeps silent is considered wise; when he closes his lips, he is deemed intelligent."

This principle is hardest to apply after being insulted. We feel honor bound to respond quickly, clearly, and harshly. Proverbs 12:16 observes, "The vexation of a fool is known at once, but the prudent ignores an insult." The more I've marinated in wisdom, the more I've discerned what insults are worthy of a response. I've also learned that the shorter the response, the sooner the tension dissipates. Often the best response is no response. According to Proverbs 26:4, "Answer not a fool according to his folly, lest you be like him yourself." Your tongue is the most important muscle *not* to exercise (12:23).

Do Hard Things First. Prudence isn't merely thinking the right thing or saying the right thing; it's doing the right thing in the right way at the right time. If there's one discipline I recommend, it's to do hard things first. Distraction and procrastination are the twin killers of a life well lived. Proverbs 10:5 says, "He who gathers in summer is a prudent son, but he who sleeps in harvest is a son who brings shame."

Here's a simple discipline that's had a great impact on my life. It's simple, though not easy: Make a daily to-do list. Then do the hardest thing first. When that's accomplished, you get a surge of energy, pride, and focus. The rest of the list feels like running downhill. The more you do hard things first, the easier hard things become.

Perceive What Is Around You; Predict What Is Ahead of You. Prudence is the ability to discern the subtleties of a situation. It's the knowledge of when to speak and when to be silent, when to save and when to spend, when to buy and when to sell. This is a choice not between good and bad but between better and best. As Paul stated, "'All things are lawful,' but not all things are helpful. 'All things are lawful,' but not all things build up" (1 Corinthians 10:23). Are you able to discern between them?

Prudence can read the signs of the times and differentiate between the important and the urgent. Anxiety, laziness, anger, and lust are discernment killers. The more triggered we are, the less discernment we have. Seeing into the future doesn't require the gift of prophecy; it requires experience aligned with analysis—the ability to think through options and potential consequences without being clouded by emotions. Proverbs 4:25–26 says, "Let your eyes look directly forward, and your gaze be straight before you. Ponder the path of your feet; then all your ways will be sure."

There's one more thing to consider. Prudence isn't merely doing what is best for you; it's aligning with God's desires and designs. It's not merely about being effective or successful; it's about being faithful. Prudence and providence flow through the same stream. How do you access that kind of wisdom? You find it through those who have gone before you!

Wisdom in Action

Prudence can be developed through the pain of personal experience or the gain of others' experiences. Why would you try to get it yourself when it can be freely given by others who already have it? That's why it's so imperative that we leverage the mentors God has provided.

Why don't we ask for advice more often? Sometimes our pride gets in the way. We don't want to appear foolish. Lean in and listen to this: Seeking counsel makes you appear wise to your counselors. Your mentors assess your intelligence by the wisdom you seek, not the wisdom you lack. Here's another important point: Seeking advice doesn't merely benefit you; it also blesses the one you ask. The person you seek advice from, like all of us, wants to be valued and valuable. By seeking their advice, you are meeting that need. They will love you for it, so learn to love seeking wisdom.

From whom should we seek advice? The short answer is *from everyone, everywhere, all the time.* The Bible recommends three particularly rich resources:

1. **Parents:** Proverbs 15:5 says, "A fool despises his father's instruction, but whoever heeds reproof is prudent." If you are blessed with wise and loving parents, even if they aren't believers, they are still God's first and most loyal mentors in your life.
2. **Spouses:** Proverbs 19:14 says, "House and wealth are inherited from fathers, but a prudent wife is from the LORD." Submitting to a spouse's advice is sometimes difficult, but not nearly as difficult as living without it.
3. **God:** James 1:5 says, "If any of you lacks wisdom, let him ask God, who gives generously to all without reproach, and it will be given him." Prayer is a particularly powerful resource for prudence.

Start here and start today. You will soon find yourself in the company of Issachar: "Issachar, men who had understanding of the times, to know what Israel ought to do" (1 Chronicles 12:32).

LINETH UNTO DEATH, AND HER PATHS UNTO THE DEAD. NONE THAT GO UNT
URN AGAIN, NEITHER TAKE THEY HOLD OF THE PATHS OF LIFE. THAT
/EST WALK IN THE WAY OF GOOD MEN, AND KEEP THE PATHS OF THE RIGH

This Week

- ☐ **Day 1:** Read this essay.
- ☐ **Day 2:** Memorize Proverbs 8:12.
- ☐ **Day 3:** Read the biography of Daniel (Daniel 1) and find one thing to apply.
- ☐ **Day 4:** Meditate on Matthew 10:16; 1 Corinthians 6:13; 10:23.
- ☐ **Day 5:** Discuss.

Group Discussion

1. Share a funny story illustrating when you lacked discretion.
2. Reflect on Proverbs 8:12. How do wisdom, prudence, knowledge, and discretion interrelate? How can we cultivate these qualities in our lives?
3. Which action step do you need to implement most: restrain your words, do hard things first, or perceive what is around you and predict what is ahead of you?
4. Who are the wisest counselors in your life right now?

Table Talk (in your home)

What are the hard things you need to do first?

Watercooler (at work or the gym)

How would you define *prudence* for a teenager?

MOUTH COMETH KNOWLEDGE AND UNDERSTANDING. HE LAYETH UP
DOM FOR THE RIGHTEOUS: HE IS A BUCKLER TO THEM THAT WALK UPRIGH
PETH THE PATHS OF JUDGMENT, AND PRESERVETH THE WAY OF HIS SAINTS

30

Moderation

Be not among drunkards or among gluttonous eaters of meat, for the drunkard and the glutton will come to poverty, and slumber will clothe them with rags.

—Proverbs 23:20–21

Everyone has something that won't make it through the night. For some, it's a tube of Pringles. Once it's opened, it will be devoured in a single sitting. For others, it's Blue Bell mint chocolate chip ice cream. I'm a bit embarrassed to tell you mine, because it's truly disgusting. Have you ever seen those orange marshmallow circus peanuts in a truck stop gas station? They have a consistency somewhere between packing peanuts and a banana peel. There's nothing appealing about them, but the tactile satisfaction of biting them in half and melting them in my mouth is cruelly addictive. It could also have something to do with the near-instant sugar coma. I won't stop until the bag is empty and my belly is distended.

We all have our vices. It could be screens or sleep, alcohol or carbs, work or "retail therapy." We can't seem to stop ourselves. In the previous chapter, we looked at prudence, the ability to do the right thing in the right way at the right time. Moderation is the other side of that coin—not doing too much of anything at any time. It's self-regulation. Self-regulation never comes naturally to children. Benevolent parents instill it despotically. Once self-regulation is instilled in even one area of your life, you can replicate it in others. Your satisfaction depends on doing just that.

"Everything in Moderation, Including Moderation"

This famous saying has been attributed to Socrates, Benjamin Franklin, Oscar Wilde, and Mark Twain. Solomon got at the heart of it in Ecclesiastes 7:16–17: "Be not overly righteous, and do not make yourself too wise. Why should you destroy yourself? Be not overly wicked, neither be a fool. Why should you die before your time?" Several hundred years later and eight hundred miles away, Aristotle wrote about the golden mean, the balance between two extremes. Ancient philosophers and modern cultural commentators alike have advised moderation.

It has been said that Americans worship their work, work at their play, and play at their worship. The statistics seem to support that. The average American spends about four hours and twenty minutes daily on their phone. That's in addition to three hours of TV and doesn't even account for non-work-related computer use.[1] Yet 37 percent of Americans are sleep deprived.[2]

Our diet is equally unbalanced. Only 9 percent of Americans eat the recommended two to three cups of vegetables daily.[3] We also consume, on average, seventeen teaspoons of added sugar a day, twice the recommendation for men and triple the recommendation for women.[4] That's partly why more than 70 percent of Americans over the age of twenty-five are overweight, with 42 percent of American adults meeting the criteria for obesity.[5] The other factor is that we are sedentary. Experts recommend 150 minutes per week of moderate aerobic activity (like walking) or 75 minutes of vigorous activity (like running) as well as strength training twice weekly. Half the population gets enough aerobic activity, but only a quarter meets the strength-training metric too.[6]

Is it any wonder that 23 percent of American adults experience some form of mental illness?[7] Meditation and medication help. Only one is free. Sixteen percent of American adults medicate for mental health.[8] Only 25 percent take the free option of attending a religious service weekly.[9]

We are out of balance. It's not so surprising that Solomon identified similar categories of imbalance nor that the New Testament touches on the same topics.

Gluttony		
Proverbs 23:1–2: "When you sit down to eat with a ruler, observe carefully what is before you, and put a knife to your throat if you are given to appetite."	**1 Corinthians 6:13:** " 'Food is meant for the stomach and the stomach for food'—and God will destroy both one and the other."	See also Proverbs 25:27; 27:7; 28:7.
Greed		
Proverbs 28:22: "A stingy man hastens after wealth and does not know that poverty will come upon him."	**Mark 8:36:** "What does it profit a man to gain the whole world and forfeit his soul?"	See also Psalm 37:16; Ecclesiastes 4:6; Luke 12:15.
Laziness		
Proverbs 5:23: "He dies for lack of discipline, and because of his great folly he is led astray."	**1 Corinthians 9:24–25:** "Run that you may obtain it. Every athlete exercises self-control in all things. They do it to receive a perishable wreath, but we an imperishable."	See also Ezekiel 16:49–50.
Pleasure (Drinking, Lust, Entertainment)		
Proverbs 21:17: "Whoever loves pleasure will be a poor man; he who loves wine and oil will not be rich."	**Luke 21:34:** "Watch yourselves lest your hearts be weighed down with dissipation and drunkenness and cares of this life, and that day come upon you suddenly like a trap."	See also Esther 1:10–12; Proverbs 23:20–21; Song of Solomon 2:7; 3:5; 8:4; Isaiah 5:11; Ephesians 5:18.

The reason balance is so important is that it creates margin. Margin is where all the good stuff in life happens. Having margin for a vacation creates your most positive memories (scroll through your photos to confirm). Having margin in finances allows you to take advantage of the best deals. Having margin in energy allows you to have that important conversation. The margin of health allows you to experience the outdoors. Balance isn't about being a boringly disciplined person. It's about being free to experience the wonder of life's margins.

Building Moderation to Grow Margin

I still have difficulty with circus peanuts. That's why I won't buy them. But I have great discipline in physical exercise and Bible study, and I always hit deadlines, but I binge TV and sugar. My discipline is strong in some areas while weak in others. That's true for you as well. Here's the good news: If you have discipline in one area, you can transfer that moderation to other areas. The following chart will help you monitor some of the main categories of moderation. After tracking these disciplines for one week, identify your strongest and weakest.

Discipline	Mon	Tues	Wed	Thurs	Fri	Sat
Hours of Sleep						
Calories Consumed						
Sugar Intake						
Caffeine Intake						
Minutes of Exercise						
TV Screen Time						
Phone or Other Screen Time						

Discipline	Mon	Tues	Wed	Thurs	Fri	Sat
Posts on Social						
Making Bed						
Flossing Teeth						
Bible Reading						
Prayer (beyond meals)						
Weekly Sabbath						
Weekly Church Attendance						

Now that you have identified strengths and weaknesses, it's time to organize your day around them. Scan this chart and create a note on your phone for future tracking. Apply the practices below to build moderation.

Wisdom in Action

Here are three practices to help you transfer moderation from one area to another:

1. **Keystone Habits.** Front-load your day with your strongest disciplines. Some habits are viral—they tend to spread to their surrounding habits. Flossing, making your bed, and morning devotions top the list.
2. **Fasting** is a biblical practice that teaches your body who's boss. It's a powerful discipline to foster delayed gratification. The Bible mentions fasting from food and water, but you can fast from any of your vices (screens, makeup, sugar, caffeine, alcohol, social media, Amazon, Pinterest, gaming, etc.).
3. **Accountability.** Where your discipline is weak, accountability is essential, whether it's exercise, financial planning, or spiritual

> disciplines. Share your goals and your schedule to increase success. In some areas, accountability can be technology. You can track calories, monitor screen time, or exercise with an app or AI assistant.

Discipline creates moderation. Moderation creates margin. Margin is where the best things in life reside.

LL KEEP THEE: TO DELIVER THEE FROM THE WAY OF THE EVIL MAN, FRO
N THAT SPEAKETH FROWARD THINGS; WHO LEAVE THE PATHS OF UPRIGH
VALK IN THE WAYS OF DARKNESS; WHO REJOICE TO DO EVIL, AND DELIGHT

This Week

- ☐ **Day 1:** Read this essay.
- ☐ **Day 2:** Memorize Proverbs 23:20–21.
- ☐ **Day 3:** Read the biography of Mordecai and Esther (Esther 4–5) and find one thing to apply.
- ☐ **Day 4:** Meditate on Mark 8:36; 1 Corinthians 9:24–25; 1 John 2:15–17.
- ☐ **Day 5:** Discuss.

Group Discussion

1. What is one area of your life where you lack self-control?
2. How does Aristotle's golden mean—finding a balance between extremes—help us lead more fulfilling and stable lives?
3. Where do you need to find more margin in your life (health, finances, time, emotional energy, etc.)?
4. If you were to fast in one area of your life, what would it be, and why?

Table Talk (in your home)

Where do you think we're most out of balance—screens, meals together, days off, house chores, diet, exercise?

Watercooler (at work or the gym)

What areas of your life would you say are most balanced, and what areas are most imbalanced?

UNTO DEATH, AND HER PATHS UNTO THE DEAD. NONE THAT GO UNTO HER
AIN, NEITHER TAKE THEY HOLD OF THE PATHS OF LIFE. THAT THOU
LK IN THE WAY OF GOOD MEN, AND KEEP THE PATHS OF THE RIGHTEOUS

31

Social Justice

When justice is done, it is a joy to the righteous
but terror to evildoers.

—Proverbs 21:15

In America, conversations around social justice tend to focus on racism, immigration, and LGBTQ. These are important (and volatile) issues. People disagree very strongly on the nature of the problems and potential solutions. There is nearly unanimous agreement, however, on other social justice issues that oppress millions, such as sex trafficking (6 million), forced labor (28 million), and forced marriages (22 million).[1] Something must be done.

Oppression of the Poor

The systemic root of injustice is not racism or even economic inequality but a lack of wisdom. Remember, wisdom isn't *knowing* the right thing; it's the skill of *doing* the right thing. Many social justice advocates have the right heart but are advocating harmful practices. This has been documented in the book *When Helping Hurts,* which describes efforts that have eroded communities.[2] Compassion has sometimes perpetuated cycles of poverty by offering handouts rather than a hand up. Helping hurts when the person offering benevolence feels good about their gift while the person receiving it is robbed of dignity and agency.

Social justice is for the good of society, not just individuals. Poverty can breed crime, abuse, greed, and tribalism. Solomon warned of the danger of perpetuating poverty in Proverbs 22:8–9: "Whoever sows injustice will reap calamity, and the rod of his fury will fail. Whoever has a bountiful eye will be blessed, for he shares his bread with the poor." You might get away with oppression in the short term, but in the long run, poverty disintegrates society, and that hurts everyone. This isn't just a warning for the rich; the poor are also prone to oppress their neighbors: "A poor man who oppresses the poor is a beating rain that leaves no food" (28:3).

Several times in the Old Testament, God commands us to care for immigrants because we too were immigrants in Egypt: "When a stranger sojourns with you in your land, you shall not do him wrong. You shall treat the stranger who sojourns with you as the native among you, and you shall love him as yourself, for you were strangers in the land of Egypt: I am the LORD your God" (Leviticus 19:33–34; see also Exodus 22:21–24; 23:9; Deuteronomy 10:18–19; 24:17–22). Concern for the poor reminds us where we came from.

There are two critically important points in these passages:

1. God connects care for the foreigner with loving our neighbor. This is one of the two primary commands of Jesus (Matthew 22:37–39). Therefore, social justice is core to being a Christian.
2. The command to love our neighbor (the foreigner) is connected to knowing God. When we know who God is, we see people through *his* eyes. They are not strangers but spiritual family.

All of us are closer to poverty than we'd like to imagine. We are just two bad decisions or one catastrophe away from being poor. In our current culture, equity for conservatives is equity of opportunity. For liberals, it's equity of outcome. For Christians, it's equity of value. Seeing others as brothers and sisters is the path to biblical justice.

Protection of the Poor

The poor are often underpaid at work and underrepresented in courts of law. Proverbs addresses both. Concerning work, Solomon wrote, "The fallow ground of the poor would yield much food, but it is swept away through injustice" (13:23). Moses was even more specific in Deuteronomy 24:14–15: "You shall not oppress a hired worker who is poor and needy. . . . You shall give him his wages on the same day, before the sun sets (for he is poor and counts on it), lest he cry against you to the LORD, and you be guilty of sin."

Biblical justice in the workplace means providing an equitable opportunity to work for a livable wage, healthcare, childcare, and safety. It acknowledges people's value to God, not just their ability to contribute to society. This differs from socialism. Socialism says, "What's yours is mine; I'll take it." Christianity says, "What's mine is God's; I'll share it." This is what families do, and Christians see the poor as family members in God's household.

Likewise, Solomon warned his son about social justice in courts of law: "A righteous man knows the rights of the poor; a wicked man does not understand such knowledge" (Proverbs 29:7). Asaph said the same thing: "Give justice to the weak and the fatherless; maintain the right of the afflicted and the destitute. Rescue the weak and the needy; deliver them from the hand of the wicked" (Psalm 82:3–4).

Moses codified social justice in the law: "If your brother becomes poor and cannot maintain himself with you, you shall support him as though he were a stranger and a sojourner, and he shall live with you" (Leviticus 25:35). The prophets carried on the call for social justice: "Learn to do good; seek justice, correct oppression; bring justice to the fatherless, plead the widow's cause" (Isaiah 1:17; see also Jeremiah 22:3). God has a special concern for the poor, immigrants, widows, orphans, and the disabled. There is no true worship of God where his children are abused or neglected. "Is not this the fast that I choose: to loose the bonds of wickedness, to undo the straps of the yoke, to let the oppressed go free, and to break every yoke? Is it not to share your bread with the hungry and bring the homeless poor into your house; when you see the naked, to cover him, and not to hide yourself from your own flesh?" (Isaiah 58:6–7).

Wisdom in Action

The problems of the world are vast. How could you possibly make a dent in human trafficking, global poverty, racism, or a host of other issues? The answer is simple, though not easy. Open your eyes to what is around you right now. Jesus gave some pretty good ideas of issues to watch for in Matthew 25:34–36:

> The King will say to those on his right, "Come, you who are blessed by my Father, inherit the kingdom prepared for you from the foundation of the world. For I was hungry and you gave me food, I was thirsty and you gave me drink, I was a stranger and you welcomed me, I was naked and you clothed me, I was sick and you visited me, I was in prison and you came to me."

You can't do everything, but neither can you do nothing. Compassion for those in need around you was the theme of Jesus's first recorded sermon (Luke 4:18–19), the point of the parable of the good Samaritan (10:36–37), and the practice of the early church (Acts 2:44–45; 4:32–35). It begins by believers supporting one another: "As we have opportunity, let us do good to everyone, and especially to those who are of the household of faith" (Galatians 6:10). From there it emanates to others around you.

Seeing the poor as brothers and sisters moves us from benevolence to inclusion. That is key to developing social justice over social service. This is a call not to welfare but to wellness that stems from treating all God's children with equity. "Religion that is pure and undefiled before God the Father is this: to visit orphans and widows in their affliction, and to keep oneself unstained from the world" (James 1:27).

LL KEEP THEE: TO DELIVER THEE FROM THE WAY OF THE EVIL MAN, FRO
N THAT SPEAKETH FROWARD THINGS; WHO LEAVE THE PATHS OF UPRIGH
WALK IN THE WAYS OF DARKNESS; WHO REJOICE TO DO EVIL, AND DELIGHT

This Week

- ☐ **Day 1:** Read this essay.
- ☐ **Day 2:** Memorize Proverbs 21:15.
- ☐ **Day 3:** Read the biography of Zacchaeus (Luke 19:1–10) and find one thing to apply.
- ☐ **Day 4:** Meditate on Romans 12:13; Galatians 6:9–10; 1 John 3:16–18.
- ☐ **Day 5:** Discuss.

Group Discussion

1. What one or two social justice issues are most important to you?
2. What individuals or groups would you have the most difficulty seeing as children of God?
3. Reflect on the idea that true religion involves caring for orphans, widows, and the poor. How can your small group or church better embody this biblical mandate?
4. How can we ensure that our efforts to help others are both compassionate and effective?

Table Talk (in your home)

What need could our family meet for someone in our neighborhood, church, or circle of influence?

Watercooler (at work or the gym)

What do you think is the most important social justice issue today?

UNTO DEATH, AND HER PATHS UNTO THE DEAD. NONE THAT GO UNTO HER
AIN, NEITHER TAKE THEY HOLD OF THE PATHS OF LIFE. THAT THOU
LK IN THE WAY OF GOOD MEN, AND KEEP THE PATHS OF THE RIGHTEOUS

32

Repentance

Whoever conceals his transgressions will not prosper, but he who confesses and forsakes them will obtain mercy.

—Proverbs 28:13

In the year A.D. 66, during the Jewish revolt against Rome, a young general of the Jewish military named Flavius Josephus confronted a warlord named Jesus (not the Nazarene, of course) in Galilee. Jesus had conspired against him, but Josephus had discovered the plot, foiled it, and managed to capture the warlord. Josephus described in his autobiography how he summoned his prisoner and confronted him with his treachery. Surprisingly, the general offered forgiveness on one condition: "Repent . . . and be faithful to me."[1]

If this sounds familiar, it's because that's strikingly similar to the phrase Jesus (the Nazarene) used to open his preaching career: "The time is fulfilled, and the kingdom of God is at hand; repent and believe in the gospel" (Mark 1:15). Jesus isn't asking us to feel bad about our sins. He's calling us to change sides—to give our loyalty to a different Lord. Biblical repentance is to pledge allegiance to the One we have fought against. It's, colloquially speaking, to make a U-turn.

U-Turns

Repentance requires humility to acknowledge our misguided direction. I know it's foolish, but I would rather go fast in the wrong direction than turn around and admit my error. Mistakes are embarrassing and a waste of time. But only by repentance can we move in the right direction. Solomon warned, "Be not wise in your own eyes; fear the LORD, and turn away from evil" (Proverbs 3:7). Repentance begins with humility and grows into fidelity.

Proverbs 16:6 says, "By steadfast love and faithfulness iniquity is atoned for, and by the fear of the LORD one turns away from evil." At first blush, it seems to mean that if you love God and are faithful to him, you will repent and be forgiven. But there is a deeper layer. It's not our faithfulness to God that leads to forgiveness but Jesus's faithfulness to us, as Romans 3:26 teaches: "This was also to demonstrate his righteousness in the present time, so that he would be just and the justifier of the one who lives because of Jesus' faithfulness" (NET).[2]

Repentance is the front door to the kingdom: "From that time Jesus began to preach, saying, 'Repent, for the kingdom of heaven is at hand'" (Matthew 4:17). That's precisely the message that John preached before him (Mark 1:4; Acts 13:24; 19:4) and the apostles after him (Mark 6:12; Acts 2:38; 3:19; 5:31; 8:22; 11:18; 17:30; 20:21; 26:20). Repentance isn't merely central to wisdom; it's core to Christianity.

This gift of repentance isn't popular. After all, who wants to admit they're going in the wrong direction? Solomon felt this resistance when he wrote in Proverbs 14:9, "Fools mock at the guilt offering, but the upright enjoy acceptance." Jesus felt it even more in the cities where he had done the most miracles: "He began to denounce the cities where most of his mighty works had been done, because they did not repent. 'Woe to you, Chorazin! Woe to you, Bethsaida! For if the mighty works done in you had been done in Tyre and Sidon, they would have repented long ago in sackcloth and ashes'"

(Matthew 11:20–21). Warning: Those who know the most about Jesus aren't always the quickest to repent.

This relates to another core truth about repentance—it's usually corporate, not individual. Churches, cities, and nations are called to repent. Who you surround yourself with may determine whether you all are able to make a U-turn.

"About Face" Is About Us

The Holy Spirit convicts the world of sin, righteousness, and judgment to come (John 16:8), and he calls us to repentance. Often he uses people around us to spur that change. For example, Proverbs 10:17 says, "Whoever heeds instruction is on the path to life, but he who rejects reproof leads others astray." Rebuke can backfire when the stiff-necked resist, resulting in more suffering: "He who is often reproved, yet stiffens his neck, will suddenly be broken beyond healing" (29:1).

This call to repentance is part of the job description of prophets, pastors, and parents, as well as teachers, coaches, and other mentors. If you are spiritually responsible for someone, this is in your job description. God described this difficult duty using the metaphor of a watchman on a wall in Ezekiel 33:6: "If the watchman sees the sword coming and does not blow the trumpet, so that the people are not warned, and the sword comes and takes any one of them, that person is taken away in his iniquity, but his blood I will require at the watchman's hand." If we don't warn people to repent, we will be held accountable.

Not many people relish confronting others' sins. We're uncomfortable with the phrase "repent or perish." It sounds judgmental and harsh, right? Except that it was Jesus who first said it—in fact, he said it *twice* (Luke 13:3, 5).

A call to repentance isn't mean or judgmental; it's kind: "Do you presume on the riches of his kindness and forbearance and patience, not knowing that God's kindness is meant to lead you to repentance?" (Romans 2:4).

It's not only kind; it's also patient: "The Lord is not slow to fulfill his promise as some count slowness, but is patient toward you, not wishing that any should perish, but that all should reach repentance" (2 Peter 3:9).

Those who call us to make a U-turn are not "traffic cops" hindering our progress but advocates pointing us to the "carpool lane." While we think of repentance as an individual act, both the Old and the New Testaments call entire groups to repentance. Perhaps the most famous passage is 2 Chronicles 7:14: "If my people who are called by my name humble themselves, and pray and seek my face and turn from their wicked ways, then I will hear from heaven and will forgive their sin and heal their land."

In the New Testament, after the first Christian sermon, Peter called the entire crowd to repent: "Repent and be baptized every one of you in the name of Jesus Christ for the forgiveness of your sins, and you will receive the gift of the Holy Spirit" (Acts 2:38). Grammatically, "be baptized" is singular. "Repent," on the other hand, is a third-person plural: "all y'all repent." It's a group activity that our own nation needs desperately.

Wisdom in Action

What does it look like to repent? Let's be clear. It's not about weeping at an altar call. Godly sorrow may lead to repentance, as 2 Corinthians 7:10 suggests: "Godly grief produces a repentance that leads to salvation without regret, whereas worldly grief produces death." But sorrow alone is *not* repentance. Judas Iscariot felt bad for what he did and hanged himself (Matthew 27:3–5). The apostle Peter, who also betrayed Jesus (albeit with a very different motive), repented and was restored (John 21:1–19).

How can we embrace true repentance? Luke 3:8 says, "Bear fruits in keeping with repentance." What does the fruit of repentance taste like? Two things: restitution and reconciliation. Restitution requires that you make right what you did wrong as much as possible. If you stole something, return it or pay it back. If you lied, tell the truth. If you harmed someone's reputation, go above and beyond to restore it. Sometimes restitution isn't possible. For example, you can't return virginity. You can't give back a year of childhood. You can't recapture innocence.

However, repentance requires you to do what you can to restore the damage you caused and reconcile where possible. Reconciliation may not mean you get back together, rejoin the team, or attend family dinners. The distance you caused may remain, but the animosity can be reduced through an admission of your guilt and an apology for the damage. This kind of reconciliation is important for your horizontal relationships on earth. It's also vital for your vertical relationship with God. The two go hand in hand. Our reconciliation with God is typically in tandem with our reconciliation with others.

LL KEEP THEE: TO DELIVER THEE FROM THE WAY OF THE EVIL MAN, FRO
N THAT SPEAKETH FROWARD THINGS; WHO LEAVE THE PATHS OF UPRIGH

This Week

- ☐ **Day 1:** Read this essay.
- ☐ **Day 2:** Memorize Proverbs 28:13.
- ☐ **Day 3:** Read the biography of Judas (Matthew 26:14–16, 20–25, 47–56; 27:3–10) and find one thing to avoid.
- ☐ **Day 4:** Meditate on Luke 13:3, 5; 15:7, 10; 17:3–4.
- ☐ **Day 5:** Discuss.

Group Discussion

1. What are some wrong directions you have taken in your life, and how did you decide to make a U-turn?
2. Who are you spiritually responsible for? Is there a need in this season to call them to repentance?
3. How does pride keep us from repenting, and what steps can we take to cultivate humility?
4. This chapter emphasizes restitution and reconciliation as the fruit of repentance. How have you seen or experienced these in your life?

Table Talk (in your home)

What does it look like to truly apologize and make things right?

Watercooler (at work or the gym)

When is it right to call someone out for a bad decision or warn them when they're heading in a destructive direction?

UNTO DEATH, AND HER PATHS UNTO THE DEAD. NONE THAT GO UNTO HER
AIN, NEITHER TAKE THEY HOLD OF THE PATHS OF LIFE. THAT THOU

33

Consequences

There is a way that seems right to a man,
but its end is the way to death.

—Proverbs 14:12

In 1915, Robert Frost concluded his most famous poem, "The Road Not Taken," with these words: "Two roads diverged in a wood, and I—/ I took the one less traveled by, / And that has made all the difference."[1] Jesus spoke a similar proverb two thousand years earlier: "Enter by the narrow gate. For the gate is wide and the way is easy that leads to destruction, and those who enter by it are many. For the gate is narrow and the way is hard that leads to life, and those who find it are few" (Matthew 7:13–14).

Throughout our lives, we come upon forks in the road. Our choice in these moments makes little difference for the first few steps. Before long, however, the distance between these divergent paths widens, eventually resulting in vastly different destinations. Few look far enough down the path to see where small steps incrementally take us. But wisdom begs us to discern the direction of our decisions. As Andy Stanley put it, "Direction—not intention—determines our destination."[2] How can we see farther down the path so "when you walk, your step will not be hampered, and if you run, you will not stumble" (Proverbs 4:12)?

Direction—Not Intention—Determines Our Destination

Robert Frost's poem reveals that the path you choose will determine your destination. Yet there is a subtler truth in the poem. We don't just choose a path; the path chooses us. Our chosen path reveals what's in us, not merely what's ahead of us. This is also the truth of Proverbs 11:3: "The integrity of the upright guides them, but the crookedness of the treacherous destroys them."

While our path isn't predetermined, the trajectory it sets us on is. Psalm 37:23–24 says, "The steps of a man are established by the LORD, when he delights in his way; though he fall, he shall not be cast headlong, for the LORD upholds his hand." This is an incredible promise. When we choose the Lord's path, even when we stumble (and we all do), he grabs our hand like a good father and keeps us from falling.

Wisdom beckons us to look far enough down the path to see where it will lead. This was partly what Moses was suggesting in some of his final words to the Israelites: "I call heaven and earth to witness against you today, that I have set before you life and death, blessing and curse. Therefore choose life, that you and your offspring may live" (Deuteronomy 30:19).

The younger we are, the more shortsighted we are. Kids seldom value brushing their teeth, doing homework, eating vegetables, showing up on time, or saying "thank you." But these micro-habits have massive directional implications. None matter much in the moment, yet they set the trajectory for our future self. Young people haven't lived enough life to see where the paths lead. Older people know that by the time you experience the effects of decisions, it's too late to undo them.

That's why elders are invaluable. They are telescopes to our decisions. While teenagers are frustrated with their parents, who can't seem to see what's happening right around them, the reality is that teens can't clearly see what's ahead of them. This truth is easy to see in others. Only wisdom helps us see it in the mirror.

Parents aren't the only telescope at our disposal, and teenagers aren't the only ones who need these telescopes. Mentors have a future perspective that can help us see which path leads to which destination. Ultimately, they are a window into God's will. Listen to his call in Isaiah 48:17–18: "I am the LORD your God, who teaches you to profit, who leads you in the way you should go. Oh that you had paid attention to my commandments! Then your peace would have been like a river, and your righteousness like the waves of the sea." Wisdom is not merely choosing the right path but inviting the right partners to journey along with us.

Words and Work Set Your Direction

Proverbs 12:14 says, "From the fruit of his mouth a man is satisfied with good, and the work of a man's hand comes back to him." Your words reveal what's in you; your work predicts what's ahead of you.

Words. Jesus said, "What comes out of the mouth proceeds from the heart, and this defiles a person. For out of the heart come evil thoughts, murder, adultery, sexual immorality, theft, false witness, slander. These are what defile a person" (Matthew 15:18–20). A modern proverb says, "The eyes are the window to the soul." More accurately, however, your mouth is the window to your soul. What comes out of your mouth reveals what's in your heart.

Parents are rightly concerned about their kids swearing. Far more damaging, however, are bragging and embellishing. Bragging is when you artificially boost your reputation with words rather than actions. Embellishing is when you add to a story to make yourself look better than you are. Both are attempts to get something for nothing. You cheat your soul of significance when you attempt to gain honor without becoming honorable. That laziness of character will erode your integrity. Proverbs 19 includes nearly identical proverbs: "A false witness will not go unpunished, and he who breathes out lies will not escape" (verse 5; see also verse 9).

Work. Physical labor (for those who are able) reveals grit. It's as true spiritually as it is physically. Romans 2:6–8 says, "He will render to each one according to his works: to those who by patience in well-doing seek for glory and honor and immortality, he will give eternal life; but for those who are self-seeking and do not obey the truth, but obey unrighteousness, there will be wrath and fury." How you work reveals your character. That's why God can judge us based on our works.

Some will object to judgment based on works, since we are saved by grace through faith (Ephesians 2:8–10). However, every scripture describing judgment says it's based on our works (Matthew 16:27; Romans 2:6; 14:12; 2 Corinthians 5:10; 1 Peter 1:17; Revelation 2:23; 20:12). While we don't earn salvation through our works, we do demonstrate our faith through our works. Works are the *result* of salvation, not the *cause* of it. How we work and the words we speak set the trajectory of this life and the next.

Wisdom in Action

We don't always consider the consequences of our work and words. When you come to a fork in the road, here are four questions to ask to help you see further ahead so you can choose the right path. You might first ask, "What would _______ choose?" Fill in the blank with a mentor you respect or someone you want to become like. Second, "Who wins in this decision—my present self or my future self?" The more you prioritize your future self, the quicker you'll become your ideal self. Third, "Who am I trying to impress—a friend, a lover, a parent, a coach, or God?" There may be multiple answers to this question, but the best rule of thumb is to impress those who are most impressive. A foolish friend will be impressed by foolishness. Finally, "Will this decision require payment now or later?" Every payment deferred, whether financial, relational, or physical, will require more interest than you estimate. Every deposit made today acquires interest—and usually more than you imagine.

If these questions guide your decisions, this proverb will be true of you: "An evil man is ensnared in his transgression, but a righteous man sings and rejoices" (Proverbs 29:6).

LL KEEP THEE: TO DELIVER THEE FROM THE WAY OF THE EVIL MAN, FRO
N THAT SPEAKETH FROWARD THINGS; WHO LEAVE THE PATHS OF UPRIGH

This Week

- ☐ **Day 1:** Read this essay.
- ☐ **Day 2:** Memorize Proverbs 14:12.
- ☐ **Day 3:** Read the biography of Adam and Eve (Genesis 3) and find one thing to avoid.
- ☐ **Day 4:** Meditate on Matthew 7:13–14; Romans 2:6–8; Galatians 6:7–8.
- ☐ **Day 5:** Discuss.

Group Discussion

1. When have the consequences of a decision been very different than you expected? (This could be a fun example.)
2. This chapter mentions that our chosen path reveals what's in us, not merely what's ahead of us. How do your past decisions reflect your inner values and priorities?
3. What practical steps can you take to anticipate the long-term consequences of your decisions?
4. How can mentors, elders, and other wise counselors help you determine the potential outcomes of your decisions? Share an example of when someone helped you avoid a bad choice.

Table Talk (in your home)

What are some future consequences you'd like to avoid?

Watercooler (at work or the gym)

What are some lessons you've learned the hard way that you'd share with a friend or new employee?

UNTO DEATH, AND HER PATHS UNTO THE DEAD. NONE THAT GO UNTO HER
AIN, NEITHER TAKE THEY HOLD OF THE PATHS OF LIFE. THAT THOU

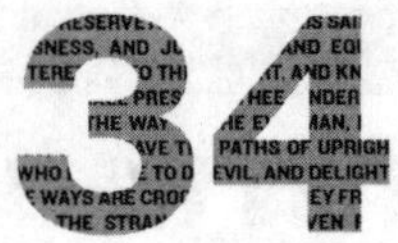

Discipline

Whoever loves discipline loves knowledge,
but he who hates reproof is stupid.

—PROVERBS 12:1

If you want to learn (in)effective strategies for child discipline, might I suggest a free parenting course at your local grocery store? Children are naturally triggered by overstimulation and simultaneous boredom. The phenomenon occurs as parents are distracted, stressed, and rushed, resulting in an interesting social experiment. You can observe the art of bribery, threats, and counting to three (multiple times). If the grocery store doesn't work for you, you could always take an overseas flight to learn about alternative parenting strategies that involve Benadryl.

Nobody appreciates an undisciplined child in public. The fault often lies more with parenting strategies than childish behaviors. Mountains of studies have been done on how unhealthy disciplinary practices affect children.[1] Without appropriate parental guidance, a child will likely struggle with insecurity, anxiety, self-regulation, and antisocial behavior. At school, undisciplined children are easily unfriended, resulting all too often in disruptive and eventually criminal behavior.

Do You Love Discipline?

Nobody naturally likes discipline, but we can grow to love it. We can love the improvement of our character more than the discomfort of correction. That's the point of Proverbs 12:1: "Whoever loves discipline loves knowledge, but he who hates reproof is stupid." The book of Hebrews agrees with Solomon: "For the moment all discipline seems painful rather than pleasant, but later it yields the peaceful fruit of righteousness to those who have been trained by it" (12:11).

We value discipline because it helps us avoid pain and poverty in the future. Proverbs 13:18 warns, "Poverty and disgrace come to him who ignores instruction, but whoever heeds reproof is honored." Children who aren't disciplined sometimes seek it out through misbehavior because discipline isn't just a sign of wisdom; it's a sign of being loved.[2]

God applies discipline for the same reason earthly parents do—he loves his children. Proverbs 3:11–12 says, "My son, do not despise the LORD's discipline or be weary of his reproof, for the LORD reproves him whom he loves, as a father the son in whom he delights." Not only does this truth appear in the wisdom literature of the Old Testament, but it's also repeated in the law, poetry, and prophecy (Deuteronomy 8:5; 11:2; Psalm 94:12; Jeremiah 31:18–19). There is no surer sign that you are loved than when you are disciplined.

Discipline is no more enjoyable for the one giving it than the one receiving it. So, if someone takes the time and the risk to discipline you, you should be incredibly grateful for the love they are showing you. Job's friend Eliphaz was right about that: "Behold, blessed is the one whom God reproves; therefore despise not the discipline of the Almighty" (Job 5:17).

As a parent, I often disciplined with mixed motives. I didn't want to be embarrassed in public or inconvenienced in private. God's motives are never mixed. His punishment is always therapeutic: "Come, let us return to the LORD; for he has torn us, that he may heal us; he has struck us down, and he will bind us up" (Hosea 6:1). There is a very real chance that without discipline our lives will end badly, not merely on this earth but in eternity: "When we are judged by the Lord, we are disciplined so that we may not be condemned along with the world" (1 Corinthians 11:32).

Jesus disciplines with love as well: "Those whom I love, I reprove and discipline, so be zealous and repent" (Revelation 3:19). Not only does Jesus discipline us as God does, but he also asks us to discipline others. That's why he gave us very clear guidelines for how to do so appropriately by going to a brother or sister privately, then following up (if needed) with witnesses, and only after that making the transgression public (Matthew 18:15–17). No one enjoys discipline, whether giving or receiving it, but it's essential to practice if we want to be like God.

Be Disciplined or Be Disciplined

You will either discipline yourself or be disciplined by others. As Paul said, "I discipline my body and keep it under control, lest after preaching to others I myself should be disqualified" (1 Corinthians 9:27). Discipline is required for excellence in sports, business, finance, and education. Those disciplined as children have a better chance of exercising discipline as adults.

Paul told his disciples Timothy and Titus to practice the discipline he modeled for them. To Timothy, he said, "Have nothing to do with irreverent, silly myths. Rather train yourself for godliness; for while bodily training is of some value, godliness is of value in every way, as it holds promise for the present life and also for the life to come" (1 Timothy 4:7–8). And to Titus, he said, "The grace of God has appeared, bringing salvation for all people, training us to renounce ungodliness and worldly passions, and to live self-controlled, upright, and godly lives in the present age" (Titus 2:11–12).

If you don't have a mentor like Paul, allow the Bible to play that role: "All Scripture is breathed out by God and profitable for teaching, for reproof, for correction, and for training in righteousness, that the man of God may be complete, equipped for every good work" (2 Timothy 3:16–17). Placing yourself in a community of believers under a qualified teacher is a preemptive discipline. Training in the Word of God can spare you from the embarrassment and pain of a necessary confrontation after wayward behavior.

No one likes to be disciplined, but we can learn to love the results. The more open we are to discipline, the easier it will be to receive it. One of the best ways to learn that kind of openness is by seeking out honest feedback after an event. Even better is to learn to seek wise counsel on the front end of a task. This kind of preemptive discipline looks way better on your résumé.

Wisdom in Action

Here are some suggestions of the most effective ways to be disciplined in various areas of your life.

Exercise. Most of us must have a plan and a partner to stay disciplined in exercise. Don't just show up at the gym and figure out what you want to do. Use AI to design a workout program to help you achieve your goals, whether losing weight, gaining strength, or improving performance. Don't show up alone. Having a partner exponentially improves your chances of reaching your goals.

Finances. Here's a simple rule: Never buy anything on credit . . . ever. The exception is a house because home values typically rise over time. The only reason to use a credit card is to avoid carrying cash. If this is your goal, you must automate paying your bill in full every month.

Diet. You will lose weight only if you're honest with yourself and keep a record of everything you eat. There are simple and effective free mobile apps that help you track and monitor your intake. You will never outrun a fork.

Time. Make a to-do list each day. Then label each item according to its priority: A, B, C, and D. Your A priority items are actions that will directly affect the kind of person you want to become. Make sure to complete all your A's every day. These are "secular" in nature but have an impact on your spiritual character. When your life is well ordered, you create space for your spirit to put down roots. Simple disciplines like diet, exercise, and rest will overflow into your spiritual disciplines of prayer, Bible reading, and worship. When you're proactive about your own discipline, you'll be disciplined by others less. That's a win for everyone.

LL KEEP THEE: TO DELIVER THEE FROM THE WAY OF THE EVIL MAN, FRO
N THAT SPEAKETH FROWARD THINGS; WHO LEAVE THE PATHS OF UPRIGH

This Week

- ☐ **Day 1:** Read this essay.
- ☐ **Day 2:** Memorize Proverbs 12:1.
- ☐ **Day 3:** Read the biography of Samson (Judges 16) and find one thing to apply or avoid.
- ☐ **Day 4:** Meditate on 1 Corinthians 9:27; 11:32; Hebrews 12:11.
- ☐ **Day 5:** Discuss.

Group Discussion

1. What discipline did you receive growing up that led to you be disciplined today?
2. How open or resistant are you to discipline now?
3. How can you discipline yourself in exercise, finances, diet, or time management?
4. Reflect on the statement "You will either discipline yourself or be disciplined by others." How does this apply to your current life situation?

Table Talk (in your home)

How can we cultivate our spiritual disciplines of Bible study, prayer, and community involvement?

Watercooler (at work or the gym)

Do you consider yourself a disciplined person? Why or why not?

UNTO DEATH, AND HER PATHS UNTO THE DEAD. NONE THAT GO UNTO HER
AIN, NEITHER TAKE THEY HOLD OF THE PATHS OF LIFE. THAT THOU

PART 5

Character

35

Love

Let not steadfast love and faithfulness forsake you; bind them around your neck; write them on the tablet of your heart.

—Proverbs 3:3

Pat Tillman entered the NFL in 1998 at age twenty-one and quickly became a standout safety for the Arizona Cardinals. He was a rising star, admired for his skill on the field and his character off the field. He had everything a man could want—fame, wealth, and a promising future. Something deeper called to him, however. After 9/11, he felt called to a higher purpose and a greater sacrifice for his country.

He chose to walk away from the life he loved for the country he loved even more. Loyalty, sacrifice, and a commitment to something greater than himself led Tillman to sign up for the Army Rangers.

On April 22, 2004, at twenty-seven, Pat Tillman paid the ultimate price for that commitment. He was killed in a remote region of Afghanistan, a victim of friendly fire during an ambush.[1] He died a world away at the hands of his own countrymen. His sacrifice is a microcosm of the major message of the Bible—love.

The Greatest of These Is Love

If there were a single word to capture the message of the entire Bible, it would be *love.* The most important verse for the Jews was Deuteronomy 6:5: "You shall love the LORD your God with all your heart and with all your soul and with all your might." The most important verse for Christians is John 3:16: "For God so loved the world, that he gave his only Son, that whoever believes in him should not perish but have eternal life." Love is the essence of the two great commands: Love God and love your neighbor (Matthew 22:37–39; Luke 10:27) and the foremost fruit of the Spirit (Galatians 5:22–23).[2] Paul offered a fitting summary in 1 Corinthians 13:13: "Faith, hope, and love abide, these three; but the greatest of these is love."

In the Old Testament, the Hebrew word for "love" is *chesed* (if you sound like you are about to spit when you say the "ch," you are pronouncing it correctly). It's not mere emotion but covenant loyalty. Forty-four times, this word *chesed* is paired with the synonym *emeth,* meaning "truth," "firmness," or "faithfulness." This common combination finds its way into Proverbs five times, as in our key verse: "Let not steadfast love and faithfulness forsake you; bind them around your neck; write them on the tablet of your heart" (Proverbs 3:3; see also 14:22; 16:6; 20:6, 28).

Love isn't just the core of the Bible. It's the core pursuit of our lives. Proverbs 19:22 is right: "What is desired in a man is steadfast love." We look for it in our spouse (5:19), family (15:17), and friends (17:17). Without love, nothing else matters. All our human relationships—spouses, siblings, friends—are training grounds for a relationship with our Father in heaven. "Anyone who does not love does not know God, because God is love" (1 John 4:8).

When God described himself to Moses, he said, "The LORD, the LORD, a God merciful and gracious, slow to anger, and abounding in steadfast love and faithfulness, keeping steadfast love for thousands" (Exodus 34:6–7).

This became the standard description of God (Numbers 14:18; 2 Chronicles 30:9; Nehemiah 9:17; Psalms 86:15; 103:8; 145:8; Joel 2:13; Jonah 4:2).

When we turn to the New Testament, love is embodied in the person of Jesus (John 3:16). Jesus sacrificed his life to pay the penalty for our sins. God didn't just love us when we were lovely: "God shows his love for us in that while we were still sinners, Christ died for us" (Romans 5:8). God loved Jesus more intensely than we can imagine. Virtually all God said about Jesus was "This is my beloved Son, with whom I am well pleased" (Matthew 3:17; 17:5; see also 12:18). Jesus knew that part of the reason God loved him so much was his willingness to lay down his life: "For this reason the Father loves me, because I lay down my life that I may take it up again" (John 10:17).

Jesus asks us to love him with that same intensity. He demands our allegiance to him above anything else (Matthew 6:24), even family loyalties: "Whoever loves father or mother more than me is not worthy of me, and whoever loves son or daughter more than me is not worthy of me" (10:37). His demands are high, but so are his rewards:

> In all these things we are more than conquerors through him who loved us. For I am sure that neither death nor life, nor angels nor rulers, nor things present nor things to come, nor powers, nor height nor depth, nor anything else in all creation, will be able to separate us from the love of God in Christ Jesus our Lord. (Romans 8:37–39)

What Does Love Look Like?

Love is the greatest of all human pursuits. However, many of us aren't adept at discerning true love. Not only are we "lookin' for love in all the wrong places" (to quote country legend Johnny Lee),[3] but we also often don't recognize authentic love when it stares us in the face. Scripture helps us see what real love looks like.

Seek love that speaks truth. We saw this in the chapter on reproof. Having hard conversations and correcting wayward actions is a sure sign of love. Proverbs 9:8 says, "Do not reprove a scoffer, or he will hate you; reprove a wise man, and he will love you." Not only will this kind of person love you, but they will also forgive you. Proverbs 10:12 reminds us that "hatred stirs up strife, but love covers all offenses."

Seek love that sacrifices self. John 3:16 defines love as God giving his one and only Son. If you are looking for that kind of love on earth, seek love from someone willing to sacrifice what is most precious to them. If you want to be that kind of person, be willing to sacrifice what is most precious to you—time, energy, finances, priorities. Jesus summarized this principle in a simple sentence: "Greater love has no one than this, that someone lay down his life for his friends" (John 15:13).

If you are looking for a checklist of love, here's a pretty good one: "Love is patient and kind; love does not envy or boast; it is not arrogant or rude. It does not insist on its own way; it is not irritable or resentful; it does not rejoice at wrongdoing, but rejoices with the truth. Love bears all things, believes all things, hopes all things, endures all things" (1 Corinthians 13:4–7).

Wisdom in Action

Jesus commanded us, above all else, to love God (Matthew 22:37). This is the whole duty of humankind (Ecclesiastes 12:13). But how? Realistically, what can we do to sacrificially serve God? After all, he needs nothing from us. Jesus answered, "A new commandment I give to you, that you love one another: just as I have loved you, you also are to love one another. By this all people will know that you are my disciples, if you have love for one another" (John 13:34–35). That "one another" is the rub.

In this world, we love people who are like us. But since God loved us as enemies, he calls us to love our enemies (Matthew 5:44). You may not be able to make yourself *feel* differently, but you can still serve sacrificially. To truly love God, we must love those he loves. How? In 1 John 3:16–17 we find the answer with clarity: "By this we know love, that he laid down his life for us, and we ought to lay down our lives for the brothers. But if anyone has the world's goods and sees his brother in need, yet closes his heart against him, how does God's love abide in him?" Seek opportunities to serve in this way, and you will love well.

LINETH UNTO DEATH, AND HER PATHS UNTO THE DEAD. NONE THAT GO UNT
URN AGAIN, NEITHER TAKE THEY HOLD OF THE PATHS OF LIFE. THAT
EST WALK IN THE WAY OF GOOD MEN, AND KEEP THE PATHS OF THE RIGHT

This Week

- ☐ **Day 1:** Read this essay.
- ☐ **Day 2:** Memorize Proverbs 3:3.
- ☐ **Day 3:** Read the biography of Ruth (Ruth 1) and find one thing to apply.
- ☐ **Day 4:** Meditate on John 3:16, 13:34–35; Romans 13:8.
- ☐ **Day 5:** Discuss.

Group Discussion

1. When did you first say "I love you" to someone outside your family? When did you last say it to someone outside your family?
2. How can Jesus's sacrificial love shape how we love others who are difficult to love?
3. Reflect on 1 Corinthians 13:4–7. Which aspect of love mentioned is most challenging for you, and why?
4. How can we balance loving those who are difficult or different while still maintaining our own boundaries and well-being?

Table Talk (in your home)

In what practical ways can we lay down our lives for others in our daily routines?

Watercooler (at work or the gym)

How would you define love?

MOUTH COMETH KNOWLEDGE AND UNDERSTANDING. HE LAYETH UP
DOM FOR THE RIGHTEOUS: HE IS A BUCKLER TO THEM THAT WALK UPRIGH
PETH THE PATHS OF JUDGMENT, AND PRESERVETH THE WAY OF HIS SAINTS

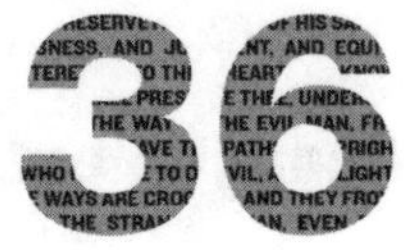

Commitment

Many a man proclaims his own steadfast love,
but a faithful man who can find?

—Proverbs 20:6

On June 6, 1944, Easy Company of the 101st Airborne Division parachuted into Normandy behind enemy lines. During the liberation of Europe, they would take 150 percent casualties. Yet their accomplishments had an outsize impact on Hitler's defeat.

In the winter of 1944, the siege of Bastogne epitomized their resolve. Surrounded by German divisions, Easy Company was a key part of the force that held the line despite being outnumbered and outgunned. Their bonds of loyalty, forged in battle, became the bedrock of their endurance. It eventually enabled them to capture Hitler's Eagle's Nest above the town of Berchtesgaden, Germany.

Easy Company's unwavering commitment to one another became legendary. Their story was immortalized in Stephen Ambrose's book *Band of Brothers,* which became a critically acclaimed miniseries in 2001. Their example demonstrates the power of commitment to preserve and protect what matters most.

God's Commitment to Us

Faithfulness is more than keeping a promise. It's covenant loyalty, what we might call "fidelity," "allegiance," or "commitment." I've chosen the word *commitment* to capture this dense and important idea. This kind of fidelity is founded on love, which is why these words stand side by side in the Bible forty-four times.

As we saw in the previous chapter, this is how God described himself to Moses: "The LORD, the LORD, a God merciful and gracious, slow to anger, and abounding in *steadfast love and faithfulness,* keeping steadfast love for thousands" (Exodus 34:6–7). David described God's faithfulness as extravagant: "Your steadfast love, O LORD, extends to the heavens, your faithfulness to the clouds" (Psalm 36:5).

God is faithful in every way, but two are particularly important for believers. First, "no temptation has overtaken you that is not common to man. God is faithful, and he will not let you be tempted beyond your ability, but with the temptation he will also provide the way of escape, that you may be able to endure it" (1 Corinthians 10:13). God always provides a way for us to live his way. And when we fail, "if we confess our sins, he is faithful and just to forgive us our sins and to cleanse us from all unrighteousness" (1 John 1:9). In other words, our faithfulness to God stands squarely on his faithfulness to us.

Not only is God faithful to us, but he is also faithful to himself. If he makes a promise, he always keeps it. That's why, when we are faithless, he will be faithful to the terms of his own covenant. Paul gave this stark warning in 2 Timothy 2:12–13: "If we deny him, he also will deny us; if we are faithless, he remains faithful—for he cannot deny himself." Because God has provided a way of escape *and* forgiveness, if we deny him, he will deny us according to the terms of the covenant.

Most of the time when the words *faithfulness* and *love* are used in tandem, they refer to God's nature, but in Proverbs, they characterize the wise:

"Let not steadfast love and faithfulness forsake you; bind them around your neck; write them on the tablet of your heart" (3:3). Our faithful love reflects what we have received from God.

Metrics for Commitment

In the Bible, our commitment to God is measured in two principle behaviors. First, we speak truth: "A faithful witness does not lie" (Proverbs 14:5), and "a wicked messenger falls into trouble, but a faithful envoy brings healing" (13:17). Our natural tendency is to bend the truth to our advantage, whether we're trying to avoid hurting someone's feelings, exaggerating our online profile, or leaving out a few details with our parents or spouse. This always creates more problems than it solves.

Because truth is so rare, it brings unprecedented refreshment. Proverbs 25:13 says, "Like the cold of snow in the time of harvest is a faithful messenger to those who send him; he refreshes the soul of his masters." For this reason, Paul charged his disciple to replicate truth through other truth-tellers in 2 Timothy 2:2: "What you have heard from me in the presence of many witnesses entrust to faithful men, who will be able to teach others also."

A second metric for commitment is money management. It may be a surprise that our financial management is a high priority with God. Wealth is one of the clearest windows into our motives—whether we trust God and love people. Solomon warned his son, "A faithful man will abound with blessings, but whoever hastens to be rich will not go unpunished" (Proverbs 28:20).

Jesus had more to say about money than even heaven or hell. Luke 16 summarizes much of his teaching:

> One who is faithful in a very little is also faithful in much, and one who is dishonest in a very little is also dishonest in much. . . . No ser-

> vant can serve two masters, for either he will hate the one and love the other, or he will be devoted to the one and despise the other. You cannot serve God and money. (verses 10, 13)

About half of Jesus's thirty-seven parables feature money.[1] The final essays of this book will have much more to say about wealth, but our commitment to honesty with words and money is the cornerstone for becoming the kind of person the Bible describes as faithful.

Who are the people described as faithful in the Bible? The list in the Old Testament is the standard who's who: Abraham (Nehemiah 9:8), Moses (Numbers 12:7), David (1 Samuel 22:14), Hezekiah (2 Kings 20:3), and Daniel (Daniel 6:4). They were key leaders and men of renown.

However, we find something striking when we turn to the New Testament. The list looks very different. These are not national leaders but local evangelists: Timothy (1 Corinthians 4:17), Tychicus (Ephesians 6:21), Epaphras (Colossians 1:7), Onesimus (Colossians 4:9), and Silvanus (1 Peter 5:12). Aside from Timothy, they are virtual unknowns. How did they get elevated to such status? The difference is Jesus. The writer of Hebrews explained why in this particularly revealing passage:

> Moses was faithful in all God's house as a servant, to testify to the things that were to be spoken later, but Christ is faithful over God's house as a son. And we are his house, if indeed we hold fast our confidence and our boasting in our hope. (3:5–6)

Moses was a mere servant, but Jesus elevated us as sons. Our commitment to God isn't the cause of our status; it's our response to it. Furthermore, our commitment to God is demonstrated in our commitment to the people around us. Our loyalty as children, siblings, spouses, workers, and citizens reflects on the good name of our God. We are, therefore, people of truth whose word is our bond.

Wisdom in Action

Lasting commitment starts with crystal-clear priorities. What matters most to you, not today, but for your future? Once you can articulate your top three priorities, you can set intentional boundaries around them. It's not how often you say yes to good things that develops commitment but how ruthlessly you say no to good things that compete with great things. Today's easy yes often becomes tomorrow's lasting regret. "No" becomes easier when you surround yourself with people who know and support your commitments. The right priorities, the right nos, and the right companions are the ingredients for the right commitments.

LINETH UNTO DEATH, AND HER PATHS UNTO THE DEAD. NONE THAT GO UNT
URN AGAIN, NEITHER TAKE THEY HOLD OF THE PATHS OF LIFE. THAT
EST WALK IN THE WAY OF GOOD MEN, AND KEEP THE PATHS OF THE RIGHT

This Week

- ☐ **Day 1:** Read this essay.
- ☐ **Day 2:** Memorize Proverbs 20:6.
- ☐ **Day 3:** Read the biography of Ittai (2 Samuel 15:13–30; 18:1–5) and find one thing to apply or avoid.
- ☐ **Day 4:** Meditate on Luke 16:10, 13; 2 Timothy 2:12–13; Revelation 17:14.
- ☐ **Day 5:** Discuss.

Group Discussion

1. What three things are you most committed to?
2. Why do you think commitment is so rare, and how can we cultivate it in our own lives?
3. Why do you think truth-telling is so vital to being a person of commitment?
4. How can you show commitment to God and others in small, everyday ways?

Table Talk (in your home)

What commitments do we want to be known for?

Watercooler (at work or the gym)

What would you say you are most committed to?

MOUTH COMETH KNOWLEDGE AND UNDERSTANDING. HE LAYETH UP
DOM FOR THE RIGHTEOUS: HE IS A BUCKLER TO THEM THAT WALK UPRIGHT
PETH THE PATHS OF JUDGMENT, AND PRESERVETH THE WAY OF HIS SAINTS

37

Joy

A joyful heart is good medicine, but a crushed spirit
dries up the bones.

—Proverbs 17:22

Joy is a complex chemical cocktail in the brain, meticulously designed by God for good. We experience joy when our brain releases a series of neurotransmitters: dopamine, serotonin, oxytocin, and endorphins.[1] Dopamine is the feel-good neurotransmitter, driving our motivation as part of the brain's reward system. Serotonin regulates our mood and emotions. Oxytocin, the "love hormone," strengths social bonds and trust. Endorphins act as natural painkillers, promoting a sense of euphoria.

Positive acts, such as kindness, gratitude, or sacrifice, release these chemicals in small doses. When the high fades, the positive behaviors are repeated to release more of the chemicals, creating an upward spiral of joy. That's God's design, and it's very effective.

This is why Proverbs describes joy as a by-product of righteous living. It's meant to be more than a momentary experience—it's a lifestyle aligned with God's wisdom. Thus, Solomon said, "All the days of the afflicted are evil, but the cheerful of heart has a continual feast" (15:15).

Joy as Fate

In wisdom literature (and Greek philosophy), joy results from what happened to you. Joy is in *godly children* (Proverbs 23:24–25; 29:3), but as every parent knows, kids have their own will. Likewise, *justice* brings joy (21:15), but it's mostly out of our control. Three times, Proverbs says something like this: "Anxiety in a man's heart weighs him down, but a good word makes him glad" (12:25; see also 15:23, 30). Good news is great to receive, but it's impossible to control. Hope brings joy, but it can also backfire according to Proverbs 13:12: "Hope deferred makes the heart sick, but a desire fulfilled is a tree of life."

Solomon had little hope that we could produce joy. His suggestions at the end of his life are thin: "I perceived that there is nothing better for them than to be joyful and to do good as long as they live; also that everyone should eat and drink and take pleasure in all his toil—this is God's gift to man" (Ecclesiastes 3:12–13). Eat, drink, and work? There has got to be more to life than that.

While the Old Testament has glimmers of joy, it has relatively little to say about how to achieve it. Yet prophecy points a way forward: "This is the day that the LORD has made; let us rejoice and be glad in it" (Psalm 118:24). "The day" describes Jesus's death—when "the stone that the builders rejected has become the cornerstone. This is the LORD's doing; it is marvelous in our eyes" (verses 22–23). Our joy comes through the coming One. Paradoxically, it's through his execution we find our greatest joy.

Joy as Faith

Like in the Old Testament, the greatest source of joy in the New Testament is good news. Unlike in the Old Testament, the good news is not about your life but about Jesus's life, death, and resurrection. The word *gospel* literally translates to "good news." Our joy comes from faith in Jesus, which gives us hope for the future and is a joy we can control.

It begins with Jesus's birth, which was pregnant with joy. The star brought joy (Matthew 2:10), the angels promised joy to Zechariah (Luke 1:14) and the shepherds (2:10), John the Baptist expressed joy about Jesus in utero (1:44), and Mary rejoiced while awaiting Jesus's birth (1:47).

None of that would matter, however, had it not been for the Resurrection. Though Jesus's death would bring great sorrow to his disciples, his resurrection would bring joy to replace mourning. Jesus predicted it before it ever happened. In John 16:22, he said, "You have sorrow now, but I will see you again, and your hearts will rejoice, and no one will take your joy from you." It's hardly surprising that joy is a prominent feature of the Resurrection accounts (Matthew 28:8; Luke 24:41, 52). Nor is it surprising that joy marked the early church (Acts 8:8; 15:3).

What makes joy for Christians unique is that joy thrives in struggle. Jesus said as much in Luke 6:22–23: "Blessed are you when people hate you and when they exclude you and revile you and spurn your name as evil, on account of the Son of Man! Rejoice in that day, and leap for joy, for behold, your reward is great in heaven." It went beyond a slogan or a suggestion. He modeled how to turn the sorrow of persecution into the celebration of resurrection. While this sounds counterintuitive, it makes sense when we understand the psychology of joy. Pleasure derives from a present experience; joy comes from hope. The good news of Jesus is all about hope—hope that our sins are forgiven, hope of seeing Jesus when he returns, hope of a reward in heaven. Present persecution may rob us of pleasure, but it reminds us of our proximity to Jesus and our future with him.

That's why we read in Hebrews 12:1–2, "Let us run with endurance the race that is set before us, looking to Jesus, the founder and perfecter of our faith, who for the joy that was set before him endured the cross, despising the shame, and is seated at the right hand of the throne of God." This change in mindset caused by the gospel's good news makes Christians virtually irrepressible. Our resilience comes from the hope that is based firmly on the historical events of the life, death, and resurrection of Jesus.

That's why James could say, "Count it all joy, my brothers, when you meet trials of various kinds" (James 1:2). That's why Jesus said, "These things I have spoken to you, that my joy may be in you, and that your joy may be full" (John 15:11). The apostle Paul modeled this transformative attitude as well as anyone, other than Jesus. He said in 2 Corinthians 7:4, "In all our affliction, I am overflowing with joy."

There is one other aspect of Christian joy that is transformative. Our joy comes not from what happens to us but from what we see happening for Jesus. As John the Baptist's fame was waning and Jesus's skyrocketing, John's disciples asked him what he would do about it. He replied, "The one who has the bride is the bridegroom. The friend of the bridegroom, who stands and hears him, rejoices greatly at the bridegroom's voice. Therefore this joy of mine is now complete. He must increase, but I must decrease" (John 3:29–30). This is the cry of every Christ follower. "Though you have not seen him, you love him. Though you do not now see him, you believe in him and rejoice with joy that is inexpressible and filled with glory" (1 Peter 1:8).

Wisdom in Action

How do we access joy in Jesus? Through the Holy Spirit, as seen in Acts 13:52: "The disciples were filled with joy and with the Holy Spirit." Paul taught in Romans 14:17, "The kingdom of God is not a matter of eating and drinking but of righteousness and peace and joy in the Holy Spirit." Romans 15:13 says, "May the God of hope fill you with all joy and peace in believing, so that by the power of the Holy Spirit you may abound in hope." This is especially true in times of trouble: "You became imitators of us and of the Lord, for you received the word in much affliction, with the joy of the

Holy Spirit" (1 Thessalonians 1:6). This was even true of Jesus: "In that same hour he rejoiced in the Holy Spirit" (Luke 10:21). The Holy Spirit is the primary driver of joy in the Christian life.

If you want more joy, get more access to the Holy Spirit. How? There are a number of possibilities, but the most accessible and practical is by gathering with God's people (Romans 15:32; 2 Corinthians 2:3; 7:13; Philippians 4:1; Philemon 7; 2 John 12). The manifold works of the Spirit manifest themselves in Christ's body. The more Christians gather for worship and service, the more fruit and gifts are expressed.

If you need more joy in your life, show up where God's Spirit is most manifest. As you serve and worship alongside other believers, you'll trigger the chemical cocktail of joy God embedded in your brain. This is his gift to you. Your joy is in your control.

LINETH UNTO DEATH, AND HER PATHS UNTO THE DEAD. NONE THAT GO UNT
URN AGAIN, NEITHER TAKE THEY HOLD OF THE PATHS OF LIFE. THAT
YEST WALK IN THE WAY OF GOOD MEN, AND KEEP THE PATHS OF THE RIGH

This Week

- ☐ **Day 1:** Read this essay.
- ☐ **Day 2:** Memorize Proverbs 17:22.
- ☐ **Day 3:** Read the biography of Hannah (1 Samuel 1:1–2:10) and find one thing to apply.
- ☐ **Day 4:** Meditate on Romans 14:17; James 1:2; 1 Peter 1:8.
- ☐ **Day 5:** Discuss.

Group Discussion

1. Describe your perfect day.
2. How does understanding how God designed you change the way you think about pursuing joy in your daily life?
3. Our greatest joy is possible because of Jesus's deepest suffering. How can this shift in perspective influence your daily actions and attitudes?
4. How can gathering with other believers amplify the joy in your life?

Table Talk (in your home)

What is the one thing we do as a family that brings you the most joy?

Watercooler (at work or the gym)

How do you think joy is different from happiness?

MOUTH COMETH KNOWLEDGE AND UNDERSTANDING. HE LAYETH UP
DOM FOR THE RIGHTEOUS: HE IS A BUCKLER TO THEM THAT WALK UPRIGH
PETH THE PATHS OF JUDGMENT, AND PRESERVETH THE WAY OF HIS SAINTS

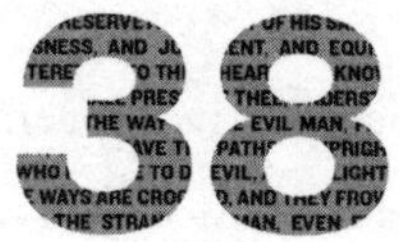

Peacemaking

Blessed is the one who finds wisdom, and the one who gets understanding. . . . Her ways are ways of pleasantness, and all her paths are peace.

—Proverbs 3:13, 17

When some hear the word *peace,* they think about internal calm. Others think about home and "If Mama ain't happy . . ." Refugees think about *peace* very differently as they dream of life after war. In Hebrew, *peace* is broader still. It encompasses physical health, spiritual calm, and community stability. It even served as something as mundane as a standard greeting. They would say hello and goodbye using the word *shalom.*[1] When they met someone under uncertain circumstances, they would ask, "Do you come in peace?"[2]

Shalom was so common it found its way into familiar names, such as Ab*salom* (who was hardly a picture of peace), Jeru*salem,* meaning "City of Peace" (Hebrews 7:2), and most famously, perhaps *Solom*on, who received his name from God when God promised David a son who would be a prince of peace: "Behold, a son shall be born to you who shall be a man of rest. I will give him rest from all his surrounding enemies. For his name shall be Solomon, and I will give peace and quiet to Israel in his days" (1 Chronicles 22:9).

Solomon was to bring peace to Jerusalem, the city of peace, though that seems paradoxical from our perspective, given the long history of war over the Holy City. Even today we should follow the words of Psalm 122:6–9: "Pray for the peace of Jerusalem! 'May they be secure who love you! Peace be within your walls and security within your towers!' For my brothers and companions' sake I will say, 'Peace be within you!' For the sake of the house of the LORD our God, I will seek your good."

Peace as a Treaty

One of the most common uses of *peace* in the Old Testament refers to a treaty between nations, as in Deuteronomy 20:10: "When you draw near to a city to fight against it, offer terms of peace to it." This was the practical peace that would keep people from being maimed in hand-to-hand combat. In the New Testament, *peace* is also used to describe a treaty—not between two warring nations, but between God and us.

Before coming to Christ, we were all part of an opposition force against God. We may not have felt it or recognized it, but our individual sin was part of a cultural assault on God. Jesus came not merely as a peace offering but as a peacemaker to pay the price for us to be reconciled to God. The word *shalom* in a verbal form means "to make payment." Peace is a product of paying the price so the treaty can be signed.

Atonement by the blood of Jesus is our peace treaty. Paul said this in both Romans and Colossians. In Romans 5:1, we read, "Since we have been justified by faith, we have peace with God through our Lord Jesus Christ." And in Colossians 1:19–20, "In him all the fullness of God was pleased to dwell, and through him to reconcile to himself all things, whether on earth or in heaven, making peace by the blood of his cross." This makes even more sense when we realize that each person of the Trinity is known for peace.

Jesus. Even before he was born, he was identified as the Prince of Peace (Isaiah 9:6). Angels announced his birth with a promise of peace in Luke 2:14: "Glory to God in the highest, and on earth peace among those with whom he is pleased!" Even as he marched to his death, the crowds acclaimed him as a royal peacemaker in Luke 19:38: "Blessed is the King who comes in the name of the Lord! Peace in heaven and glory in the highest!" Even the night before Jesus died, he promised peace to his followers amid tribulation: "I have said these things to you, that in me you may have peace. In the world you will have tribulation. But take heart; I have overcome the world" (John 16:33).

Given that Jesus was known for peace, it's stunning that he said, "Do not think that I have come to bring peace to the earth. I have not come to bring peace, but a sword" (Matthew 10:34). How can Jesus be the Prince of Peace if he causes so much division? Because the peace Jesus brings is a peace treaty between humanity and God. Those who reject the treaty declare war against God.

God the Father. Jesus's penchant for peace reflects the nature of his Father. It's somewhat surprising how often God is characterized by peace. Here are several examples: "God is not a God of confusion but of peace" (1 Corinthians 14:33). "May the God of peace himself sanctify you completely" (1 Thessalonians 5:23). Or my favorite, "The God of peace will soon crush Satan under your feet. The grace of our Lord Jesus Christ be with you" (Romans 16:20).

The Holy Spirit. If the Father and Son are bent on peace, is it surprising that this also describes the Holy Spirit? Romans 8:6 says, "To set the mind on the flesh is death, but to set the mind on the Spirit is life and peace." Ephesians 4:3 urges us to be "eager to maintain the unity of the Spirit in the bond of peace." And Romans 14:17 tells us, "The kingdom of God is not a matter of eating and drinking but of righteousness and peace and joy in the Holy Spirit." If this is the nature of the Trinity, then Christians must be bent on making peace.

Blessed Are the Treaty Makers

Wise people are known for their ability to bring peace to difficult situations. Proverbs 16:7 says, "When a man's ways please the LORD, he makes even his enemies to be at peace with him." King David, the fabled warrior, repeatedly praised peacemakers: "Turn away from evil and do good; seek peace and pursue it" (Psalm 34:14). "The meek shall inherit the land and delight themselves in abundant peace" (37:11). "Mark the blameless and behold the upright, for there is a future for the man of peace" (37:37). The New Testament joins the chorus in James 3:17–18: "The wisdom from above is first pure, then peaceable, gentle, open to reason, full of mercy and good fruits, impartial and sincere. And a harvest of righteousness is sown in peace by those who make peace."

The most famous statement about peacemakers comes from Jesus: "Blessed are the peacemakers, for they shall be called sons of God" (Matthew 5:9). To be called someone's son means that you reflect their nature and character—"like father, like son." Since peacemaking is the very nature of God the Father, Son, and Holy Spirit, it's an essential characteristic of Jesus's disciples. Peacemaking is in our spiritual DNA. It's our mandate, not merely from Lady Wisdom, but from the entire Trinity. So "let him seek peace and pursue it" (1 Peter 3:11).

Wisdom in Action

Jesus followed the beatitude "Blessed are the peacemakers" with "Blessed are those who are persecuted" (Matthew 5:9–10). One leads directly into the other. Becoming a peacemaker isn't about being "nice." It's about standing up for those who lack *shalom* in their lives. It's about standing in the face of social injustice and saying, "Not on my watch." This could include defending someone being bullied at school, helping an awkward newbie at work, or fighting for legislation to right social wrongs. Peacemaking may require tearing down walls before building bridges, which often draws fire.

More than social justice, peacemaking is about making God's grace accessible to an ever-widening circle of humanity. The ultimate peace we bring is spiritual. We go behind enemy lines and free captives of the Evil One. How? Simply by sharing the good news of Jesus, who came to die for our sins and pay the ransom to free us from our spiritual captivity. Again, this may not make you popular with your peers. However, as Jesus's followers, we seek *his* approval, first and foremost. If you're not ready to be persecuted for the kingdom of God, you can still be saved. You just won't earn the title "son of God."

LINETH UNTO DEATH, AND HER PATHS UNTO THE DEAD. NONE THAT GO UNT
URN AGAIN, NEITHER TAKE THEY HOLD OF THE PATHS OF LIFE. THAT
EST WALK IN THE WAY OF GOOD MEN, AND KEEP THE PATHS OF THE RIGH

This Week

- ☐ **Day 1:** Read this essay.
- ☐ **Day 2:** Memorize Proverbs 3:13, 17.
- ☐ **Day 3:** Read the biography of Abigail (1 Samuel 25:18–35) and find one thing to apply or avoid.
- ☐ **Day 4:** Meditate on Romans 5:1; 12:18; Colossians 3:15.
- ☐ **Day 5:** Discuss.

Group Discussion

1. When you think of peace, is there a place that comes to mind (real or imaginary)? What is that place like?
2. How does the Hebrew concept of *shalom* differ from the common understanding of peace today?
3. How can we become peacemakers in our communities?
4. How have God, Jesus, and the Holy Spirit brought peace into your life?

Table Talk (in your home)

How could our home become a place of peace—for ourselves and our guests?

Watercooler (at work or the gym)

What do you think it means to be a peaceful person?

MOUTH COMETH KNOWLEDGE AND UNDERSTANDING: HE LAYETH UP
DOM FOR THE RIGHTEOUS: HE IS A BUCKLER TO THEM THAT WALK UPRIGH
PETH THE PATHS OF JUDGMENT, AND PRESERVETH THE WAY OF HIS SAINTS

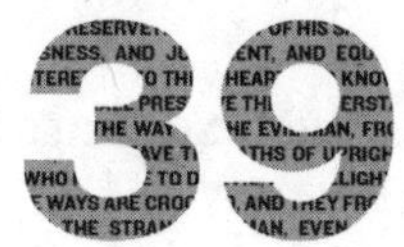

Patience

With patience a ruler may be persuaded, and a soft tongue will break a bone.

—Proverbs 25:15

The average load time for a webpage is two and a half seconds,[1] yet almost half of all users abandon the page if it takes longer than three seconds to load. Most people who click on a video drop it in the first few seconds if it doesn't capture their interest.[2] Those who continue watching average only 2.7 minutes.[3] Online shopping has made us impatient with in-store shopping. We want zero-wait self-checkouts. "Snail mail," which takes up to five business days, has been replaced with email. Yet increasingly, people prefer to text so they don't have to wait as long for a response.

Ad-free, on-demand streaming services are costly but save us a few seconds of ads. Venmo and Zelle, Lyft and Uber, DoorDash and Grubhub deliver instant gratification. The speed of technology has been a cancer to patience.

Our modern proverb "Haste makes waste" is reflected in the ancient dictum "Whoever makes haste with his feet misses his way" (Proverbs 19:2). Our hurried lives create harried souls. Without patience, we're unlikely to master the most important skills for character development: delayed gratification, grit, and steadfastness. The best things in life take time. The breadth of your influence is dependent on the length of your patience.

Patience Was Rare Before Jesus

Given the importance of patience for character development, it's stunning that it's almost exclusively an attribute of God, not of humans. Solomon recognizes the power of patience: "With patience a ruler may be persuaded, and a soft tongue will break a bone" (Proverbs 25:15). Yet outside Proverbs, only one other passage from Solomon urges us to develop patience: "Better is the end of a thing than its beginning, and the patient in spirit is better than the proud in spirit" (Ecclesiastes 7:8).

Apart from a verse in Job (discussed below), the only other exhortation to patience comes from two psalms, which encourage us to wait on the Lord. Psalm 37:7 says, "Be still before the LORD and wait patiently for him" (see also 40:1). This is a key to understanding patience. *Without hope for a positive outcome in the future, there's no reason to develop patience.* Those who believe that God cares for us have ample reason to patiently wait for him to do his work in his timing. Although patience isn't talked about frequently in the Old Testament, this hopeful patience was modeled by Abraham and Job:

> Be patient, therefore, brothers, until the coming of the Lord. See how the farmer waits for the precious fruit of the earth, being patient about it, until it receives the early and the late rains. . . . You have heard of Job's perseverance and have seen what the Lord finally brought about." (James 5:7, 11)

For many, suffering on earth creates space for patience to grow. That was Job's story. We talk about Job's patience, but he started to lose faith in God's faithfulness when his suffering lasted too long. He complained, "What is my strength, that I should wait? And what is my end, that I should be patient?"

(Job 6:11). Christians have the advantage of looking to Jesus's faithfulness in his sufferings as a model for our own. Regardless of what we're going through, we can remember 1 Peter 2:21: "Christ also suffered for you, leaving you an example, so that you might follow in his steps."

Patience is a pillar virtue for the Christian. Without patience, we can't love others as Christ has loved us. The Greek word can be translated "long-suffering." Any of us married or raising children realize there's no love without suffering long. That's why it's the first attribute of love in 1 Corinthians 13: "Love is patient" (verse 4). Patience is central to the fruit of the Spirit in Galatians 5:22–23: "The fruit of the Spirit is love, joy, peace, patience, kindness, goodness, faithfulness, gentleness, self-control." Patience isn't merely a personal virtue; it's an essential skill for meaningful relationships.

Patience as Endurance

There's a second Greek word for "patience"—*hypomonē.* This is not patience with people but patience in suffering. It's what the Bible calls "steadfastness." The foundation of patience with people is love and humility. The foundation of endurance is faith and hope—believing that God will ultimately protect and provide for you. Both kinds of patience are essential for Christians, and both have sparse examples in the Old Testament.

One would think endurance would be a common virtue in the Old Testament, but it's not. It's featured in only one proverb: "A man's spirit will endure sickness, but a crushed spirit who can bear?" (Proverbs 18:14). Outside this proverb, the only place endurance is esteemed is in Exodus 18:23: "If you do this, God will direct you, you will be able to endure, and all this people also will go to their place in peace."

Why is patience with people or problems rare in the Old Testament but common in the New? Because patience depends on Jesus's model of living. His sacrifice demonstrates how to prioritize other people, and his endurance inspires us to look forward in hope to his return. This endurance is essential for our salvation. As Jesus said, “By your endurance you will gain your lives” (Luke 21:19). Paul said the same thing in Romans 2:7: “To those who by patience in well-doing seek for glory and honor and immortality, he will give eternal life.”

We don’t merely endure suffering; we embrace it. Romans 5:3–4 teaches, “We rejoice in our sufferings, knowing that suffering produces endurance, and endurance produces character, and character produces hope.” And in Colossians 1:11, Paul prayed that we would be “strengthened with all power, according to his glorious might, for all endurance and patience with joy.”

Patient endurance can’t stand alone. It stands on the shoulders of other virtues. This becomes clear when you see a cluster of character traits that tend to build on one another. The following passages include patient endurance in a list of virtues: Ephesians 4:2; 1 Timothy 6:11; 2 Timothy 3:10–11; and 2 Peter 1:5–7. The virtues of faith and love are frequently found with patience. When our faith in God grows, so too will our love for people. That’s when we become patient with them.

Virtue stacking eventually results in spiritual maturity: “Make every effort to supplement your faith with virtue, and virtue with knowledge, and knowledge with self-control, and self-control with steadfastness, and steadfastness with godliness, and godliness with brotherly affection, and brotherly affection with love” (2 Peter 1:5–7).

Wisdom in Action

Patience is developed most efficiently through suffering. That’s the bad news. Here’s the good news: Since patience is so rare these days, even a little bit will set you apart in a big way. Your goal should be twofold. First, develop patience with people by loving them sacrificially as Christ has loved you. Second, develop endurance by embracing suffering, which is the only path to grit, or, as the Bible calls it, “steadfastness.” The key is following in the footsteps of those before you and keeping your eyes on the Lord above you. Hebrews 12:1–2 says:

Therefore, since we are surrounded by so great a cloud of witnesses, let us also lay aside every weight, and sin which clings so closely, and let us run with endurance the race that is set before us, looking to Jesus, the founder and perfecter of our faith, who for the joy that was set before him endured the cross, despising the shame, and is seated at the right hand of the throne of God (Hebrews 12:1–2).

If you can do that, your practiced wisdom will set you apart, making you more resilient than those around you.

LINETH UNTO DEATH, AND HER PATHS UNTO THE DEAD. NONE THAT GO UN
URN AGAIN, NEITHER TAKE THEY HOLD OF THE PATHS OF LIFE. THAT
EST WALK IN THE WAY OF GOOD MEN, AND KEEP THE PATHS OF THE RIGH

This Week

- ☐ **Day 1:** Read this essay.
- ☐ **Day 2:** Memorize Proverbs 25:15.
- ☐ **Day 3:** Read the biography of Job (Job 42) and find one thing to apply or avoid.
- ☐ **Day 4:** Meditate on Colossians 1:11; 2 Timothy 3:10–11; James 5:11.
- ☐ **Day 5:** Discuss.

Group Discussion

1. What challenges your patience most (traffic, kids, laziness, incompetence, etc.)?
2. How can patience be a powerful tool in influencing others, as Proverbs 25:15 suggests?
3. How does patient endurance differ from patience with people, and why are both important for spiritual growth?
4. How has your patience grown through suffering?

Table Talk (in your home)

How can we practice more patience with one another as a family?

Watercooler (at work or the gym)

Why do you think people are less patient than ever?

MOUTH COMETH KNOWLEDGE AND UNDERSTANDING. HE LAYETH UP
DOM FOR THE RIGHTEOUS: HE IS A BUCKLER TO THEM THAT WALK UPRIGH
PETH THE PATHS OF JUDGMENT, AND PRESERVETH THE WAY OF HIS SAINTS

40

Goodness

A good name is to be chosen rather than great riches,
and favor is better than silver or gold.

—Proverbs 22:1

Goodness has gotten a bad rap. It's often equated with antiquated morality—quaint and cute but hardly formidable. Occasionally, a figure arises to dispel cultural prejudices against goodness. One such person was born in Pennsylvania in 1928. His childhood was fraught with illness, which left him isolated but planted seeds of empathy toward the lonely or overlooked. By age thirty-four, he had earned two degrees—one in music and another in theology—preparing him for ordination as a Presbyterian minister. But that's not what he's known for.

In 1966, at age thirty-eight, he launched a television program for children focused on moral training rather than the typically loud and colorful characters common in children's television. Through simple conversations, puppet stories, and calm explanations, he taught children about kindness, empathy, and self-worth. *Mister Rogers' Neighborhood* ran for thirty-one seasons, ending in 2001 when Fred Rogers was seventy-three years old. He passed away less than two years later.[1]

Fred Rogers didn't just entertain; he nurtured children's souls. His gentleness and unwavering commitment to goodness made him an iconic figure in children's television and American culture. In 2019, his goodness was enshrined in a major motion picture, *A Beautiful Day in the Neighborhood,* featuring Tom Hanks.

Goodness Versus Righteousness

Righteousness is what Jesus provided through his sacrifice. Goodness is what we offer him in response. Our good works are an effect of salvation, not the cause of it. It's what some theologians call "sanctification." This oversimplification of the biblical doctrine of goodness may help us understand the process: Righteousness comes from God and establishes our relationship with him, while goodness is our response to God and affects our relationship with others.

Paul spelled this out clearly in Ephesians 2:8–10: "By grace you have been saved through faith. And this is not your own doing; it is the gift of God, not a result of works, so that no one may boast. For we are his workmanship, created in Christ Jesus for good works, which God prepared beforehand, that we should walk in them."

People of goodness are described several ways in Scripture: blameless, upright, people of integrity, or even as the righteous. While none of us can claim to have achieved goodness, we are called to walk on its path. Goodness is a journey in the book of Proverbs: "So you will walk in the way of the good and keep to the paths of the righteous" (2:20). Therefore, the question is not whether you are good but whether you are heading down the good path.

Our culture often scoffs at the idea of goodness, considering it soft, naïve, or gullible. We may not adore the label we receive for being good, but we value the results. As Solomon said, "A good man will be filled with the fruit of his ways" (14:14). He also gave several examples of what that fruit looks like: "A good man obtains favor from the LORD" (12:2). "A good man leaves an inheritance to his children's children" (13:22). "Whoever pursues righteousness and kindness will find life, righteousness, and honor" (21:21). Who doesn't want that?

The rest of the Old Testament confirms that the way of goodness leads to good things. For ancient Israel, it allowed them to possess the promised land (Deuteronomy 6:18). In the New Testament, the stakes are even higher. Rather than land, you possess and protect the very reputation of Jesus Christ "so that the name of our Lord Jesus may be glorified in you, and you in him, according to the grace of our God and the Lord Jesus Christ" (2 Thessalonians 1:12). As 1 Peter 2:15 says, "This is the will of God, that by doing good you should put to silence the ignorance of foolish people." If this is the path you want, Proverbs shows you how to find it.

Progress on the Path

This may come as a surprise, but progress in goodness doesn't come through religious activities. As Proverbs 21:3 says, "To do righteousness and justice is more acceptable to the LORD than sacrifice." Going to church, reading your Bible, and praying are helpful, but it's our actions that matter (not mere words or intentions), as Proverbs 20:11 affirms: "Even a child makes himself known by his acts, by whether his conduct is pure and upright."

Jesus "went about doing good and healing all who were oppressed by the devil" (Acts 10:38). That's as good a place to start as any. We may not have the ability to physically heal sickness or cast out demons, but we can use what we have to alleviate the suffering of those around us. That's why Paul told Timothy to tell the wealthy in his church "to do good, to be rich in good works, to be generous and ready to share" (1 Timothy 6:18).

That's not just for the rich but for anyone with more than they need. If you have more time than you need, use it to meet a need. If you have more talent or more of some other resource than you need, use it to meet a need.

Goodness comes down to a simple mindset that will change your behavior: God blesses funnels, not buckets. He doesn't put his resources in buckets to be carried; instead, he puts them in funnels to be distributed. If God has blessed you, he wants you to bless others.

What could this look like? The Bible calls several people "good." By looking at how they lived, we can build a working model of goodness. Noah was good (Genesis 6:9) because he followed God even when those around him didn't. Abraham was good (Genesis 15:6; 18:19; James 2:23) because he believed God even when he couldn't see the promise fulfilled. Job was good (Job 1:1) because he held on to God's goodness even when his life wasn't good. David was good (2 Samuel 22:21, 24; 1 Kings 9:4) because he put God above his own ambitions. Daniel was good (Daniel 6:4) because he refused to abandon God's values in a culture that had no respect for them.

When we come to the New Testament, Joseph was good (Matthew 1:19) because he wouldn't publicly dishonor Mary. Zechariah and Elizabeth were good (Luke 1:6), as was Simeon (Luke 2:25), because he believed in God's promise against all hope. Cornelius was good (Acts 10:22) because he believed in God when no one believed he belonged to God's people. Barnabas was good (Acts 9:27; 11:24) because he believed in Paul when no one else did.

That's quite a list. It's also striking that no single behavior stands out. They all did good things because of the good hearts they had. Their faith in God drove their actions. This seems to be what 3 John 11 is getting at: "Beloved, do not imitate evil but imitate good. Whoever does good is from God; whoever does evil has not seen God."

Wisdom in Action

Righteousness is what you receive from God; goodness is what you offer to others because of what you have received from God. What has God given you that he might be asking you to give to someone in need? This could be a physical possession, a talent, time, an open ear, or a hand up. The expressions of goodness are infinite though they come from a single source.

Here's the secret to achieving goodness: Most opportunities for goodness will feel like an interruption. Preparing for interruptions is the only way to capitalize on those unexpected opportunities God provides to demonstrate goodness to others. Are you ready?

LINETH UNTO DEATH, AND HER PATHS UNTO THE DEAD. NONE THAT GO UNT
URN AGAIN, NEITHER TAKE THEY HOLD OF THE PATHS OF LIFE. THAT
EST WALK IN THE WAY OF GOOD MEN, AND KEEP THE PATHS OF THE RIGH

This Week

- ☐ **Day 1:** Read this essay.
- ☐ **Day 2:** Memorize Proverbs 22:1.
- ☐ **Day 3:** Read the biography of Cornelius (Acts 10) and find one thing to apply.
- ☐ **Day 4:** Meditate on Galatians 5:22–23; 2 Thessalonians 1:11–12; 1 Peter 2:15.
- ☐ **Day 5:** Discuss.

Group Discussion

1. Who in your life embodies goodness? Why?
2. How does the distinction between righteousness and goodness change your perspective on the Christian life and your responsibility toward others?
3. Which biblical figure known for goodness resonates most with you, and why?
4. If goodness grows through kindness to others even more than religious activities, how can you expand your focus from "huddle activities" (such as prayer and church attendance) to practical actions that involve social service?

Table Talk (in your home)

If we are to move from buckets to funnels, what is one thing we could give to someone or do for someone in need that would help them experience God's grace?

Watercooler (at work or the gym)

What does having a good name mean, and why is that important?

MOUTH COMETH KNOWLEDGE AND UNDERSTANDING. HE LAYETH UP
DOM FOR THE RIGHTEOUS: HE IS A BUCKLER TO THEM THAT WALK UPRIGH
PETH THE PATHS OF JUDGMENT, AND PRESERVETH THE WAY OF HIS SAINTS

41

Gentleness

A gentle tongue is a tree of life, but perverseness in it breaks the spirit.

—Proverbs 15:4

Ulysses S. Grant was born in 1822, the son of a tanner. This Ohio native served in the army during the Mexican-American War, then retired from service in 1854 as a captain. Seven years later, however, Confederate forces attacked Fort Sumter in Charleston, initiating the Civil War. Grant rejoined the army in 1861 to serve his country in its time of need.

By the war's end, he had risen to the highest position in the U.S. Army, leading the Union forces to ultimate victory. Grant's refusal to negotiate with enemies earned him the nickname "Unconditional Surrender." Off the battlefield, however, he was very different. Grant was a devoted husband to Julia Dent and a doting father to their four children—Frederick, Ulysses Jr., Ellen, and Jesse. His tender letters to his wife reveal a gentle affection markedly different from the steely image of the lieutenant general.

His gentleness extended even to his enemies. On April 9, 1865, Robert E. Lee surrendered to Grant at Appomattox Court House, marking the end of the Civil War. Grant displayed extraordinary respect, allowing the Confederate officers to keep their horses and sidearms, and officers and soldiers to return home instead of being sent to prison camps.[1] This act of dignity helped pave the way for reconciliation in the war-torn nation. Grant's ability to be a resolute warrior and a gentle leader highlights the nature of true strength. Meekness isn't weakness; it's strength restrained. In the Bible, gentleness is, surprisingly, a characteristic of warriors who use their strength to protect the most vulnerable.

The Nature of Gentleness

I asked ChatGPT, "What is gentle?" and received these responses: a mother's touch, a light breeze, a feather, cotton fabric. These all pertain to touch. Solomon described only one object as gentle—the tongue (Proverbs 15:4). I know, gross. But it's not really about the tongue, it's about the heart. A tender heart touches people through words spoken. As we've established earlier in this book, Solomon had much to say about our words, like in Proverbs 12:18: "There is one whose rash words are like sword thrusts, but the tongue of the wise brings healing." Or this bit of wisdom in Proverbs 17:27: "Whoever restrains his words has knowledge, and he who has a cool spirit is a man of understanding."

Who are these gentle giants that Solomon could call "men of understanding"? Only three men are labeled gentle in all the Old Testament. David described himself as gentle in 2 Samuel 3:39, which is odd given how much blood he had on his hands. Moses made that claim in one of his final speeches in Deuteronomy 32:2 (again, a bit odd given how he beat water out of rock). Jeremiah joined them in Jeremiah 11:19. Other than these three, only God is described as gentle.

Here's what's weird: When God is described as gentle, it's in the context of war. Psalm 45:4 says, "In your majesty ride out victoriously for the cause of truth and meekness and righteousness; let your right hand teach you awesome deeds!" The same paradox is true for King David. He was a gentle general. Moses, likewise, was a man of war, yet Numbers 12:3 says, "The man Moses was very meek, more than all people who were on the face of the earth." Clearly, meekness isn't weakness. Their strength was reserved for their foes. Their friends, however, were privy to their gentleness.

One powerful way to embody gentleness is by sympathizing with the suffering. This posture is beautifully captured in a poetic prophecy about Jesus: "A bruised reed he will not break, and a faintly burning wick he will not quench; he will faithfully bring forth justice" (Isaiah 42:3). This idea of gentle strength is the key to understanding the most famous statement about meekness in the Bible: "Blessed are the meek, for they shall inherit the earth" (Matthew 5:5).

The Meek Shall Inherit the Earth

This beatitude quotes from King David's Psalm 37:11. It's a battle cry, a song instructing Israel to wait on the Lord and refrain from anger against the unrighteous. In due time God would destroy their enemies and grant the land to the meek who trusted in him. It was a battle cry for Jesus as well when his enemies surrounded him.

In your battles, you can rest in his strength. Jesus bids us, "Take my yoke upon you, and learn from me, for I am gentle and lowly in heart, and you will find rest for your souls" (Matthew 11:29). It takes strength to be gentle. And when your strength fails, you can stand on his. Jesus is a gentle warrior. At his triumphal entry, he rode a humble donkey, not a warhorse (Matthew 21:5, citing Zechariah 9:9).

In the Old Testament, gentleness required waiting on God to overthrow your enemies. Christians have an altogether different approach. We approach our enemies with a gentle tongue to share the message of Christ. In 1 Peter 3:15, it says, "In your hearts honor Christ the Lord as holy, always being prepared to make a defense to anyone who asks you for a reason for the hope that is in you; yet do it with gentleness and respect." In this way, we befriend our enemies, hoping to welcome them into the kingdom as brothers and sisters.

In the family of God, our gentleness includes how we discipline an erring brother or sister: "Brothers, if anyone is caught in any transgression, you who are spiritual should restore him in a spirit of gentleness" (Galatians 6:1). Paul modeled this as well as anyone: "We were gentle among you, like a nursing mother taking care of her own children" (1 Thessalonians 2:7).

This is far easier said than done. Perhaps that's why gentleness seldom stands alone in the New Testament. It's included in collections of virtues like the fruit of the Spirit (Galatians 5:22–23).

We discover something interesting if we compare this with other passages that list gentleness among other virtues (Ephesians 4:2; Colossians 3:12–14; 1 Timothy 6:11). The symbiotic virtues are love and gentleness (four times each), followed by patience (three times), then humility, kindness, and faithfulness (two times each). Your gentleness grows in direct proportion to your love for people and your patience with them. These stand on the shoulders of your humility, kindness, and faithfulness. Gentleness grows from and along with these other virtues.

Wisdom in Action

In a world that is anything but gentle, how can we develop gentleness? Three specific practices are captured in a single concise paragraph in the letter of James. First, gentle words must flow from a gentle life: "Who is wise and understanding among you? By his good conduct let him show his works in the meekness of wisdom" (3:13). Self-promotion and aggression undermine a soft tongue.

Second, avoid comparison: "If you have bitter jealousy and selfish ambition in your hearts, do not boast and be false to the truth. This is not the wisdom that comes down from above, but is earthly, unspiritual, demonic. For where jealousy and selfish ambition exist, there will be disorder and every vile practice" (verses 14–16). Jealousy and selfish ambition will extinguish gentleness. But if you stop feeding them through comparison, they'll wither.

Finally, stack virtues: "The wisdom from above is first pure, then peaceable, gentle, open to reason, full of mercy and good fruits, impartial and sincere" (verse 17). Gentleness grows in the environment of other attributes such as peace, humility, kindness, love, joy, and patience. Start with your character strengths and incrementally add gentleness to them. Our best (and worst) qualities aren't separate from one another. As one increases, so do others that are associated with it. When you practice gentleness, other powerful qualities flourish as well.

LINETH UNTO DEATH, AND HER PATHS UNTO THE DEAD. NONE THAT GO UNT
URN AGAIN, NEITHER TAKE THEY HOLD OF THE PATHS OF LIFE. THAT
EST WALK IN THE WAY OF GOOD MEN, AND KEEP THE PATHS OF THE RIGHT

This Week

- ☐ **Day 1:** Read this essay.
- ☐ **Day 2:** Memorize Proverbs 15:4.
- ☐ **Day 3:** Read the biography of Jezebel (1 Kings 21:1–24) and find one thing to avoid.
- ☐ **Day 4:** Meditate on Matthew 5:5; 11:29; James 3:13.
- ☐ **Day 5:** Discuss.

Group Discussion

1. Who have you known that is both powerful and gentle? Describe what it's been like to be in their presence.
2. The New Testament highlights gentleness alongside other virtues like love and patience. How have you seen gentleness, love, and patience work together to grow character?
3. Where or with whom do you need to be gentler?
4. In what practical ways can you nurture gentleness in your speech and actions, especially when dealing with difficult people?

Table Talk (in your home)

When can we be gentler with our words?

Watercooler (at work or the gym)

Do you perceive gentle people as weak?

MOUTH COMETH KNOWLEDGE AND UNDERSTANDING. HE LAYETH UP
DOM FOR THE RIGHTEOUS: HE IS A BUCKLER TO THEM THAT WALK UPRIGHT
PETH THE PATHS OF JUDGMENT, AND PRESERVETH THE WAY OF HIS SAINTS

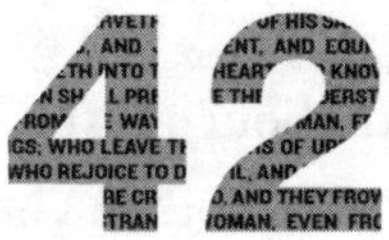

Self-Control

Better a patient person than a warrior, one with self-control than one who takes a city.

—Proverbs 16:32, NIV

In her book *The Cost of Control,* Sharon Miller described how little we have control over. We have no control over the weather, the economy, politics, culture wars, or even our bodies. Yet we try to control them all as if we were God—a problem that goes back to our primordial parents. When we try to wrestle control from God's hands, there's a high cost.

Miller made two striking observations. First, every time we try to take control over a relationship or an event, we make matters worse. She labeled this a Faustian deal with the devil, because control promises us what it can never deliver. We can't change other people or the future. Our attempts to manipulate lead only to tension and resentment. Second, she pointed out that while we don't have control, we *do* have agency. We can take responsibility for ourselves and our responses.[1]

We've already discussed two forms of agency in previous chapters: moderation (deliberately doing less than we want to do) and discipline (purposely doing more than we think we can do). Moderation is agency over excess; discipline is agency over neglect. Another form of agency, self-control, is the final fruit of the Holy Spirit, which makes it especially important.

In this book, we've talked about the fruit of the Spirit, though we've ordered them differently than Paul does in Galatians 5:22–23 because we've approached them through Solomon's lens of wisdom rather than Paul's. This chart shows which chapters cover each fruit of the Spirit and the labels Proverbs gives them.

Fruit of the Spirit	Chapter
Love	**35** Love
Kindness	**35** Included with Love
Faithfulness	**36** Commitment
Joy	**37** Joy
Peace	**38** Peacemaking
Patience	**39** Patience
Goodness	**40** Goodness
Gentleness	**41** Gentleness
Self-Control	**42** Self-Control

Why Self-Control Is Rare in the Old Testament

Interestingly, the term *self-control* is mentioned only once in the Old Testament in the ESV (Proverbs 25:28). Even so, Solomon encouraged self-control in three main areas. First, we should carefully control our words: "Whoever guards his mouth preserves his life; he who opens wide his lips comes to ruin" (13:3). Second, self-control should shape our diet: "Be not among drunkards or among gluttonous eaters of meat, for the drunkard and the glutton will come to poverty, and slumber will clothe them with rags" (23:20–21). Third, we should control our bodily urges, particularly our sexual urges: "Like a bird that strays from its nest is a man who strays from his home" (27:8).

Paul likewise counseled sexual self-control for both married and unmarried. To the married, he said, "Do not deprive one another, except perhaps by agreement for a limited time, that you may devote yourselves to prayer; but then come together again, so that Satan may not tempt you because of your lack of self-control" (1 Corinthians 7:5). To singles, he said, "If they cannot exercise self-control, they should marry. For it is better to marry than to burn with passion" (verse 9).

Because our culture has inappropriately equated sexual expression with our personal identity, sex has been elevated to who we are, not just what we do. At the same time, culture has reduced sexual expression to a bodily function, not a spiritual connection. Therefore, sex has become psychologically essential and morally inconsequential. It's assumed that everyone will be sexually active in whatever expression is convenient and personally pleasing with no regard for spiritual consequences. Add to this the ubiquitous access to pornography through technology, and you have a recipe for disaster in sexual self-control.

One of the notable indicators of the last days is a lack of self-control. People will be "heartless, unappeasable, slanderous, without self-control, brutal, not loving good" (2 Timothy 3:3). Our demand for immediate gratification has made us emotionally and spiritually fragile. The good news for believers is that the bar is set so low that even minimal growth will set you apart from your peers.

Why Self-Control Is Common in the New Testament

When the apostle Paul was in the custody of Felix, governor of Judea, they were at odds politically and theologically. Regardless, Paul captured his attention: "As he reasoned about *righteousness and self-control and the coming judgment,* Felix was alarmed and said, 'Go away for the present. When I get an opportunity I will summon you'" (Acts 24:25). He was overwhelmed by guilt and shame over his own lack of self-control. He dismissed Paul to squelch his own conscience.

Self-control is essential for every person who is saved by the grace of

Jesus: "Every athlete exercises self-control in all things. They do it to receive a perishable wreath, but we an imperishable" (1 Corinthians 9:25). Self-control isn't what we muster as much as what the Holy Spirit imbues. It's a gift from God. Second Timothy 1:7 says, "God gave us a spirit not of fear but of power and love and self-control." However, we must exercise and nourish it for it to have full effect. Peter devoted a lengthy passage to this. Read carefully how it progresses:

> His divine power has granted to us all things that pertain to life and godliness, through the knowledge of him who called us to his own glory and excellence, by which he has granted to us his precious and very great promises, so that through them you may become partakers of the divine nature, having escaped from the corruption that is in the world because of sinful desire. For this very reason, make every effort to supplement your faith with virtue, and virtue with knowledge, and knowledge with self-control, and self-control with steadfastness, and steadfastness with godliness, and godliness with brotherly affection, and brotherly affection with love. (2 Peter 1:3–7)

Notice that self-control follows knowledge. Once you know the right way to live, self-control is required to carry it out.

Wisdom in Action

The first step in building self-control is to recognize that the only thing you can control is yourself. Release the rest to God. If we attempt to control the weather, our future, or other people, we will be frustrated and disillusioned when things don't go our way. But once we relinquish control to God, we can focus on the tasks and circumstances he's given us to steward. In the two previous chapters dealing with moderation and discipline, we discussed some practical advice about self-control. Here I would like to suggest two additional ways to build self-control.

Do one more rep. If you're at the gym, do one more rep of each exercise. Take one more lap. If you're at work, answer one more email. Make one more call. Over time, if you slowly increase your effort, the long-term impact will surprise you.

Choose one hard thing. They tell me that the cold plunge is good for me. I hate it. That's why I've started doing the cold plunge after every workout—three minutes at forty-eight degrees. It's not just because I'm convinced of the medical benefits, which I believe are substantial. It's because when you willingly embrace difficulty, you won't be overwhelmed when trials and challenges come. Choose to do one hard thing every day, and your resilience will grow. As your resilience grows, so does your self-control.

LINETH UNTO DEATH, AND HER PATHS UNTO THE DEAD. NONE THAT GO UNT
URN AGAIN, NEITHER TAKE THEY HOLD OF THE PATHS OF LIFE. THAT
EST WALK IN THE WAY OF GOOD MEN, AND KEEP THE PATHS OF THE RIGH

This Week

- ☐ **Day 1:** Read this essay.
- ☐ **Day 2:** Memorize Proverbs 16:32 (NIV).
- ☐ **Day 3:** Read the biography of John the Baptist (John 3:22–36) and find one thing to apply.
- ☐ **Day 4:** Meditate on 1 Corinthians 9:25; 2 Timothy 1:7; 2 Peter 1:3–7.
- ☐ **Day 5:** Discuss.

Group Discussion

1. What's one area of your life where you could be considered a control freak?
2. How has trying to control things outside your power caused frustration? What has helped you release control of those things?
3. In what ways is our culture lacking in self-control?
4. What practices, such as "do one more rep" and "choose one hard thing," would you suggest to help build self-control?

Table Talk (in your home)

Identify one area where you would like to have more self-control.

Watercooler (at work or the gym)

In what ways would you like to see people around you have more self-control?

MOUTH COMETH KNOWLEDGE AND UNDERSTANDING. HE LAYETH UP
DOM FOR THE RIGHTEOUS: HE IS A BUCKLER TO THEM THAT WALK UPRIGH
PETH THE PATHS OF JUDGMENT, AND PRESERVETH THE WAY OF HIS SAINTS

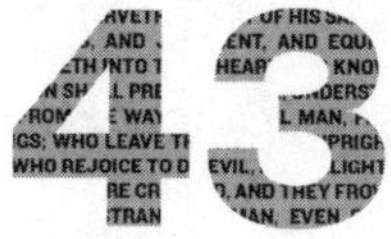

Pride

Pride goes before destruction, and a haughty spirit before a fall.

—Proverbs 16:18

The 2006 blockbuster movie *300* is based on a true story. The Spartans stood firm at Thermopylae against the overwhelming force of the Persian king Xerxes (480 B.C.). Though defeated, they gave Xerxes a black eye and ample impetus to ravage Greece in revenge. Xerxes's backstory is told in the biblical book of Esther, but neither the movie nor the Bible tells what happened next. For that, we turn to the ancient historian Herodotus.[1]

Despite a warning from one of his advisers, Xerxes, blinded by pride, sent his fleet to sea in an effort to crush continuing Greek resistance. His fleet was the most powerful of the ancient world and could have easily defeated the Greek navy, except for one admiral, Themistocles.

Themistocles was a brilliant strategist who knew that the Greeks' best hope was to fight in the straits of Salamis, so he baited Xerxes's fleet with a false message about chaos and support for the Persians within the Greek navy. Once the armada pursued the Greek ships into the straits, their sheer numbers made maneuvering difficult. The Greek triremes exploited the cramped conditions, inflicting heavy losses on the Persian fleet.

From his golden throne on the shoreline, Xerxes watched the catastrophic consequences of his arrogance. His naval power was broken; his pride was crushed.

Why God Hates Pride

"Pride goes before destruction, and a haughty spirit before a fall" (Proverbs 16:18). That is an apt description of the fall of Adam and Eve in the garden. The serpent tempted Eve with the beauty of the fruit, but that wasn't what seduced her. Nor was it the lust of the flesh, even though the fruit was good for food. Rather, it was the boastful pride of life that drove Eve to take a bite and pass it on to Adam (1 John 2:16). Satan promised that this trespass would make her "like God" (Genesis 3:5). That intoxicating temptation triggered the Fall.

Satan knew the power of this seduction well. It was, in fact, what caused his own demise. That is, if Isaiah 14:12–15 is taken as a description of Lucifer's fall from heaven:

> How you are fallen from heaven,
> O Day Star, son of Dawn!
> How you are cut down to the ground,
> you who laid the nations low!
> You said in your heart,
> "I will ascend to heaven;
> above the stars of God
> I will set my throne on high;
> I will sit on the mount of assembly
> in the far reaches of the north;
> I will ascend above the heights of the clouds;
> I will make myself like the Most High."
> But you are brought down to Sheol,
> to the far reaches of the pit.

Pride has been the root of our sin problem ever since the garden. We exalt ourselves as idolatrous substitutes for God. We want control of our lives. This same proclivity manifests itself in toddlers who obstinately proclaim, "I can do it myself," "That's *mine*," or simply "No." This infantile insistence grows in adulthood, precipitating an avalanche of abuse, violence, greed, and deception. It's the cause of war, poverty, crime, and slavery. Is it any wonder that God hates pride?

Pride is a transgression God takes seriously. Proverbs 16:5 proclaims, "Everyone who is arrogant in heart is an abomination to the LORD; be assured, he will not go unpunished." It may not happen today or even tomorrow, but God has fixed a day for judgment when he will humble all who exalt themselves: "The LORD of hosts has a day against all that is proud and lofty, against all that is lifted up—and it shall be brought low" (Isaiah 2:12).

However, God doesn't have to wait for Judgment Day to repay the proud. The principle of reversal is embedded throughout the Bible. Proverbs 3:34 says, "Toward the scorners he is scornful, but to the humble he gives favor." Both James and Peter paraphrased the principle: "God opposes the proud but gives grace to the humble" (James 4:6; 1 Peter 5:5). Since they use identical wording, this was likely a common saying in the early church. Perhaps it's a paraphrase of Jesus himself, who said, "Whoever exalts himself will be humbled, and whoever humbles himself will be exalted" (Matthew 23:12; see also Luke 14:11; 18:14).

If God is this serious about pride, we should be too. Certainly, we despise pride in other people. It's off-putting in athletes, politicians, CEOs, pastors, and entertainers.

It's easy to see and despise pride in the rich and famous. It marked many kings of old, including Uzziah (2 Chronicles 26:16) and Hezekiah (32:25–26). And God said to the king of Tyre, "Because your heart is proud, and you have said, 'I am a god, I sit in the seat of the gods, in the heart of the seas,' yet you are but a man, and no god, though you make your heart like the heart of a god . . . therefore, behold, I will bring foreigners upon you, the most ruthless of the nations" (Ezekiel 28:2, 7). We love seeing the haughty humbled, but when it comes to seeing pride in ourselves, it's a bit trickier.

How to Recognize Pride in the Mirror

Pride isn't a rich person's problem; it's a problem we all possess. Paul offered this description of people in the last days—see if any of this sounds familiar: "People will be lovers of self, lovers of money, proud, arrogant, abusive, disobedient to their parents, ungrateful, unholy" (2 Timothy 3:2). If you read this and thought, *Yeah, those people are bad,* beware! We are all "those people." Look in the mirror before you look at others.

Proverbs offers three ways to detect pride in yourself. First, consider how often you mock others: " 'Scoffer' is the name of the arrogant, haughty man who acts with arrogant pride" (21:24). Second, consider how often you promote your opinions: "Do you see a man who is wise in his own eyes? There is more hope for a fool than for him" (26:12). Third, consider how often you feel superior to others: "There are those who are clean in their own eyes but are not washed of their filth. There are those—how lofty are their eyes, how high their eyelids lift!" (30:12–13). Now, through these filters, go take another hard look in the mirror.

Wisdom in Action

Here's my confession: The most common criticism I've gotten throughout my career is that I come across as arrogant. Here's the truth: It's not arrogance people detect; it's insecurity. My bravado is a thin veil of self-protection to conceal my deep sense that I'm not enough. My greatest fear is that you will think of me what I think of myself. When this fear consumes me, I conceal it with confidence, bold speech, and self-congratulatory stories.

Chances are your arrogance is insecurity in disguise. Accomplishments will never nullify your feelings of insufficiency. Only God's approval can elevate your self-perception, because he declares you good by the very nature of your creation. Your goodness is embedded in your physical and spiritual DNA. It can't be altered by sin or circumstances. Therefore, the way to demolish pride is to receive the affirmation of your heavenly Father. This happens through praying, reading God's promises in Scripture, and receiving encouragement from fellow Christians. When you believe what God says about you, strivings cease. That's good news because then you can use your energy for your purpose in life, not self-promotion or self-protection.

How can you achieve that kind of transformation? Here's a simple tip—one that's sustained countless believers through the ages: Read Romans 8 every day until you believe it. I challenge you to memorize it word for word. Over time, you will learn to see yourself through God's eyes.

LINETH UNTO DEATH, AND HER PATHS UNTO THE DEAD. NONE THAT GO UNT
URN AGAIN, NEITHER TAKE THEY HOLD OF THE PATHS OF LIFE. THAT
EST WALK IN THE WAY OF GOOD MEN, AND KEEP THE PATHS OF THE RIGH

This Week

- ☐ **Day 1:** Read this essay.
- ☐ **Day 2:** Memorize Proverbs 16:18.
- ☐ **Day 3:** Read the biography of the king of Babylon, an image of Satan (Isaiah 14:1–23), and find one thing to avoid.
- ☐ **Day 4:** Meditate on Matthew 23:12; Galatians 3:3; James 4:6.
- ☐ **Day 5:** Discuss.

Group Discussion

1. Describe a moment when your own pride led to a negative consequence. What did you learn from that experience?
2. How have you seen insecurity manifest itself as arrogance?
3. What, if anything, *should* we be prideful about? When does that become dangerous?
4. How can you recognize when you're being prideful?

Table Talk (in your home)

What should we take pride in as a family, and when should we call out pride?

Watercooler (at work or the gym)

Why do you think prideful people are off-putting?

MOUTH COMETH KNOWLEDGE AND UNDERSTANDING. HE LAYETH UP
DOM FOR THE RIGHTEOUS: HE IS A BUCKLER TO THEM THAT WALK UPRIGH
PETH THE PATHS OF JUDGMENT, AND PRESERVETH THE WAY OF HIS SAINTS

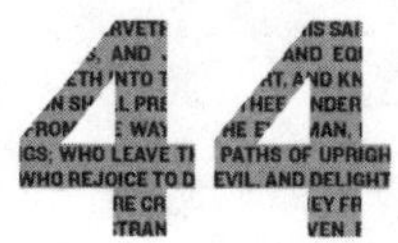

Humility

It is better to be of a lowly spirit with the poor than to divide the spoil with the proud.

—Proverbs 16:19

"I'm going to take my talents to South Beach." That's what LeBron James said when leaving Cleveland for Miami.[1] As you can imagine, that sparked controversy and accusations that he was self-centered and arrogant. James later confessed, "I was very immature."[2] Granted, he has a right to be a bit cocky on the court. Some (incorrectly) argue he's the best ever to play the game. Most people don't know that off the court his actions display humility, not arrogance.

James is deeply involved with his hometown of Akron, Ohio. He doesn't just make donations; he shows up. He has personally invested in the youth there. He opened the I Promise School, which offers at-risk youth education, meals, and counseling.[3] His philanthropy is backed by real relationships. It's not uncommon to see James at the school. He encourages students and follows their progress. His I PROMISE initiative has made a powerful impact for families in Akron.

This illustrates how humility is less about diminishing yourself than about elevating others. LeBron James's humility is measured by how he treats those in need. This is the essence of true humility.

Reversal Part 2

In the previous chapter, we examined pride. This chapter will examine humility. Here's the difference: Pride is primarily a preoccupation with self. Humility, however, is a preoccupation with helping others. Both pride and humility prompt God to reverse a person's fortunes. We saw in the last chapter how common it is for God to turn the tables on pride: "Pride goes before destruction, and a haughty spirit before a fall" (Proverbs 16:18; see also 3:34; 11:2; 18:12; 29:23; Isaiah 2:11; Matthew 23:12; Luke 14:11; 18:14; James 4:6; 1 Peter 5:5). God is equally eager to reverse the fortunes of those who exercise humility by treating the most vulnerable with deference and compassion.

David taught this principle of reversal for the humble (Psalm 18:27), as did Jesus's mother (Luke 1:52) and Jesus himself (Matthew 18:4). Jesus's half brother James stated it clearly in two separate passages: "Let the lowly brother boast in his exaltation, and the rich in his humiliation, because like a flower of the grass he will pass away" (James 1:9–10) and "Humble yourselves before the Lord, and he will exalt you" (4:10).

We hate being humbled, and I suspect few enjoy being humble. It may feel demeaning in the moment, but it yields great advantages. For example, Proverbs 22:4 says, "The reward for humility and fear of the LORD is riches and honor and life." If riches, honor, and life seem attractive, let's consider how we can humble ourselves.

How Do We Humble Ourselves?

The most prominent example of this principle in the Bible is Pharaoh. God called Moses to confront Pharaoh and demand he release the Israelites. Nine times he and Aaron confronted Pharaoh with God's demands: "Thus says the LORD, the God of the Hebrews, 'How long will you refuse to humble yourself before me? Let my people go, that they may serve me'" (Exodus 10:3). Ten times Pharaoh refused. He exalted himself, and in response, God humbled and humiliated him.

Pharaoh, of course, wasn't the only one humbled in the Bible. This was a common theme for kings, including Ahab (1 Kings 21:29), Rehoboam (2 Chronicles 12:6–7), Hezekiah (2 Chronicles 32:26), Manasseh (2 Chronicles 33:12), and Josiah (2 Chronicles 34:27). There is a crucial warning here. You and I may not be kings, but we are still prone to exalt ourselves through prominence, power, or wealth. More dangerously, we give people the impression that we alone are responsible for our success, which is an invitation for God to humble us.

This call to humble ourselves applies to nations as well as individuals, as is famously recorded in 2 Chronicles 7:14: "If my people who are called by my name humble themselves, and pray and seek my face and turn from their wicked ways, then I will hear from heaven and will forgive their sin and heal their land." This national prayer of repentance is desperately overdue.

Humbling ourselves isn't easy. It flies in the face of our sinful nature. While Pharaoh is an example of God humbling the proud, Jesus is an example of God exalting the humble.

Jesus's humility is described most famously in Paul's poetic passage in Philippians 2, and Paul calls us to imitate him: "Do nothing from selfish ambition or conceit, but in humility count others more significant than yourselves. Let each of you look not only to his own interests, but also to the interests of others" (verses 3–4).

Jesus's self-humiliation had the most striking consequence: "Being found in human form, he humbled himself by becoming obedient to the point of death, even death on a cross" (verse 8). How did God respond when Jesus humbled himself in the most abject way? He exalted him to the highest degree: "Therefore God has highly exalted him and bestowed on him the name that is above every name, so that at the name of Jesus every knee should bow, in heaven and on earth and under the earth, and every tongue confess that Jesus Christ is Lord, to the glory of God the Father" (verses 9–11).

Wisdom in Action

It came as quite a shock when I learned that biblical humility is more about how I treat others than how I think about myself. It was liberating because I have difficulty altering my emotions at will. You probably do too. My actions, however, are well within my control. I can alter how I treat people more easily than I can change my feelings. Therefore, humility doesn't have to be artificially contrived through self-deprecation.

Humility is well within reach for all of us. It can be as simple as taking out the trash, letting someone go ahead of us in line, taking time to listen to a child's story, or doing someone else's chores around the house. Every day, likely every hour, if our eyes are open, we'll see opportunities to prioritize the person in front of us.

Paul modeled this well. Although he was an elite Jew with the best education, he served the church sacrificially. He poured into younger men like Timothy and Titus. He worked with his hands while planting churches. He wrote letters of encouragement and prayed unceasingly for those churches. Occasionally, he even allowed himself to be beaten to progress the gospel. This line, which he said to the elders in Ephesus, sums up his ministry: "Serving the Lord with all humility and with tears and with trials that happened to me through the plots of the Jews" (Acts 20:19).

In the previous chapter I confessed how my insecurity made humility difficult to practice. I'm happy to report that, through some accountability and rebuke, I've made some progress. I discovered something that took my breath away. When I openly confessed struggles in public, people praised me behind my back. Previously, when I was the hero of my own stories, people criticized me behind my back. Likewise, the more I served selflessly, the more compliments I received. Previously, the higher I placed myself publicly, the more potshots people took. I'm still a work in progress, but this stunning observation gave me motivation. When we humble ourselves, the Lord *will* exalt us, often through people right around us.

LINETH UNTO DEATH, AND HER PATHS UNTO THE DEAD. NONE THAT GO UNT
URN AGAIN, NEITHER TAKE THEY HOLD OF THE PATHS OF LIFE. THAT
EST WALK IN THE WAY OF GOOD MEN, AND KEEP THE PATHS OF THE RIGH

This Week

- ☐ **Day 1:** Read this essay.
- ☐ **Day 2:** Memorize Proverbs 16:19.
- ☐ **Day 3:** Read the biography of Jesus (Philippians 2:1–11) and find one thing to apply.
- ☐ **Day 4:** Meditate on Matthew 18:4; Acts 20:19; James 4:10.
- ☐ **Day 5:** Discuss.

Group Discussion

1. Who in your life exemplifies biblical humility by treating others with dignity?
2. Scripture says humility can lead to riches, honor, and life (Proverbs 22:4). How has humility created positive outcomes in your relationships or career?
3. Does insecurity ever prompt you to present yourself as more put together than you are? What problems has that caused you?
4. Philippians 2:3 calls us to "count others more significant than yourselves." How can you apply this principle practically to your relationships at work, in your family, or in your community?

Table Talk (in your home)

In this home, how can you put someone else's needs before your own?

Watercooler (at work or the gym)

In what occupations do people struggle the most with humility?

MOUTH COMETH KNOWLEDGE AND UNDERSTANDING. HE LAYETH UP
DOM FOR THE RIGHTEOUS: HE IS A BUCKLER TO THEM THAT WALK UPRIGH
PETH THE PATHS OF JUDGMENT, AND PRESERVETH THE WAY OF HIS SAINTS

PART 6

Wealth

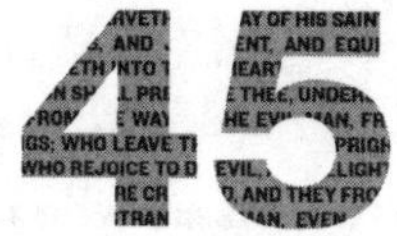

Money

Whoever trusts in his riches will fall, but the righteous will flourish like a green leaf.

—Proverbs 11:28

"In God We Trust" first appeared on U.S. coins in 1864 during the Civil War. It was a way to affirm the nation's dependence on divine providence during a crisis. It would be nearly a century (1956) before Congress passed a resolution to adopt these words as the national motto.

By 1966, "In God We Trust" was added to all U.S. currency.[1] The intention was to declare trust in God, not in material wealth. What a paradox: Despite the fact that our money declares faith in God, we've put our faith in money.

What Good Is Money?

Money isn't the problem. "The *love* of money is a root of all kinds of evils" (1 Timothy 6:10). The love of money comes from our hearts. Money is a gift from God's hand: "The blessing of the Lord makes rich" (Proverbs 10:22). Even our ability to make money is from God. He created the earth from which our resources originate. He created our hands with the ability to till the ground and our minds with the skill to reshape its materials. "You shall remember the LORD your God, for it is he who gives you power to get wealth" (Deuteronomy 8:18). So regardless of how you make a living, the credit belongs to the Lord.

With this mindset, we can do much good with money:

Money can provide security through the purchase of a home, tools for a trade, clothes, and medical care. Proverbs 10:15 says, "A rich man's wealth is his strong city; the poverty of the poor is their ruin." Our financial security can extend even to our grandchildren: "A good man leaves an inheritance to his children's children, but the sinner's wealth is laid up for the righteous" (13:22).

Money can be used for worship. Ezra 7:17 instructed the returning exiles, "With this money, then, you shall with all diligence buy bulls, rams, and lambs, with their grain offerings and their drink offerings, and you shall offer them on the altar of the house of your God that is in Jerusalem."

Money can help the hurting. God's greatest priority for our money is to help the hurting. God commanded Israel, "If you lend money to any of my people with you who is poor, you shall not be like a moneylender to him, and you shall not exact interest from him" (Exodus 22:25). Jesus went further when he told his disciples, "Sell your possessions, and give to the needy. Provide yourselves with moneybags that do not grow old, with a treasure in the heavens that does not fail, where no thief approaches and no moth destroys" (Luke 12:33). Our money is a gift from God to test and grow our spiritual wealth.

Discontentment keeps our money from doing the good it could. Rather than us mastering money, money will master us. Proverbs has this to say about contentment: "Better is a little with the fear of the LORD than great treasure and trouble with it" (15:16). Contentment comes down to faith. Do you believe that God will provide? That is, after all, his pledge to us in Hebrews 13:5: "Keep your life free from love of money, and be content with what you have, for he has said, 'I will never leave you nor forsake you.' "

Through faith, we can be content in any circumstance. Paul famously said, "I can do all things through him who strengthens me" (Philippians 4:13). He was talking not about miracles or leaping tall buildings in a single bound but about financial contentment. Sometimes Paul's ministry was well funded. Other times he had practically nothing. At all times, he was content because he knew that God would always provide all his needs. With this kind of contentment, money can be a tool rather than a temptation.

The Lies Money Tells You

Money is an incorrigible liar. Here are three of its favorite lies:

1. *You earned me; I'm yours.* No, you didn't. God gave you wealth and the ability to generate it. Therefore, it all belongs to him. As soon as you think you own wealth, wealth owns you.
2. *I'm not enough; you need more.* As soon as you achieve any financial goal—a specific salary or amount saved—greed attempts to consume contentment. You instinctively feel you need more.
3. *I will always be here to protect you.* Not true. Wealth has wings and wanderlust. Proverbs 27:24 says, "Riches do not last forever; and does a crown endure to all generations?" Nor can wealth save you when life takes a disastrous turn: "Riches do not profit in the day of wrath, but righteousness delivers from death" (11:4). Even billionaires die.

This is why Jesus spoke so forthrightly and so frequently about the danger of wealth. He warned his followers, "The cares of the world and the deceitfulness of riches and the desires for other things enter in and choke the word" (Mark 4:19). Later he again warned them, "How difficult it will be for those who have wealth to enter the kingdom of God!" (10:23).

What can we do to protect ourselves from the wiles of wealth? Jesus weighed in with wisdom: "Take care, and be on your guard against all covetousness, for one's life does not consist in the abundance of his possessions" (Luke 12:15). How do we guard against covetousness? We use our wealth to help others rather than to protect ourselves. As Jesus said to the rich young ruler, "If you would be perfect, go, sell what you possess and give to the poor, and you will have treasure in heaven" (Matthew 19:21). I love how practically Paul said it:

> Godliness with contentment is great gain, for we brought nothing into the world, and we cannot take anything out of the world. But if we have food and clothing, with these we will be content. But those who desire to be rich fall into temptation, into a snare, into many senseless and harmful desires that plunge people into ruin and destruction. For the love of money is a root of all kinds of evils. (1 Timothy 6:6–10)

Wisdom in Action

Jesus warns us not to worry about money (Matthew 6:25). That's easier said than done, of course. These three simple practices will reduce your worry and increase your enjoyment of wealth. First, if you haven't already, create a budget. The first 10 percent you earn goes to the local church as a tithe. This does more for your spiritual growth than any other discipline. Save the next 10 percent for your future. Avoid get-rich-quick schemes. Automatically invest this amount in a mutual fund and forget about it. If you do this, you will never have to worry about your retirement. The remaining 80 percent is for you to live on.

Second, don't buy anything on credit (except a house). That includes cars, clothes, computers, or cellphones. If you can't pay cash, God probably wouldn't approve your purchase. If you have the slightest qualms about a purchase, postpone it for twenty-four hours. This eliminates most impulse purchases.

Third, seek opportunities to be radically generous (this comes from the remaining 80 percent). This could include leaving a 50 percent tip, giving away a prized possession, paying for someone else's car repair, or sponsoring a child in another country. This is how we follow Jesus's most important advice about money: "Do not lay up for yourselves treasures on earth, where moth and rust destroy and where thieves break in and steal, but lay up for yourselves treasures in heaven, where neither moth nor rust destroys and where thieves do not break in and steal. For where your treasure is, there your heart will be also" (Matthew 6:19–21). Money is neither good nor evil, but it reveals what's in you, whether good or evil.

LINETH UNTO DEATH, AND HER PATHS UNTO THE DEAD. NONE THAT GO UN
URN AGAIN, NEITHER TAKE THEY HOLD OF THE PATHS OF LIFE. THAT
EST WALK IN THE WAY OF GOOD MEN, AND KEEP THE PATHS OF THE RIGH

This Week

☐ **Day 1:** Read this essay.

☐ **Day 2:** Memorize Proverbs 11:28.

☐ **Day 3:** Read the biography of the rich young ruler (Matthew 19:16–30) and find one thing to apply or avoid.

☐ **Day 4:** Meditate on Matthew 6:19–21, 25, 33.

☐ **Day 5:** Discuss.

Group Discussion

1. Who taught you how to manage money wisely? If no one did, what do you wish someone had taught you?
2. How do you actively seek God more than wealth?
3. Money tells three lies: "You earned me," "I'm not enough," and "I will always be here to protect you." Which lie do you wrestle with the most?
4. If a teenager asked you, "How can I learn to be content with what I have?" what would you tell them?

Table Talk (in your home)

How can we practice contentment in our home?

Watercooler (at work or the gym)

Why do you think people struggle to be content with what they have?

MOUTH COMETH KNOWLEDGE AND UNDERSTANDING. HE LAYETH UP
DOM FOR THE RIGHTEOUS: HE IS A BUCKLER TO THEM THAT WALK UPRIGH
PETH THE PATHS OF JUDGMENT, AND PRESERVETH THE WAY OF HIS SAINTS

46

Dishonest Gain

Treasures gained by wickedness do not profit,
but righteousness delivers from death.

—Proverbs 10:2

If you want to get rich quickly and don't care how many people you cheat or lie to, there are plenty of options. For instance, once hailed as a Wall Street darling, Enron used deceptive accounting practices to inflate its profits while hiding massive debts, allowing executives to make millions. When the company filed for bankruptcy in 2001, employees and shareholders were left with nothing.[1]

Countrywide Financial, once the largest mortgage lender in the United States, offered risky loans to people they knew couldn't afford them, with the executives who pushed these loans profiting handsomely. These subprime mortgages contributed to the housing bubble that burst in 2007, leaving many Americans in financial ruin.[2]

Apple was accused of planned obsolescence when they deliberately slowed older iPhones through software updates. While Apple claimed this was to lengthen the phone's lifespan as the battery aged, many saw it as a deliberate tactic to drive sales of newer devices.[3]

Companies like Sensa have made exaggerated claims about the effectiveness of their weight-loss products.[4] Consumers buy in, hoping to slim down. For many, the only reduction they see is in their bank account.

In May 2015, the U.S. Department of Justice indicted fourteen FIFA officials and corporate executives for paying or accepting bribes and kickbacks in exchange for lucrative rights related to media, marketing, and hosting the World Cup. The charges, which spanned twenty-four years, included racketeering, wire fraud, and money laundering.[5] Dishonest gain may offer quick rewards, but the consequences are long-lasting.

Three Options for Bad Gains

Financial growth can be a slow and difficult process. That's why so many people look for shortcuts through dishonest gain. Proverbs describes several options, the most popular of which is **deception**. You lie about your intention, your resources, or the value of the product. Have you ever known someone who boasted about haggling? They acted like they didn't like a product and then bragged about the swindle. Solomon has a humorous description of what we have all experienced: "'Bad, bad,' says the buyer, but when he goes away, then he boasts" (20:14). While it seems like easy money, ill-gotten gain vanishes quickly: "The getting of treasures by a lying tongue is a fleeting vapor and a snare of death" (21:6). Jeremiah 17:11 makes the same observation: "Like the partridge that gathers a brood that she did not hatch, so is he who gets riches but not by justice; in the midst of his days they will leave him, and at his end he will be a fool."

One specific form of deception is a **false balance**. When they measured goods in the market, some used a rigged scale so they could charge more while giving customers less. Four times, Solomon warned how abominable this practice is to the Lord: "Unequal weights and unequal measures are both alike an abomination to the LORD" (Proverbs 20:10; see also 11:1; 16:11; 20:23).

A **bribe** is another age-old trick of the trade. A payment to officials under the table can shortcut fees and regulations. It's not legal, but it works like magic according to Proverbs 17:8: "A bribe is like a magic stone in the eyes of the one who gives it; wherever he turns he prospers." Bribes work, but not for long. As every charmer can attest, if you handle snakes long enough, you'll get bitten.

Extortion is the final tool. You threaten people with exposure or violence to get them to pay what you want (Psalm 62:10). The problem is, extortion makes enemies as quickly as it makes money. And it's abhorrent to the Lord: "Whoever oppresses the poor to increase his own wealth, or gives to the rich, will only come to poverty" (Proverbs 22:16).

These strategies may help you gain wealth dishonestly, but since they oppress the poor and provoke the Lord, the consequences are bleak.

How Dishonest Gain Gets You

"Honesty is the best policy" may sound trite, but it's exceedingly true. Solomon said, "Better is a poor man who walks in his integrity than a rich man who is crooked in his ways" (Proverbs 28:6). It's easy to covet your neighbor's house, wife, servants, ox, donkey, and other possessions (to borrow the categories of the Ten Commandments). He looks so happy with his manicured lawn on the other side of the fence (or on Instagram). Greener grass makes you green with envy, but in reality, money doesn't make you happy.

Obviously, poverty is no pleasure either. However, research from 2008 and 2009 confirmed that above about $75,000 (equivalent to $110,000 today), any increase in annual income has no emotional benefits, and that wealth even tends to fight against your contentment.[6] That's why Proverbs includes this prayer: "Remove far from me falsehood and lying; give me neither poverty nor riches; feed me with the food that is needful for me" (30:8).

Here's the paradox: Those who deceive others to gain wealth find that their wealth deceives them. Jesus pointed out this problem in Matthew 13:22: "As for what was sown among thorns, this is the one who hears the word, but the cares of the world and the deceitfulness of riches choke the word, and it proves unfruitful." That's why God warns you to "keep your life free from love of money, and be content with what you have, for he has said, 'I will never leave you nor forsake you'" (Hebrews 13:5). If God will never leave nor forsake us, there is no need to pursue ill-gotten gain.

This is a non-negotiable requirement for any church leader. Paul charged that any potential elder of the church must not be "a drunkard, not violent but gentle, not quarrelsome, not a lover of money" (1 Timothy 3:3). Likewise, deacons "must be dignified, not double-tongued, not addicted to much wine, not greedy for dishonest gain" (verse 8). You may not plan on leading a church, but all spiritual maturity takes seriously these cautions about wealth.

Wisdom in Action

If you want to be wise, money management isn't optional. Your financial integrity and spiritual maturity are intertwined. Moreover, what tempted you yesterday may not today, but every time you level up financially or move laterally, there are new temptations. So be alert.

Moving away from dishonest gain begins not with Herculean leaps but with small steps. Be sensible with cents, and you can be disciplined with dollars. Jesus put it this way: "One who is faithful in a very little is also faithful in much, and one who is dishonest in a very little is also dishonest in much. If then you have not been faithful in the unrighteous wealth, who will entrust to you the true riches?" (Luke 16:10–11). If you are faithful with little, the Lord will trust you with much (not to mention that your parents, your boss, and your spouse will too).

If your income, status, or responsibility grows, make sure your innocence and shrewdness keep pace. Jesus told a parable about a servant who got caught skimming off the top. His master demanded that he settle accounts, and showed him the exit. While his hourglass was emptying, he talked with several debtors and used his vanishing position to do them financial favors. Of course, he was looking for a future patron in the process. Jesus concluded this tale in a striking way: "The master commended the dishonest manager for his shrewdness. For the sons of this world are more shrewd in dealing with their own generation than the sons of light" (Luke 16:8). The point is, like this manager in the parable, all of us will have to account for how we used the Lord's resources when we meet him face-to-face.

LINETH UNTO DEATH, AND HER PATHS UNTO THE DEAD. NONE THAT GO UNT
URN AGAIN, NEITHER TAKE THEY HOLD OF THE PATHS OF LIFE. THAT
YEST WALK IN THE WAY OF GOOD MEN, AND KEEP THE PATHS OF THE RIGH

This Week

☐ **Day 1:** Read this essay.

☐ **Day 2:** Memorize Proverbs 10:2.

☐ **Day 3:** Read the biography of Ananias and Sapphira (Acts 5:1–11) and find one thing to apply or avoid.

☐ **Day 4:** Meditate on Mark 4:19; Luke 16:10–11; Hebrews 13:5.

☐ **Day 5:** Discuss.

Group Discussion

1. Share a story about a time someone took advantage of you financially.
2. Why is dishonesty so tempting when it comes to financial gain?
3. Give an example of how this proverb has played out in real life: "Treasures gained by wickedness do not profit, but righteousness delivers from death" (Proverbs 10:2).
4. Why is contentment the antidote for dishonest gain?

Table Talk (in your home)

Where would you be most tempted to cut corners to gain financially?

Watercooler (at work or the gym)

Have you ever been tempted to cut corners to gain financially?

MOUTH COMETH KNOWLEDGE AND UNDERSTANDING. HE LAYETH UP
DOM FOR THE RIGHTEOUS: HE IS A BUCKLER TO THEM THAT WALK UPRIGH
PETH THE PATHS OF JUDGMENT, AND PRESERVETH THE WAY OF HIS SAINTS

47

Greed

Such are the ways of everyone who is greedy for unjust gain;
it takes away the life of its possessors.

—Proverbs 1:19

The American household is deep in debt, much of it driven by greed. The average American household holds $7,951 in credit card debt with an average interest rate at 21 percent.[1] An average auto loan for a used car was $26,144 at an interest rate of 10 percent (conservatively).[2] If you have a student loan, you are looking at an average of $38,375 as of 2023 with an interest rate of 5.5 percent, if you are lucky.[3] The interest alone, excluding your mortgage, is $6,395 per year. Unfortunately, this is only part of the problem.

In addition to debt, unnecessary expenses often contribute to financial strain. The average household spends around $141 monthly for cellphone service when much cheaper options are available.[4] Streaming services cost an average of $69 per month.[5] And we are Eating out more than ever before to the tune of $374 per month. These three alone add an annual upcharge of $7,008.

If you cut these three expenses in half and then add just half of your annual interest to it, you could invest $9,899 per year in a mutual fund. Let's say you started at age twenty-five and the mutual fund grows by 6 percent a year (a reasonable estimate); at age thirty, your $49,495 investment would be worth $59,150. At fifty, you would have put in $247.475, but it would be worth $575,690. By seventy, you would have invested $445,455 but could retire with $2,376,736 and live off the interest. That is the price tag for greed over a lifetime.

The Problem of Greed

The Greek word for "greed" can be translated as "wanting-more-ish-ness." That describes all of us, at least a little. Culturally, greed is ubiquitous. It's so common that it's difficult for us to perceive—like a fish not realizing it's wet. Greed is nothing new. Jeremiah 6:13 says, "From the least to the greatest of them, everyone is greedy for unjust gain; and from prophet to priest, everyone deals falsely." Today we tout consumerism as a moral good because it drives the economy. That's not totally false. However, the Bible warns about the danger of greed.

Greed is more likely to lead to poverty than to wealth according to Proverbs 28:22: "A stingy man hastens after wealth and does not know that poverty will come upon him." It's worse than that, however, because it destroys your relationships, not just your accounts: "A greedy man stirs up strife, but the one who trusts in the LORD will be enriched" (verse 25). It gets even worse. When God wants to punish his people, he uses the greed of their enemies to motivate the attack: "Behold, therefore, I stretched out my hand against you and diminished your allotted portion and delivered you to the greed of your enemies" (Ezekiel 16:27).

Greed is a black hole. The Bible reminds us multiple times and with curious metaphors how greed is never satisfied. Proverbs 27:20 says, "Sheol and Abaddon are never satisfied, and never satisfied are the eyes of man." Proverbs 30:15–16 adds, "The leech has two daughters: Give and Give. Three things are never satisfied; four never say, 'Enough': Sheol, the barren womb, the land never satisfied with water, and the fire that never says,

'Enough.'" When you give in to greed, it will take over your life. Be wise and avoid it at all costs.

Avoid Greed and the Greedy

Avoiding greed is difficult, thanks to endless advertising, buy-now offers, and a culture of consumerism. According to Dr. Jean Twenge in *Generation Me,* "Research shows that the more television you watch, the more materialistic you are."[6] Once you get on the merry-go-round of greed, jumping off is nearly impossible. It's dizzying! Solomon rightly warned, "Do not toil to acquire wealth; be discerning enough to desist. When your eyes light on it, it is gone, for suddenly it sprouts wings, flying like an eagle toward heaven" (Proverbs 23:4–5). Jesus offered a similar caution: "Take care, and be on your guard against all covetousness, for one's life does not consist in the abundance of his possessions" (Luke 12:15). The things we possess easily possess us.

The cost of a car is far greater than the purchase price. There is insurance, taxes, accessories, fuel, and repairs. For almost anything you own, there is an additional 20 percent cost of ownership. When was the last time you upgraded your smartphone? You likely also purchased a protective case, a screen protector, apps, a monthly service plan, and accessories like earbuds or chargers. If it breaks, the repair or replacement can break your budget. Then there are RVs and boats. It's said that the two happiest days for a boat owner are the day they buy it and the day they sell it.

With our increasing demand for products and the rise of inflation, it's easy to get lured into get-rich-quick schemes. They will drain your time, resources, attention, and dreams. They're a scourge you should avoid: "Wealth gained hastily will dwindle, but whoever gathers little by little will increase it" (Proverbs 13:11).

There are telltale signs that help us recognize swindlers who will try to seduce us with get-rich-quick schemes.

The quickest way is through their *flattery.* They will tell you exactly what you want to hear so you will forfeit precisely what they want to take. Notice the company kept by the greedy in 1 Corinthians 6:10: "Nor thieves, nor the greedy, nor drunkards, nor revilers, nor swindlers will inherit the kingdom of God." For this same reason, 2 Peter 2:3 warns, "In their greed they will exploit you with false words. Their condemnation from long ago is not idle, and their destruction is not asleep." If someone is buttering you up, keep your hand on your wallet.

Another telltale sign is *sexual immorality.* Three passages connect it with greed (1 Corinthians 5:10–11; 6:9–10; Ephesians 4:19; 2 Peter 2:14). It's wise to avoid getting into bed financially with those who use their bed immorally. The lust of the flesh and greed for gain sprout from the same root.

Caution: Some of the most dangerous swindlers are the most religious. Even back in Jesus's day he warned, "Woe to you, scribes and Pharisees, hypocrites! For you clean the outside of the cup and the plate, but inside they are full of greed and self-indulgence" (Matthew 23:25).

Wisdom in Action

Jesus's warning cuts close to the bone for me. This isn't easy to admit, but greed is a real temptation for me. I began to realize this character flaw in my mid-twenties when I went out to eat with friends. When the bill came, I acted like I didn't see the check, waiting for others to pick it up. I hated that about myself, so I determined to do something about it. I decided that I would always try to be the first to pull out my credit card. Obviously, there are times when it's appropriate to let others pay, but I never again wanted to be cheap, greedy, or selfish. It was excruciating at first. Over time, however, my heart changed. Now I relish generosity. A second step I took was to shop for clothes at Goodwill. I did that for decades. Although I could afford costlier clothes, I couldn't afford blindness to those who couldn't. Being around people who had little financial margin made me aware of how blessed I was and how beautiful generosity is.

Here are some other practical things you can do to short-circuit greed:

1. Make a list of all your subscriptions; then cut them in half.
2. Monitor how often you eat out; then cut it in half.
3. Stay off the internet two hours before going to bed to eliminate impulse shopping online.
4. When you do purchase something, get the second best—car, computer, phone, tool. Not only is this financially wise; it's also a deliberate act of humility that cultivates contentment.

LINETH UNTO DEATH, AND HER PATHS UNTO THE DEAD. NONE THAT GO UNT
URN AGAIN, NEITHER TAKE THEY HOLD OF THE PATHS OF LIFE. THAT

This Week

- ☐ **Day 1:** Read this essay.
- ☐ **Day 2:** Memorize Proverbs 1:19.
- ☐ **Day 3:** Read the biography of Achan (Joshua 7) and find one thing to avoid.
- ☐ **Day 4:** Meditate on Matthew 23:25; Luke 12:15; 2 Peter 2:14.
- ☐ **Day 5:** Discuss.

Group Discussion

1. Why do you think greed is so prevalent in our culture?
2. Proverb 1:19 says greed "takes away the life of its possessors." How do you see greed robbing people of life?
3. If you used the Greek definition for "greed"—"wanting-more-ish-ness"—where would it most apply to your life?
4. What practices might help you grow in contentment?

Table Talk (in your home)

What is one change we can make in our spending habits to reduce unnecessary expenses?

Watercooler (at work or the gym)

Do you feel pressure to keep up with others in terms of material possessions?

DOM FOR THE RIGHTEOUS: HE IS A BUCKLER TO THEM THAT WALK UPRIGH
PETH THE PATHS OF JUDGMENT, AND PRESERVETH THE WAY OF HIS SAINTS

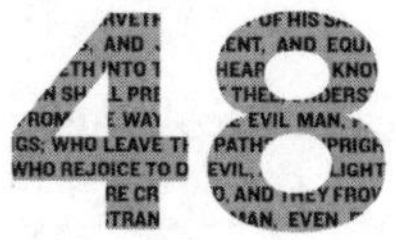

Debt

The rich rules over the poor, and the borrower is the slave of the lender.

—Proverbs 22:7

What do Mike Tyson, Nicolas Cage, MC Hammer, and Johnny Depp all have in common? Despite once being wildly wealthy, each has faced financial woes. They once had millions of dollars, yet their extravagant lifestyles and poor choices led to staggering debts.

Mike Tyson earned about $400 million during his boxing career yet filed for bankruptcy in 2003 with debts of $23 million.[1] In 2010, Nicolas Cage, an Oscar-winning actor, reportedly owed about $14 million in back taxes after overspending on luxury items like castles and rare collectibles.[2] MC Hammer filed for bankruptcy in 1996 after having made more than $30 million from his music career.[3] Clearly, it's not the amount of money but the decisions you make that determine your debt.

Debt Makes You a Slave

Among the ancient Jews, indentured servitude was a painful reality for many. Most of the population lived on the edge of subsistence. One bad crop, a single natural disaster, or a misguided gamble could throw you on the mercy of a lender, as Solomon explained: "The rich rules over the poor, and the borrower is the slave of the lender" (Proverbs 22:7).

That's why we're instructed to pay our debts as soon as possible. Proverbs 3:27–28 says, "Do not withhold good from those to whom it is due, when it is in your power to do it. Do not say to your neighbor, 'Go, and come again, tomorrow I will give it'—when you have it with you." Romans 13:7–8 echoes the command: "Pay to all what is owed to them: taxes to whom taxes are owed, revenue to whom revenue is owed, respect to whom respect is owed, honor to whom honor is owed. Owe no one anything, except to love each other, for the one who loves another has fulfilled the law."

Because debt was so common and such a burden, people would frequently ask friends and family to put up security for their debts. Solomon advised against using your property for others' security deposit: "Be not one of those who give pledges, who put up security for debts. If you have nothing with which to pay, why should your bed be taken from under you?" (Proverbs 22:26–27). Avoiding debt is so important that Solomon devoted an extended paragraph to it in Proverbs 6:1–5:

> My son, if you have put up security for your neighbor, have given your pledge for a stranger, if you are snared in the words of your mouth, caught in the words of your mouth, then do this, my son, and save yourself, for you have come into the hand of your neighbor: go, hasten, and plead urgently with your neighbor. Give your eyes no sleep and your eyelids no slumber; save yourself like a gazelle from the hand of the hunter, like a bird from the hand of the fowler.

Debt is bondage. It cripples your independence, consumes your thoughts, and shackles your soul. Since debt is so oppressive, it's surprising the Bible doesn't mention it more often (see Proverbs 6:1–5; 11:15; 17:18; 22:7, 26–27; and Romans 13:7–8). Instead, the primary focus is on helping others get out of debt.

Liberate Others from Debt

From the Roman world to medieval Europe and into the modern West, Jews have excelled financially as a people group despite relentless persecution. Their secret is twofold: work hard and care for your fellow citizens. This goes all the way back to the book of Exodus when God forbade his people from charging interest to other Jews. Exodus 22:25 says, "If you lend money to any of my people with you who is poor, you shall not be like a moneylender to him, and you shall not exact interest from him." They could charge interest to foreigners but not to other Hebrews (Deuteronomy 23:19–20).

Leviticus 25:35 goes even further: "If your brother becomes poor and cannot maintain himself with you, you shall support him as though he were a stranger and a sojourner, and he shall live with you." God's blessing on the land was tied to how the poor were treated.

God also mandated two provisions to protect against generational poverty. First, every seven years, debts were to be canceled (Deuteronomy 15:1–2). Second, every fifty years (the Year of Jubilee), all ancestral lands were returned to the families: "You shall consecrate the fiftieth year, and proclaim liberty throughout the land to all its inhabitants. It shall be a jubilee for you, when each of you shall return to his property and each of you shall return to his clan" (Leviticus 25:10).

These provisions became the foundation of generosity in the New Testament, but Jesus extended them considerably. The Old Testament allowed only foreigners to be charged interest. Jesus, however, prohibited lending at all. His unprecedented policy was for us to pay the debts of both friend and foe: "If you lend to those from whom you expect to receive, what credit is that to you? Even sinners lend to sinners, to get back the same amount. But love your enemies, and do good, and lend, expecting nothing in return, and your reward will be great, and you will be sons of the Most High, for he is kind to the ungrateful and the evil" (Luke 6:34–35).

At first, this seems like an unrealistic expectation until we realize it reflects what God did for us spiritually. We get a glimpse of this radical release in the Lord's Prayer: "Forgive us our debts, as we also have forgiven our debtors" (Matthew 6:12). It's fully illustrated, however, in two parables about moneylenders canceling debts (Matthew 18:23–34; Luke 7:41–43). God's radical release of our debts obligates us to do the same for others. These stories feel fictional until we see them embodied in Jesus on the cross. That's what Paul meant when he wrote in Colossians 2:13–14, "You, who were dead in your trespasses and the uncircumcision of your flesh, God made alive together with him, having forgiven us all our trespasses, by canceling the record of debt that stood against us with its legal demands. This he set aside, nailing it to the cross."

God paid our spiritual debt in full so that, in response to his grace, we can release others from their financial burdens as a reflection of God's grace. This was the reality for the early church, as seen in Acts 2:44–45: "All who believed were together and had all things in common. And they were selling their possessions and belongings and distributing the proceeds to all, as any had need." Additionally, Acts 4:34 says, "There was not a needy person among them, for as many as were owners of lands or houses sold them and brought the proceeds of what was sold."

This isn't to be confused with communism. Communism forces redistribution of personal possessions. Christians practice stewardship of God's property through generosity. It's an obligation out of gratitude to God, not an imposition of governmental power.

Wisdom in Action

If you have debt, you can never release others' debts. Therefore, get out of debt as soon as possible. How? First, start tithing. I know—that makes no sense since you're already in debt. I'll say more about this in our final chapter, but for now, here's the principle: 90 percent with God goes further than

100 percent without him. Divine math doesn't follow the logic of this world. But if you're in debt, *your* math isn't making much sense either.

Second, attack your smallest debt first. This also seems counterintuitive, but the thrill of paying off a debt gives you a sense of agency that extends to other debts. You attack all your debts by setting a budget and paying cash for everything. Swiping plastic or using Apple Pay isn't "real money." When you're forced to let go of a physical bill, it suddenly becomes real.

Third, eliminate all unnecessary expenses. To quote Dave Ramsey, "If you will live like no one else now, later you can live and give like no one else!"[4] You can get out of debt sooner than you think. The moment you do, you can start helping others on their journey to financial freedom.

LINETH UNTO DEATH, AND HER PATHS UNTO THE DEAD. NONE THAT GO UNT
URN AGAIN, NEITHER TAKE THEY HOLD OF THE PATHS OF LIFE. THAT
/EST WALK IN THE WAY OF GOOD MEN, AND KEEP THE PATHS OF THE RIGH

This Week

- ☐ **Day 1:** Read this essay.
- ☐ **Day 2:** Memorize Proverbs 22:7.
- ☐ **Day 3:** Read the parables of the unmerciful servant (Matthew 18:23–35) and the two debtors (Luke 7:41–43) and find one thing to apply or avoid.
- ☐ **Day 4:** Meditate on Luke 6:34–35; Acts 2:44–45; Romans 13:7–8.
- ☐ **Day 5:** Discuss.

Group Discussion

1. How did your parents talk about bills and debt when you were growing up?
2. Does the advice you received about debt from your parents align with the wisdom of the Bible? Explain.
3. How does debt make us slaves, as Proverbs 22:7 suggests?
4. What could this group do to help relieve others' debt?

Table Talk (in your home)

What's the first debt we should pay off as a family?

Watercooler (at work or the gym)

What's the most practical advice you've received about debt?

MOUTH COMETH KNOWLEDGE AND UNDERSTANDING. HE LAYETH UP
DOM FOR THE RIGHTEOUS: HE IS A BUCKLER TO THEM THAT WALK UPRIGH
PETH THE PATHS OF JUDGMENT, AND PRESERVETH THE WAY OF HIS SAINTS

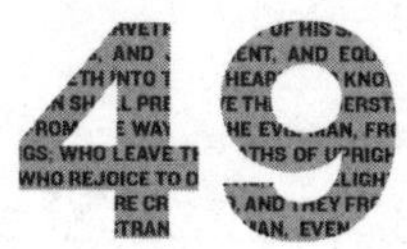

Laziness

How long will you lie there, O sluggard? When will you arise from your sleep? A little sleep, a little slumber, a little folding of the hands to rest, and poverty will come upon you like a robber, and want like an armed man.

—Proverbs 6:9–11

Comedy loves a lovable lazy character. They play the role of the adorable loafer who works hard to avoid work. In my childhood, it was Shaggy. He and his dog, Scooby-Doo, helped his friends solve mysteries. But Shaggy was a lot more motivated by snacks than by a desire to catch the culprit.

The king of the sloths, however, is Homer Simpson. In the longest-running sitcom in U.S. history, this iconic TV dad spends most of his time avoiding work at the nuclear plant and napping at his desk. The only thing he works hard at is acquiring his next doughnut. His consistent disregard for responsibility has made him an enduring symbol of "lovable laziness." Sloths make for good TV, but they are terrible teammates.

The Lazy Are Laughable

Laziness is easy to laugh at. Even Solomon used lazy people as fodder for humor. His descriptions of them are ludicrous: "The sluggard says, 'There is a lion in the road! There is a lion in the streets!' As a door turns on its hinges, so does a sluggard on his bed. The sluggard buries his hand in the dish; it wears him out to bring it back to his mouth" (Proverbs 26:13–15).

The apostle Paul also used a comical quip about sluggards: "One of the Cretans, a prophet of their own, said, 'Cretans are always liars, evil beasts, lazy gluttons' " (Titus 1:12). Years ago, I was leading a group of students in Turkey to visit the churches Paul had established. Our guide was a wonderfully fun Muslim woman named Tansu. She told me she was originally from Crete. I thoughtlessly blurted out, "Oh, the apostle Paul quoted a Cretan poet in one of his letters." That sparked her curiosity. She perked up with interest and asked, "Really? What did he say?" It was then that I realized this might be insulting to our guide. I couldn't back out at that point, so I turned to the biblical passage and showed her the quote. To my relief, she responded with a belly laugh and replied, "It's still true today!"

In real life, laziness is no laughing matter. Solomon even said hyperbolically that laziness can kill you (Proverbs 21:25). While it won't likely kill you literally, it will kill your contentment. It will rob you of opportunities. Laziness will cause pain to you and to those who entrust you with a task, as Proverbs 10:26 says: "Like vinegar to the teeth and smoke to the eyes, so is the sluggard to those who send him."

The Cost of Sloth

Our key passage highlights two costs of laziness: hunger and shame. "How long will you lie there, O sluggard? When will you arise from your sleep? A little sleep, a little slumber, a little folding of the hands to rest, and poverty will come upon you like a robber, and want like an armed man" (Proverbs 6:9–11). Lazy people in the Western world may not experience literal hunger, but they will bemoan their level of living (13:4; 19:15; 20:13). Solomon described this with several metaphors:

- *The Hunter:* "Whoever is slothful will not roast his game, but the diligent man will get precious wealth" (12:27).
- *The Farmer:* "The sluggard does not plow in the autumn; he will seek at harvest and have nothing" (20:4).
- *The Thief:* "A little sleep, a little slumber, a little folding of the hands to rest, and poverty will come upon you like a robber, and want like an armed man" (24:33–34).

The second consequence of sloth is shame. In Solomon's day, your debts could cause you to be sold into slavery or, more precisely, indentured servitude. Proverbs 12:24 warns, "The hand of the diligent will rule, while the slothful will be put to forced labor." The costs of sloth are significant, but the solutions are relatively simple.

Solutions to Laziness

How do you diagnose laziness in the mirror? Ask yourself three questions and answer them honestly:

1. *Are you working as hard as those around you?* Solomon says, "Go to the ant, O sluggard; consider her ways, and be wise. Without having any chief, officer, or ruler, she prepares her bread in summer and gathers her food in harvest" (Proverbs 6:6–8). What do you notice in ants? They don't arrive late or leave early. They are self-starters. Once they finish one task, they go on to the next. If these three metrics mark your work, you can avoid the costs of laziness.
2. *Do you make excuses for not doing your work?* That's a telltale sign of a sluggard. I've never heard anyone confess the sin of sloth. I've had a ton of people give excuses for not doing their work.

Jesus told a parable about a servant who made excuses for his negligence (Matthew 25:14–30). His excuses sound just like ours. Sluggards say things like "But you didn't tell me." "But you didn't finish *your* work." "But you're not being fair." Any response that attacks another is simply an excuse for your own negligence.

3. *Do you gossip about others?* What does gossip have to do with your work ethic? Surprisingly, a lot. Second Thessalonians 3:11 and 1 Timothy 5:13 both describe lazy people as gossips. It's a favorite pastime of sluggards because it justifies their laziness. In their own minds, their slander of others mitigates their obligation to be productive.

What should you do with lazy people? Let's always begin here: "Judge not, that you be not judged" (Matthew 7:1). Some people are accused of being lazy when they are actually being oppressed. Pharaoh accused the enslaved Israelites of sloth (Exodus 5:8, 17). Jesus told a parable about workers standing idle in the marketplace (Matthew 20:1–16). They weren't lazy; they were unemployed. Let's not accuse the economically disadvantaged of laziness when we've not given them the opportunity for gainful employment.

If, however, you have moral or legal authority over someone as a parent, teacher, mentor, or coach, you have an obligation to "admonish the idle, encourage the fainthearted, help the weak, be patient with them all" (1 Thessalonians 5:14). It's a great kindness to teach others the value and dignity of hard work. If they don't accept the kindness, then you "keep away from any brother who is walking in idleness and not in accord with the tradition that you received from us" (2 Thessalonians 3:6). This isn't cruel; it's wise because laziness is contagious.

Wisdom in Action

Second Thessalonians 3:6–13 is packed with wisdom regarding work. Without citing the entire passage, here are several excerpts you should add to your arsenal of wisdom.

First, avoid lazy people because they will rub off on you (verse 6). We all must monitor our closest friendships. How much time are our friends spending scrolling on their phones or playing video games? The priorities of those around us will always influence ours.

Second, mimic the people you respect most. Who in your life looks like the person you want to become? Examine their work ethic and follow their lead. Paul told the Thessalonians he worked hard while among them "to give you in ourselves an example to imitate" (verse 9). Who is that example for you?

Third, "if anyone is not willing to work, let him not eat" (verse 10). That may sound harsh, but it's kind because there's no "free lunch." The cost of idleness is that freeloaders become frauds. It's unhealthy to be unhelpful. Hard work bolsters your self-esteem, honors the name of the Lord you bear, and provides opportunities for you to help the less fortunate. This is the kind of person you want to be.

LINETH UNTO DEATH, AND HER PATHS UNTO THE DEAD. NONE THAT GO UN
URN AGAIN, NEITHER TAKE THEY HOLD OF THE PATHS OF LIFE. THAT
EST WALK IN THE WAY OF GOOD MEN, AND KEEP THE PATHS OF THE RIGH

This Week

- ☐ **Day 1:** Read this essay.
- ☐ **Day 2:** Memorize Proverbs 6:10–11.
- ☐ **Day 3:** Read the biography of the Thessalonians (2 Thessalonians 3:6–13) and find one thing to apply or avoid.
- ☐ **Day 4:** Meditate on Romans 12:11; 1 Thessalonians 5:14; 1 Timothy 5:13.
- ☐ **Day 5:** Discuss.

Group Discussion

1. What evidence of laziness do you find in yourself? If you're comfortable, please share.
2. How can we distinguish between lazy people and those who are oppressed or disadvantaged? How do we balance accountability with compassion?
3. What's the difference between healthful rest and laziness? How do we know when we've crossed the line from one to the other?
4. How can we encourage diligence where we have influence?

Table Talk (in your home)

What parameters should we establish to make our home a place of deep rest *and* hard work?

Watercooler (at work or the gym)

How can leaders encourage a strong work ethic without burning out their teams?

MOUTH COMETH KNOWLEDGE AND UNDERSTANDING. HE LAYETH UP
DOM FOR THE RIGHTEOUS: HE IS A BUCKLER TO THEM THAT WALK UPRIGH
PETH THE PATHS OF JUDGMENT, AND PRESERVETH THE WAY OF HIS SAINTS

50

Work

Whoever works his land will have plenty of bread, but he who follows worthless pursuits lacks sense.

—Proverbs 12:11

Different generations view work differently, often making an employer's job more like alchemy than management. Supervisors need to know what motivates, inspires, and fulfills their employees. Here's a cheat sheet:

Generation	Characteristics	Biblical Virtue
Baby Boomers (1946–64)	Strong work ethic, loyal, and dedicated. They prioritize professional success and putting in a full day's work to earn their keep.	**Diligence**
Gen X (1965–80)	Self-reliant and autonomous. They value work-life balance and fulfillment. They are adaptable but more prone to question authority.	**Balance**
Millennials (1981–96)	They prioritize meaningful work and security. They value flexibility, growth opportunities, and strong company culture.	**Purpose**

Generation	Characteristics	Biblical Virtue
Gen Z **(1997–2012)**	Technologically adept, innovative, and self-expressive. They value stability, inclusivity, and social impact.	**Community**
Gen Alpha **(2013–25)**	Expected to be tech-integrated and environmentally conscious. They will likely emphasize adaptability, creativity, and collaborative problem-solving.	**Stewardship**

A Theology of Work

We consider work a burden, but God created it to be a blessing. It was part of the beauty of Eden. God created us in his image and with his purpose—to care for the world he created. He told us in Genesis 1:28, "Be fruitful and multiply and fill the earth and subdue it, and have dominion over the fish of the sea and over the birds of the heavens and over every living thing that moves on the earth." Some read this as if God gave us resources to use at will and abuse when necessary. That isn't God's intent. Genesis 2:15 says, "The LORD God took the man and put him in the garden of Eden to work it and keep it." Those two terms, "work" and "keep," are the words for "serve" and "guard." Our created role is not to ravage the earth for resources but to serve it and guard it as stewards. Therefore, we should be asking, "What kind of world are we creating with the resources God gave us?"

Before the first sin, our work was a joyful partnership with God. But after our disobedience, that work became odious. That's when God said to Adam,

> Because you have listened to the voice of your wife
>   and have eaten of the tree
> of which I commanded you,
>   "You shall not eat of it,"

cursed is the ground because of you;
in pain you shall eat of it all the days of your life;
thorns and thistles it shall bring forth for you;
and you shall eat the plants of the field.
By the sweat of your face
you shall eat bread,
till you return to the ground,
for out of it you were taken;
for you are dust,
and to dust you shall return. (3:17–19)

Adam was exiled from the garden "to work the ground from which he was taken" (verse 23). Yet in God's grace, he left us one vestige of Eden—the day of rest. God modeled rest in Genesis 2:2–3 and then embedded it in the Ten Commandments for us: "Six days you shall labor, and do all your work, but the seventh day is a Sabbath to the LORD your God. On it you shall not do any work, you, or your son, or your daughter, your male servant, or your female servant, or your livestock, or the sojourner who is within your gates" (Exodus 20:9–10).

Interestingly, two of the Ten Commandments take up 62 percent of the words, which shows us that not all commands are equally easy to understand or obey. The two most heavily freighted in God's instructions speak about *the day of rest* and *idolatry.* Why? Because we tend to make our work an idol. We worship our work rather than God. Just as Adam and Eve betrayed God out of self-reliance, we continue to do the same today. That's why people speak of work as oppressive.

However, God protected our Edenic rest through the rule of Sabbath. Likewise, Jesus fulfilled the Sabbath by saying, "Come to me, all who labor and are heavy laden, and I will give you rest" (Matthew 11:28). This wasn't so we could avoid work, as the next verse is an invitation to get in the yoke with Jesus: "Take my yoke upon you, and learn from me, for I am gentle and lowly in heart, and you will find rest for your souls" (verse 29). We join his work just as Jesus joined his Father's perpetual labor: "My Father is working until now, and I am working" (John 5:17). This is the secret to sanctifying work: "Whatever you do, work heartily, as for the Lord and not for men" (Colossians 3:23).

A Strategy for Work

At the end of his life, Solomon reflected on the joy he got from work: "I perceived that there is nothing better for them than to be joyful and to do good as long as they live; also that everyone should eat and drink and take pleasure in all his toil—this is God's gift to man" (3:12–13; see also 2:24; 3:22; 5:18–19).

Work gives us value because our work makes us valuable to others. Proverbs 22:29 says, "Do you see a man skillful in his work? He will stand before kings; he will not stand before obscure men." While many presume men gain value from work and women gain it from relationships, the book of Proverbs says more about women being valued for their work than men. The last chapter describes the noble woman and how her value is seen in public by her provisions for her family. Here's the last verse of the entire book: "Give her of the fruit of her hands, and let her works praise her in the gates" (31:31).

God created us for work, which gives us dignity and purpose. However, when we devote our work to God, it gives dignity and purpose to others. Here are some biblical principles for work:

1. *Our work can dignify God* in the eyes of a watching world according to 1 Thessalonians 4:11–12: "Aspire to live quietly, and to mind your own affairs, and to work with your hands, as we instructed you, so that you may walk properly before outsiders and be dependent on no one."

2. *Our work can provide for our families,* as Paul pointed out in 1 Timothy 5:8: "If anyone does not provide for his relatives, and especially for members of his household, he has denied the faith and is worse than an unbeliever."
3. *Our work can meet needs around us,* as Titus 3:14 teaches: "Let our people learn to devote themselves to good works, so as to help cases of urgent need, and not be unfruitful." Work is wisdom in action.

Wisdom in Action

Proverbs 14:23 says, "In all toil there is profit, but mere talk tends only to poverty." Let's do more than talk about it. Here are four suggestions to make your work *work* for you:

1. *Work hard when there is work to be had.* Proverbs 10:5 says, "He who gathers in summer is a prudent son, but he who sleeps in harvest is a son who brings shame." We have a similar adage: "Strike while the iron is hot." With few exceptions, working harder is working smarter.
2. *Invest in your future through self-denial.* Proverbs 24:27 says, "Prepare your work outside; get everything ready for yourself in the field, and after that build your house." When you invest in your work, you are pampering your future self.
3. *Improve processes more than products.* If you want to excel in your job, work toward a future that helps everyone win through each business cycle. The best employees act like owners. Here's the difference: Employees work *for* the business; owners work *on* the business. As Proverbs 27:23–26 says, "Know well the condition of your flocks, and give attention to your herds, for riches do not last forever; and does a crown endure to all generations? When

the grass is gone and the new growth appears and the vegetation of the mountains is gathered, the lambs will provide your clothing, and the goats the price of a field."

4. Most importantly, *worship God through your work.* If you treat your work as sacred, you can "commit your work to the LORD, and your plans will be established" (16:3). Our work is a gift from Eden so we can serve and protect our environment and our people.

LL KEEP THEE: TO DELIVER THEE FROM THE WAY OF THE EVIL MAN, FRO
N THAT SPEAKETH FROWARD THINGS; WHO LEAVE THE PATHS OF UPRIGH

This Week

- ☐ **Day 1:** Read this essay.
- ☐ **Day 2:** Memorize Proverbs 12:11.
- ☐ **Day 3:** Read the biography of the noble woman (Proverbs 31) and find one thing to apply.
- ☐ **Day 4:** Meditate on Ephesians 4:28; Colossians 3:23; 2 Timothy 2:6.
- ☐ **Day 5:** Discuss.

Group Discussion

1. Who is the hardest-working person you've ever met? Who is the "smartest"-working person you've ever met?
2. What impact does your faith have on your view of work?
3. How can our work be used to reflect God's glory and provide for others, within both our family and our community?
4. How can we pursue excellence in our work without turning work into an idol? What practical steps help you maintain a healthy balance?

Table Talk (in your home)

How can we honor God through our daily tasks?

Watercooler (at work or the gym)

What advice do you have for balancing hard work and personal well-being?

UNTO DEATH, AND HER PATHS UNTO THE DEAD. NONE THAT GO UNTO HER
AIN, NEITHER TAKE THEY HOLD OF THE PATHS OF LIFE. THAT THOU

51

Plans

The plans of the diligent lead surely to abundance, but everyone who is hasty comes only to poverty.

—Proverbs 21:5

The modern equivalent of this proverb is "If you fail to plan, you plan to fail." This adage played out in the 2008 financial crisis. In the years leading up to the crisis, financial institutions and homeowners alike grew careless. They rode the wave of a steadily rising housing market. The inflated prices inflated egos. Wall Street executives leveraged their companies to pursue profits. What they perceived to be a foolproof plan turned out to be foolish. When housing prices tanked, mortgages went unpaid. The house of cards crashed.

I felt this crash personally, having invested in a real-estate deal that should have been a sure thing. It was a planned development off the first exit west of the Hoover Dam. It was a great location, and the expansion was needed at the time. It was *almost* one of the best investments I ever made. The $25,000 I invested in 2005 should have—and typically would have—doubled or tripled in three years. By 2008, however, the investment went belly up. I lost every penny. This goes to show that sometimes your good plans can get caught in the crossfire of others' foolish decisions.

Plans of Humans

Part of what makes humans unlike other animals is our ability to plan. You won't catch a chimpanzee playing chess or a wombat planning a wedding. Animals live life; humans make life happen. We have all kinds of plans. There are business plans, travel plans, retirement plans, meal plans, exercise plans, and lesson plans. People make careers out of planning weddings, buildings, marketing, cities, curricula, and churches. Many even plan their own funerals!

Planning is such an integral part of our nature that we do practically nothing without plans. My guess is that you are reading this very book right now because you planned to. Most of us are less aware of how our plans, which seem so deliberate to us, are actually determined by the Lord.

Solomon observed, "The heart of man plans his way, but the LORD establishes his steps" (Proverbs 16:9). This is what theologians mean when they talk about the sovereignty of God. Some see God's sovereignty in hindsight, frequently far removed from the event. But each time the Bible reveals a specific plan, it demonstrates how the Lord ultimately directed the outcome. When Paul was shipwrecked on Malta, twice we read about the plans of men being altered by the hand of God (Acts 27:12, 39). They made their plans, but God determined their destination.

Paul became acutely aware of God's sovereignty in his missionary journeys. He wrote to the Corinthians, "I wanted to visit you on my way to Macedonia, and to come back to you from Macedonia and have you send me on my way to Judea. Was I vacillating when I wanted to do this? Do I make my plans according to the flesh, ready to say 'Yes, yes' and 'No, no' at the same time?" (2 Corinthians 1:16–17). Paul knew his own desires were subject to God's sovereign plans.

Plans and Plots

When people refuse to submit their plans to God, they typically become plots against other people. God's nature in us, without God's will over us, will create trauma around us. God put in our hearts a desire and ability to plan. Yet outside God's will, those plans become evil plots. Solomon said one of the seven things God hates most is "a heart that devises wicked plans" (Proverbs 6:18).

The two most prominent accounts of human machinations are found in the story of Esther and the life of Christ. In the book of Esther, the wicked Haman plotted a genocide against the Jews, which Esther thwarted through her courage and her cousin's counsel (8:3, 5; 9:25). In the gospel of John, the chief priests plotted to execute Jesus (11:53; 12:10). In a surprising twist, Peter later pointed out in Acts 2:23 that these events were part of the bigger plan of God: "This Jesus, delivered up according to the definite plan and foreknowledge of God, you crucified and killed by the hands of lawless men."

In another twist, the Jewish leaders plotted Peter's demise as well (5:33). He was rescued when the famed rabbi named Gamaliel (Paul's mentor) spoke up, reminding them of the wisdom we've just read from Solomon. He said, " 'In the present case I tell you, keep away from these men and let them alone, for if this plan or this undertaking is of man, it will fail; but if it is of God, you will not be able to overthrow them. You might even be found opposing God!' So they took his advice" (verses 38–39).

Gamaliel knew that human plans are ultimately subjugated to the plans of God. If Peter's preaching of Jesus was God's will, they couldn't stop it. If it wasn't from God, it would fail. This is one of the most important insights in the Bible. We fret over our plans because we believe we are more responsible than God for bringing about a desired future. This futile fretting applies to election cycles, natural disasters, and culture wars. Yes, our plans are important, even godly, but only when submitted to God.

The Sovereignty of God

Scripture is clear: Plans belong to God. No fewer than six proverbs teach this truth. For example, Proverbs 16:1 says, "The plans of the heart belong to man, but the answer of the tongue is from the LORD" (see also 5:21; 16:9, 33; 19:21). This is true even of governing officials: "The king's heart is a stream of water in the hand of the LORD; he turns it wherever he will" (21:1). The prophets and poets of the Old Testament applied this principle most frequently to the wicked: "He frustrates the devices of the crafty, so that their hands achieve no success" (Job 5:12; see also Psalm 33:10–11; Jeremiah 6:19; 18:11–12). To his own people, however, God says things like "In him we have obtained an inheritance, having been predestined according to the purpose of him who works all things according to the counsel of his will" (Ephesians 1:11).

Wisdom in Action

Planning is part of the *imago Dei* (image of God) in us. Though God's plans will always overrule our own, he invites us to partner with him. How can we align our plans with God's? It begins by submitting those plans to him. Proverbs 16:3 says, "Commit your work to the LORD, and your plans will be established." How do we submit our plans to God? By submitting them to wise counsel. The more advisers you have on earth, the more likely you will align with God's will in heaven. Proverbs 15:22 observes, "Without counsel plans fail, but with many advisers they succeed."

One more strategy will give your plans the greatest chance of success. Rather than planning for your own good future, plan for the good of others.

God granted success to this kind of plan when Barnabas fought for John Mark to rejoin him on a second missionary journey (Acts 15:37). Paul adamantly refused. Their argument was so fierce, they ended up parting ways. Barnabas's plan to validate John Mark resulted in him writing the first gospel under Peter's tutelage. It ultimately led Paul to call for this valuable asset in his final imprisonment (2 Timothy 4:11). When we plan for the good of others, God elevates the priority of our plans.

LL KEEP THEE: TO DELIVER THEE FROM THE WAY OF THE EVIL MAN, FRO
N THAT SPEAKETH FROWARD THINGS; WHO LEAVE THE PATHS OF UPRIGH
WALK IN THE WAYS OF DARKNESS; WHO REJOICE TO DO EVIL, AND DELIGHT

This Week

- ☐ **Day 1:** Read this essay.
- ☐ **Day 2:** Memorize Proverbs 21:5.
- ☐ **Day 3:** Read the biography of Haman (Esther 7) and find one thing to avoid.
- ☐ **Day 4:** Meditate on Acts 2:23; Ephesians 1:11; Hebrews 6:17.
- ☐ **Day 5:** Discuss.

Group Discussion

1. In what area of your life are you best at making plans (budget, schedule, business, vacation, projects, etc.)?
2. When have you seen God redirect your plans? How did you react at first?
3. How has wise counsel altered your plans (relationships, retirement, education, child-rearing, profession, etc.)?
4. How can we incorporate the needs of others into our own plans, and why might this align us more closely with God's will?

Table Talk (in your home)

What personal or family goals should we commit to the Lord in prayer?

Watercooler (at work or the gym)

Do you typically seek advice from others before making big decisions?

UNTO DEATH, AND HER PATHS UNTO THE DEAD. NONE THAT GO UNTO HER
AIN, NEITHER TAKE THEY HOLD OF THE PATHS OF LIFE. THAT THOU
LK IN THE WAY OF GOOD MEN, AND KEEP THE PATHS OF THE RIGHTEOUS

52

Generosity

One gives freely, yet grows all the richer; another withholds what he should give, and only suffers want.

—Proverbs 11:24

John builds dump trucks for work and makes a very good living. He takes raw sheet metal and framing material to weld the bed to each order's specific size, weight, and strength. Who knew dump trucks were so specialized or profitable? Last year, his profit was upward of $1,000,000.

When John and his wife took us to dinner, they told us about his business. I was mesmerized not merely by his profession but by how he spent his profit. John shared his income not to boast about how much he made but to explain how much he was giving away. John and his wife (who is the *major* impetus of their generosity) gave well beyond a tithe. In fact, they gave about $800,000 to projects they believed in at the church. They celebrated giving away 80 percent of their earnings the previous year.

On top of that, they gave nearly $200,000 in outrageous tips to servers, incredible bonuses to his lowest-paid employees, and stunning benevolence to people in need. This past year, they gave away everything they made that year and lived on savings. His greatest joy is buying cars for single moms. Right after our dinner together, I got a call from a woman asking for prayer, specifically because she couldn't afford to repair her vehicle. I called John right away. Like a bulldog on a bone, he wouldn't stop until her needs were met. The joy they give to those who feel forgotten is exceeded only by the joy they receive by being a conduit for God's blessing. They are the best proof I've seen of Jesus's principle of generosity: "It is more blessed to give than to receive" (Acts 20:35).

Generosity and Justice

We typically think of generosity as a character trait that makes us better. However, the Bible speaks of generosity as an ethical issue that makes our community better. This ethical obligation to be generous is peppered throughout Proverbs. For example, Proverbs 14:31 says, "Whoever oppresses a poor man insults his Maker, but he who is generous to the needy honors him" (see also 14:21; 19:17; 22:9; 28:27). Generosity is a moral obligation because we don't actually own anything. We are merely stewards of God's resources: "The silver is mine, and the gold is mine, declares the LORD of hosts" (Haggai 2:8).

Prior to Proverbs, generosity was a legal obligation in the Mosaic law. Deuteronomy 15:7–8 offers one of many examples: "If among you, one of your brothers should become poor, in any of your towns within your land that the LORD your God is giving you, you shall not harden your heart or shut your hand against your poor brother, but you shall open your hand to him and lend him sufficient for his need, whatever it may be."

The New Testament adopts the same view of generosity and explains why it's such an important issue to God. Here are three of the most critical principles for Christian generosity:

1. **The Principle of Abundance.** Jesus said, "Give, and it will be given to you. Good measure, pressed down, shaken together, running over, will be put into your lap. For with the measure you use it will be measured back to you" (Luke 6:38). This isn't a

reward for moral behavior. God puts his resources in funnels, not buckets. He wants to bless you to bless others so they will bless God (2 Corinthians 9:11).

2. **The Principle of Paying It Forward.** Jesus famously said, "Do not lay up for yourselves treasures on earth, where moth and rust destroy and where thieves break in and steal, but lay up for yourselves treasures in heaven, where neither moth nor rust destroys and where thieves do not break in and steal" (Matthew 6:19–20). In other words, "You can't take it with you, but you can send it on ahead." Was Jesus teaching salvation by works? No. This is not works leading to salvation but works being manifested out of salvation.

   Jesus clarified what he meant in the next verse: "For where your treasure is, there your heart will be also" (verse 21). Your money doesn't follow your heart. Your heart follows your money. If you want your heart focused on heaven, invest it in things that help others get there. The connection between our generosity and our eternity is most apparent in 1 John 3:17: "If anyone has the world's goods and sees his brother in need, yet closes his heart against him, how does God's love abide in him?"

3. **The Principle of Sacrifice.** Those with fewer resources may feel disadvantaged because they can't invest as much in their eternal 401(k). However, it's not how much you give but how much you keep. One day, as Jesus sat across from the temple treasury, a widow dropped in two mites—basically a penny. The clink of the widow's coins was barely perceptible, but it rang loud in Jesus's ears.

Calling his disciples to attention, he said, "Truly, I say to you, this poor widow has put in more than all those who are contributing to the offering box. For they all contributed out of their abundance, but she out of her poverty has put in everything she had, all she had to live on" (Mark 12:43–44). Jesus is concerned not with the number of zeros at the end of your gift but with the amount of faith it took to give it.

Generosity Follows the Tithe

Tithing helps us see that God owns everything. This keeps your possessions from possessing you. Tithing fertilizes the soil of your soul so generosity can grow. When your generosity grows, God invests more in you as a wise steward of his resources. Solomon affirmed this principle, saying, "Honor the LORD with your wealth and with the firstfruits of all your produce; then your barns will be filled with plenty, and your vats will be bursting with wine" (Proverbs 3:9–10).

For Israel, this wasn't just wisdom; it was the law. Leviticus 27:30 says, "Every tithe of the land, whether of the seed of the land or of the fruit of the trees, is the LORD's; it is holy to the LORD." It was 10 percent off the top. Ten percent on the back end of your budget is a tip, not a tithe. A tip tells God, "Thank you for serving me." A tithe is a declaration that you will trust and serve him. It's a bigger deal than we think. Neglecting to tithe is called thievery in Malachi 3:8: "Will man rob God? Yet you are robbing me. But you say, 'How have we robbed you?' In your tithes and contributions."

Whenever our church uses this passage in a sermon, we get emails declaring, "That's Old Testament, and we don't live by the law." That's true—we don't live by the law, but neither did Abraham. He lived *before* the law.

The tithe began with Abraham, not Moses. He gave 10 percent of the spoils of his rescue operation to the king of Jerusalem. This mystical figure was named Melchizedek (Genesis 14:18–20). Abraham gave him a tenth of everything, establishing a precedent for the Jewish nation. Jesus affirmed tithing in Luke 11:42: "Woe to you Pharisees! For you tithe mint and rue and every herb, and neglect justice and the love of God. *These you ought to have done,* without neglecting the others."

If we lay Luke 11:42 alongside Hebrews 7, something striking emerges. Melchizedek (whose name means "king of righteousness") is a Christ figure or, perhaps, even an appearance of Jesus. Therefore, the first tithe in the Bible was paid to Jesus by Abraham. Like Abraham's initial tithe, our tithe is to the King of Righteousness. This noble practice is the foundation of generosity because it recognizes the lordship of Jesus.

Wisdom in Action

Generosity, like the tithe, must be budgeted to become habitual. All of us are moved at moments to give the spare change in our pockets. That kind of benevolence is good, but it's meager and inconsistent. It won't develop the kind of generosity that transforms your community.

When you recognize God is the owner of everything, budgeted generosity becomes habitual and transformational. We use what God entrusts to us to bless people who need to trust God. Historically, this kind of compassionate generosity has been the church's most powerful apologetic, silencing those opposed to Christ. Generosity is a powerful act of worship. This takes us full circle to the beginning of wisdom—namely, fearing God, which enables us to live skillfully in his Spirit of Wisdom.

LL KEEP THEE: TO DELIVER THEE FROM THE WAY OF THE EVIL MAN, FRO
N THAT SPEAKETH FROWARD THINGS; WHO LEAVE THE PATHS OF UPRIGH
WALK IN THE WAYS OF DARKNESS; WHO REJOICE TO DO EVIL, AND DELIGHT

This Week

- ☐ **Day 1:** Read this essay.
- ☐ **Day 2:** Memorize Proverbs 11:24.
- ☐ **Day 3:** Read the biography of Melchizedek (Hebrews 7) and find one thing to apply.
- ☐ **Day 4:** Meditate on Matthew 6:21; Luke 6:38; Acts 20:35.
- ☐ **Day 5:** Discuss.

Group Discussion

1. How have you experienced joy and freedom through giving? (See Acts 20:35.)
2. What causes most inspire you toward generosity?
3. How can you align your financial decisions with your eternal goals?
4. Have you set goals for tithing and additional generosity? If yes, how can you expand them? If no, what plan can you make?

Table Talk (in your home)

What causes or individuals can we bless this month?

Watercooler (at work or the gym)

Do you believe that generosity is a moral responsibility?

UNTO DEATH, AND HER PATHS UNTO THE DEAD. NONE THAT GO UNTO HER
AIN, NEITHER TAKE THEY HOLD OF THE PATHS OF LIFE. THAT THOU
LK IN THE WAY OF GOOD MEN, AND KEEP THE PATHS OF THE RIGHTEOUS

Conclusion

Wisdom doesn't dwell in marble halls or sacred spires—it lives in the boardrooms of business, the bustling square of the city, and the chaos of your kitchen. It reveals itself in split-second decisions and private acts of compassion. Our yearlong exploration of Proverbs has shown wisdom to be practical and skillful, not theoretical or mystical.

Standing at this vantage point, we can trace our path like cartographers of the soul. We've navigated the forest of discernment, wandered through the delicate valleys of words and relationships, scaled the rugged cliffs of behavior and character, reaching the summit where wealth meets generosity. Yet this summit serves not as our destination but as our launching point.

Solomon, whose wisdom drew admirers from distant shores, understood that wisdom grows over time: "The path of the righteous is like the light of dawn, which shines brighter and brighter until full day" (Proverbs 4:18). Each proverb we've examined has added another beam to illuminate our way forward.

In our digital age, where we have instant access to information, we realize that wisdom will never come from ChatGPT. It's the gritty art and disciplined act of living well. While knowledge multiplies exponentially, wisdom is stubbornly and resiliently fixed. It's timeless teaching woven into the DNA of daily life. It grows through our choices, echoing generationally beyond us. It's the spiritual sinew that connects heavenly truths and earthly reality.

This journey through Proverbs shows how wisdom is both a divine gift and a human pursuit. Like morning dew, it comes freely to those who seek it with open hearts (James 1:5), yet like a garden, it requires constant tending. Solomon's life teaches us that wisdom must be lived, not merely learned. The cautionary tale of his son Rehoboam warns us that wisdom must be both inherited and inhabited. You can have the wisest father in the world, but if you don't live it out yourself, your deaf ears will result in a daft heart.

As you turn this final page, reflect on your transformation. Maybe you've finally learned when to keep quiet (that's huge!), or fortified your relationships, or learned to steward resources with insight and integrity. Remember—this conclusion is merely a comma, not an exclamation point.

The real test lies ahead: How will these ancient words continue to reshape your modern life? What ripples will your wisdom create in the lives around you and beyond you? You are the embodied book of Proverbs to friends and family. What they read will affect their destiny.

You've invested twelve months in pursuing wisdom—that's a good start to sculpting a life into the masterpiece God envisioned. This is life's greatest pursuit: "How much better to get wisdom than gold! To get understanding is to be chosen rather than silver" (Proverbs 16:16).

APPENDIX

Proverbs Arranged by Category

DISCERNMENT

Topic	Proverbs	Others
Wisdom	**2:6:** "The Lord gives wisdom; from his mouth come knowledge and understanding." **3:35:** "The wise will inherit honor, but fools get disgrace." **4:6–7:** "Do not forsake her, and she will keep you; love her, and she will guard you. The beginning of wisdom is this: Get wisdom, and whatever you get, get insight." **8:1–4:** "Does not wisdom call? Does not understanding raise her voice? On the heights beside the way, at the crossroads she takes her stand; beside the gates in front of the town, at the entrance of the portals she cries aloud: 'To you, O men, I call, and my cry is to the children of man.' " **9:1–3:** "Wisdom has built her house; she has hewn her seven pillars. She has slaughtered her beasts; she has mixed her wine; she has also set her table. She has sent out her young women to call from the highest places in the town." **13:20:** "Whoever walks with the wise becomes wise, but the companion of fools will suffer harm." **16:16:** "How much better to get wisdom than gold! To get understanding is to be chosen rather than silver."	1:2–3, 5–6, 20–21, 24–26 2:2–5, 7, 10 3:7, 13, 15, 19–21 4:5, 8–9, 11, 13 5:1 6:6, 20–23 7:4 8:5–36 9:4–6, 12 10:1, 8, 13–14, 23, 31 11:2, 29–30 12:15, 18 13:1, 10, 14–15 14:1, 3, 6–8, 16, 24, 33 15:2, 7, 12, 14, 20, 31, 33 16:14, 21, 23 17:2, 16, 24, 28 18:4, 15 19:8, 20, 27 20:1, 18, 26, 29 21:11, 20, 22, 30 22:17–20 23:12, 15, 19, 23 24:3, 5–7, 13–14, 23 25:12

Topic	Proverbs	Others
Fear of the Lord	**1:7:** "The fear of the Lord is the beginning of knowledge; fools despise wisdom and instruction." **2:5:** "Then you will understand the fear of the Lord and find the knowledge of God." **9:10:** "The fear of the Lord is the beginning of wisdom, and the knowledge of the Holy One is insight." **15:33:** "The fear of the Lord is instruction in wisdom, and humility comes before honor." **22:4:** "The reward for humility and fear of the Lord is riches and honor and life." **29:25:** "The fear of man lays a snare, but whoever trusts in the Lord is safe."	1:29 3:7 8:13 10:27 14:2, 26–27 15:16 16:6 19:23 23:17 24:21 28:14 31:30
Mentors	**11:14:** "Where there is no guidance, a people falls, but in an abundance of counselors there is safety." **12:15:** "The way of a fool is right in his own eyes, but a wise man listens to advice." **15:22:** "Without counsel plans fail, but with many advisers they succeed." **19:20:** "Listen to advice and accept instruction, that you may gain wisdom in the future." **20:5:** "The purpose in a man's heart is like deep water, but a man of understanding will draw it out."	1:5 9:9 12:18, 26 13:10 20:18 24:6 27:9

Topic	Proverbs	Others
Fools	**10:23:** "Doing wrong is like a joke to a fool, but wisdom is pleasure to a man of understanding." **12:16:** "The vexation of a fool is known at once, but the prudent ignores an insult." **17:12:** "Let a man meet a she-bear robbed of her cubs rather than a fool in his folly." **17:24:** "The discerning sets his face toward wisdom, but the eyes of a fool are on the ends of the earth." **18:2:** "A fool takes no pleasure in understanding, but only in expressing his opinion." **26:1:** "Like snow in summer or rain in harvest, so honor is not fitting for a fool." **26:6:** "Whoever sends a message by the hand of a fool cuts off his own feet and drinks violence." **26:11:** "Like a dog that returns to his vomit is a fool who repeats his folly." **27:3:** "A stone is heavy, and sand is weighty, but a fool's provocation is heavier than both." **29:9:** "If a wise man has an argument with a fool, the fool only rages and laughs, and there is no quiet." **30:21–22:** "Under three things the earth trembles; under four it cannot bear up: a slave when he becomes king, and a fool when he is filled with food . . ."	1:7, 22, 32 3:35 8:5 10:1, 8, 10, 14, 18, 21 11:29 12:15, 23 13:16, 19–20 14:3, 7–9, 16–17, 24, 33 15:2, 5, 7, 14, 20 16:22

Topic	Proverbs	Others
Wicked vs. Righteous	**3:33:** "The Lord's curse is on the house of the wicked, but he blesses the dwelling of the righteous." **10:2:** "Treasures gained by wickedness do not profit, but righteousness delivers from death." **10:16:** "The wage of the righteous leads to life, the gain of the wicked to sin." **10:25:** "When the tempest passes, the wicked is no more, but the righteous is established forever." **12:7:** "The wicked are overthrown and are no more, but the house of the righteous will stand." **14:11:** "The house of the wicked will be destroyed, but the tent of the upright will flourish." **15:8:** "The sacrifice of the wicked is an abomination to the Lord, but the prayer of the upright is acceptable to him." **29:2:** "When the righteous increase, the people rejoice, but when the wicked rule, the people groan."	3:32 4:18–19 10:3, 6–7, 11, 20, 24, 28–32 11:5, 8–11, 18, 21, 23, 31 12:3, 5–6, 10, 12–13, 21, 26 13:9, 17, 21–22, 25 15:6, 9, 28–29 17:15 18:5 21:8, 15, 18, 29 24:15–16 28:1, 10, 12, 18, 28 29:6–7, 16, 27

Topic	Proverbs	Others
Wicked	**2:22:** "The wicked will be cut off from the land, and the treacherous will be rooted out of it." **4:19:** "The way of the wicked is like deep darkness; they do not know over what they stumble." **10:27:** "The fear of the Lord prolongs life, but the years of the wicked will be short." **16:4:** "The Lord has made everything for its purpose, even the wicked for the day of trouble." **17:23:** "The wicked accepts a bribe in secret to pervert the ways of justice." **18:3:** "When wickedness comes, contempt comes also, and with dishonor comes disgrace." **24:19–20:** "Fret not yourself because of evildoers, and be not envious of the wicked, for the evil man has no future; the lamp of the wicked will be put out."	1:16, 29 3:25 4:14–17 5:22 6:12–15, 18 9:7 11:7 15:26 17:4 19:28 20:26 21:4, 7, 10, 12, 27 24:24–25 26:26 28:4, 15 29:12
Righteous	**4:18:** "The path of the righteous is like the light of dawn, which shines brighter and brighter until full day." **9:9:** "Give instruction to a wise man, and he will be still wiser; teach a righteous man, and he will increase in learning." **18:10:** "The name of the Lord is a strong tower; the righteous man runs into it and is safe." **19:1:** "Better is a poor person who walks in his integrity than one who is crooked in speech and is a fool." **20:7:** "The righteous who walks in his integrity—blessed are his children after him!"	2:20 10:21 11:28, 30 16:13, 17, 31 17:26 21:26 23:17–18, 24 25:5, 26

WORDS

Topic	Proverbs	Others
Truth	**8:7:** "My mouth will utter truth; wickedness is an abomination to my lips." **12:17:** "Whoever speaks the truth gives honest evidence, but a false witness utters deceit." **12:19:** "Truthful lips endure forever, but a lying tongue is but for a moment." **13:2:** "From the fruit of his mouth a man eats what is good, but the desire of the treacherous is for violence." **23:23:** "Buy truth, and do not sell it; buy wisdom, instruction, and understanding." **24:26:** "Whoever gives an honest answer kisses the lips."	8:8–9 12:22 14:5, 25 15:7 16:11, 20 18:20 20:15, 28 22:21 23:16 28:20 29:14
Lies	**19:28:** "A worthless witness mocks at justice, and the mouth of the wicked devours iniquity." **20:17:** "Bread gained by deceit is sweet to a man, but afterward his mouth will be full of gravel." **21:6:** "The getting of treasures by a lying tongue is a fleeting vapor and a snare of death." **24:28:** "Be not a witness against your neighbor without cause, and do not deceive with your lips." **26:18–19:** "Like a madman who throws firebrands, arrows, and death is the man who deceives his neighbor and says, 'I am only joking!' " **31:30:** "Charm is deceitful, and beauty is vain, but a woman who fears the Lord is to be praised."	4:24 6:16–19 10:10, 18 12:5, 19–20, 22 13:5 14:5, 25 17:4, 7 19:5, 9, 22 21:28 25:18 26:24–26, 28 29:12 30:6–8

Topic	Proverbs	Others
Mockery	**15:12:** "A scoffer does not like to be reproved; he will not go to the wise." **17:5:** "Whoever mocks the poor insults his Maker; he who is glad at calamity will not go unpunished." **21:24:** " 'Scoffer' is the name of the arrogant, haughty man who acts with arrogant pride." **22:10:** "Drive out a scoffer, and strife will go out, and quarreling and abuse will cease." **24:9:** "The devising of folly is sin, and the scoffer is an abomination to mankind."	1:22, 26 3:34 9:7–8, 12 13:1 14:6, 9 19:25, 28–29 20:1 21:11 29:8 30:17
Slander	**11:13:** "Whoever goes about slandering reveals secrets, but he who is trustworthy in spirit keeps a thing covered." **20:19:** "Whoever goes about slandering reveals secrets; therefore do not associate with a simple babbler." **25:23:** "The north wind brings forth rain, and a backbiting tongue, angry looks." **26:2:** "Like a sparrow in its flitting, like a swallow in its flying, a curse that is causeless does not alight." **30:10:** "Do not slander a servant to his master, lest he curse you, and you be held guilty."	10:18 11:9, 13

Topic	Proverbs	Others
Gossip	**16:28:** "A dishonest man spreads strife, and a whisperer separates close friends." **18:8:** "The words of a whisperer are like delicious morsels; they go down into the inner parts of the body." **26:20:** "For lack of wood the fire goes out, and where there is no whisperer, quarreling ceases."	6:12–15 17:4, 9 25:9–10 26:22–23
Quarreling	**3:30:** "Do not contend with a man for no reason, when he has done you no harm." **15:1:** "A soft answer turns away wrath, but a harsh word stirs up anger." **26:4:** "Answer not a fool according to his folly, lest you be like him yourself." **26:17:** "Whoever meddles in a quarrel not his own is like one who takes a passing dog by the ears." **26:21:** "As charcoal to hot embers and wood to fire, so is a quarrelsome man for kindling strife." **29:9:** "If a wise man has an argument with a fool, the fool only rages and laughs, and there is no quiet."	15:18 17:14 18:6–7, 18–19 19:13 20:3 21:9, 19 22:10 23:29–30 25:24 26:5, 20 27:3, 15
Flattery	**26:28:** "A lying tongue hates its victims, and a flattering mouth works ruin." **27:21:** "The crucible is for silver, and the furnace is for gold, and a man is tested by his praise." **28:23:** "Whoever rebukes a man will afterward find more favor than he who flatters with his tongue."	2:16 6:24 7:5, 21 26:24–26 29:5

Topic	Proverbs	Others
Boasting	**25:14:** "Like clouds and wind without rain is a man who boasts of a gift he does not give." **27:2:** "Let another praise you, and not your own mouth; a stranger, and not your own lips." **30:32:** "If you have been foolish, exalting yourself, or if you have been devising evil, put your hand on your mouth."	17:19 20:14 27:1
Reproof	**3:11–12:** "My son, do not despise the Lord's discipline or be weary of his reproof, for the Lord reproves him whom he loves, as a father the son in whom he delights." **9:7–8:** "Whoever corrects a scoffer gets himself abuse, and he who reproves a wicked man incurs injury. Do not reprove a scoffer, or he will hate you; reprove a wise man, and he will love you." **17:10:** "A rebuke goes deeper into a man of understanding than a hundred blows into a fool." **25:12:** "Like a gold ring or an ornament of gold is a wise reprover to a listening ear."	1:23, 25, 30 5:12–14 6:23 9:9 10:17 12:1 13:1, 18 15:5, 12, 31–32 19:25 24:25 27:5 28:23 29:15 30:6
Encourage-ment	**12:25:** "Anxiety in a man's heart weighs him down, but a good word makes him glad." **16:24:** "Gracious words are like a honey-comb, sweetness to the soul and health to the body." **25:25:** "Like cold water to a thirsty soul, so is good news from a far country."	15:23

RELATIONSHIPS

Topic	Proverbs	Others
Parents	**1:8:** "Hear, my son, your father's instruction, and forsake not your mother's teaching." **10:1:** "A wise son makes a glad father, but a foolish son is a sorrow to his mother." **13:22:** "A good man leaves an inheritance to his children's children, but the sinner's wealth is laid up for the righteous." **13:24:** "Whoever spares the rod hates his son, but he who loves him is diligent to discipline him." **17:6:** "Grandchildren are the crown of the aged, and the glory of children is their fathers." **20:20:** "If one curses his father or his mother, his lamp will be put out in utter darkness." **22:6:** "Train up a child in the way he should go; even when he is old he will not depart from it." **29:15:** "The rod and reproof give wisdom, but a child left to himself brings shame to his mother." **30:17:** "The eye that mocks a father and scorns to obey a mother will be picked out by the ravens of the valley and eaten by the vultures."	1:1, 10 2:1 3:1, 11–12 4:1–4, 10, 20–22 5:1, 7 6:20 7:1–3, 24 10:5 11:29 13:1 15:5, 20 17:2, 21, 25 19:13, 18, 26–27 20:7 22:15 23:13–16, 19, 22–26 27:11 28:7, 24 29:3, 17 30:11 31:2, 28
Siblings	**17:17:** "A friend loves at all times, and a brother is born for adversity." **18:19:** "A brother offended is more unyielding than a strong city, and quarreling is like the bars of a castle."	17:2 18:24 19:7 27:10

Topic	Proverbs	Others
Spouses	**5:18–19:** "Let your fountain be blessed, and rejoice in the wife of your youth, a lovely deer, a graceful doe. Let her breasts fill you at all times with delight; be intoxicated always in her love." **12:4:** "An excellent wife is the crown of her husband, but she who brings shame is like rottenness in his bones." **18:22:** "He who finds a wife finds a good thing and obtains favor from the Lord." **30:18–19:** "Three things are too wonderful for me; four I do not understand: the way of an eagle in the sky, the way of a serpent on a rock, the way of a ship on the high seas, and the way of a man with a virgin." **31:10:** "An excellent wife who can find? She is far more precious than jewels."	11:16 14:1 19:13–14 21:9, 19 25:24 27:15–16 30:21–23 31:11–31
Friends	**22:11:** "He who loves purity of heart, and whose speech is gracious, will have the king as his friend." **27:6:** "Faithful are the wounds of a friend; profuse are the kisses of an enemy." **27:9–10:** "Oil and perfume make the heart glad, and the sweetness of a friend comes from his earnest counsel. Do not forsake your friend and your father's friend, and do not go to your brother's house in the day of your calamity. Better is a neighbor who is near than a brother who is far away." **27:17:** "Iron sharpens iron, and one man sharpens another."	12:26 14:20 16:19, 28 17:9, 17 18:1, 24 19:4, 6–7 22:24–25

Topic	Proverbs	Others
Influencers	**1:10:** "My son, if sinners entice you, do not consent." **3:31:** "Do not envy a man of violence and do not choose any of his ways." **4:14–15:** "Do not enter the path of the wicked, and do not walk in the way of the evil. Avoid it; do not go on it; turn away from it and pass on." **16:29:** "A man of violence entices his neighbor and leads him in a way that is not good."	1:14–15 2:12–15 12:26 13:20 14:7 22:24 24:21–22 29:24
Neighbors	**3:28–29:** "Do not say to your neighbor, 'Go, and come again, tomorrow I will give it'—when you have it with you. Do not plan evil against your neighbor, who dwells trustingly beside you." **21:10:** "The soul of the wicked desires evil; his neighbor finds no mercy in his eyes." **22:28:** "Do not move the ancient landmark that your fathers have set." **25:17:** "Let your foot be seldom in your neighbor's house, lest he have his fill of you and hate you." **27:14:** "Whoever blesses his neighbor with a loud voice, rising early in the morning, will be counted as cursing."	3:27 6:1–3 11:9, 12 12:26 14:20–21, 31 16:29 17:18 24:28 25:8–9, 18 26:18–19 27:10 29:5

Topic	Proverbs	Others
Enemies	**16:7:** "When a man's ways please the Lord, he makes even his enemies to be at peace with him." **24:17–18:** "Do not rejoice when your enemy falls, and let not your heart be glad when he stumbles, lest the Lord see it and be displeased, and turn away his anger from him." **25:21–22:** "If your enemy is hungry, give him bread to eat, and if he is thirsty, give him water to drink, for you will heap burning coals on his head, and the Lord will reward you." **27:6:** "Faithful are the wounds of a friend; profuse are the kisses of an enemy."	16:28 26:24–26
God	**3:5–6:** "Trust in the Lord with all your heart, and do not lean on your own understanding. In all your ways acknowledge him, and he will make straight your paths." **8:17:** "I love those who love me, and those who seek me diligently find me." **9:10:** "The fear of the Lord is the beginning of wisdom, and the knowledge of the Holy One is insight." **16:2:** "All the ways of a man are pure in his own eyes, but the Lord weighs the spirit." **17:3:** "The crucible is for silver, and the furnace is for gold, and the Lord tests hearts." **18:24:** "A man of many companions may come to ruin, but there is a friend who sticks closer than a brother."	3:32 5:21 6:16–19 10:29 11:20 12:2, 22 15:3, 9 18:10, 22 19:3, 23 20:27 21:2, 30–31 22:2 28:5, 14, 25 30:1–9

Topic	Proverbs	Others
Leadership	**11:14:** "Where there is no guidance, a people falls, but in an abundance of counselors there is safety." **16:10:** "An oracle is on the lips of a king; his mouth does not sin in judgment." **19:12:** "A king's wrath is like the growling of a lion, but his favor is like dew on the grass." **20:2:** "The terror of a king is like the growling of a lion; whoever provokes him to anger forfeits his life." **20:28:** "Steadfast love and faithfulness preserve the king, and by steadfast love his throne is upheld." **21:1:** "The king's heart is a stream of water in the hand of the Lord; he turns it wherever he will." **28:2:** "When a land transgresses, it has many rulers, but with a man of understanding and knowledge, its stability will long continue." **29:18:** "Where there is no prophetic vision the people cast off restraint, but blessed is he who keeps the law."	12:24 14:28, 35 15:22 16:12–15 17:7 19:10 20:8, 26 25:17, 15 27:18 27:18 28:15–16 29:2, 4, 12, 14, 26 30:21–22 31:1–4

BEHAVIOR

Topic	Proverbs	Others
Adultery	**6:29:** "So is he who goes in to his neighbor's wife; none who touches her will go unpunished." **6:32:** "He who commits adultery lacks sense; he who does it destroys himself." **22:14:** "The mouth of forbidden women is a deep pit; he with whom the Lord is angry will fall into it." **23:27–28:** "A prostitute is a deep pit; an adulteress is a narrow well. She lies in wait like a robber and increases the traitors among mankind."	2:16–20 5:3–23 6:24–28, 30–31, 33–35 7:5–27 9:13–18 29:3 30:20 31:3
Drinking	**20:1:** "Wine is a mocker, strong drink a brawler, and whoever is led astray by it is not wise." **23:21:** "The drunkard and the glutton will come to poverty, and slumber will clothe them with rags." **23:35:** " 'They struck me,' you will say, 'but I was not hurt; they beat me, but I did not feel it. When shall I awake? I must have another drink.' "	23:20, 29–34 31:4–7

Topic	Proverbs	Others
Scheming	**1:18:** "These men lie in wait for their own blood; they set an ambush for their own lives." **6:16, 18:** "There are six things that the Lord hates, seven that are an abomination to him: . . . a heart that devises wicked plans." **16:27:** "A worthless man plots evil, and his speech is like a scorching fire." **24:8–9:** "Whoever plans to do evil will be called a schemer. The devising of folly is sin, and the scoffer is an abomination to mankind."	1:11–12, 17, 31 4:24 6:12–19 11:6 12:2, 6, 20 14:2, 17, 22 16:30 24:1–2 25:19 29:10, 25 30:32
Anger	**14:29:** "Whoever is slow to anger has great understanding, but he who has a hasty temper exalts folly." **15:18:** "A hot-tempered man stirs up strife, but he who is slow to anger quiets contention." **27:4:** "Wrath is cruel, anger is overwhelming, but who can stand before jealousy?" **29:22:** "A man of wrath stirs up strife, and one given to anger causes much transgression."	14:17 15:1 16:32 19:11–12, 19 20:2–3 21:14 22:24 25:23 30:33
Revenge	**6:34:** "Jealousy makes a man furious, and he will not spare when he takes revenge." **20:22:** "Do not say, 'I will repay evil'; wait for the Lord, and he will deliver you." **24:29:** "Do not say, 'I will do to him as he has done to me; I will pay the man back for what he has done.' "	19:11 25:21–22

Topic	Proverbs	Others
Prudence	**3:21–22:** "My son, do not lose sight of these—keep sound wisdom and discretion, and they will be life for your soul and adornment for your neck." **4:25–26:** "Let your eyes look directly forward, and your gaze be straight before you. Ponder the path of your feet; then all your ways will be sure." **10:5:** "He who gathers in summer is a prudent son, but he who sleeps in harvest is a son who brings shame." **11:22:** "Like a gold ring in a pig's snout is a beautiful woman without discretion." **13:16:** "Every prudent man acts with knowledge, but a fool flaunts his folly." **14:15:** "The simple believes everything, but the prudent gives thought to his steps." **22:3; 27:12:** "The prudent sees danger and hides himself, but the simple go on and suffer for it." **26:4–5:** "Answer not a fool according to his folly, lest you be like him yourself. Answer a fool according to his folly, lest he be wise in his own eyes."	1:4 2:11 5:2 8:5, 12 10:19 12:8, 11, 16, 23 14:8, 12, 18, 35 15:5, 24 16:21–23 18: 13, 17 19:14, 25 20:25 21:16 23:9 25:20 28:2 30:24–28
Moderation	**25:16:** "If you have found honey, eat only enough for you, lest you have your fill of it and vomit it." **25:27:** "It is not good to eat much honey, nor is it glorious to seek one's own glory." **28:7:** "The one who keeps the law is a son with understanding, but a companion of gluttons shames his father."	21:17, 20 23:1–2, 20–21 27:7

Topics	Proverbs	Others
Social Justice	**11:26:** "The people curse him who holds back grain, but a blessing is on the head of him who sells it." **13:23:** "The fallow ground of the poor would yield much food, but it is swept away through injustice." **14:31:** "Whoever oppresses a poor man insults his Maker, but he who is generous to the needy honors him." **22:22–23:** "Do not rob the poor, because he is poor, or crush the afflicted at the gate, for the Lord will plead their cause and rob of life those who rob them." **24:11:** "Rescue those who are being taken away to death; hold back those who are stumbling to the slaughter." **31:8–9:** "Open your mouth for the mute, for the rights of all who are destitute. Open your mouth, judge righteously, defend the rights of the poor and needy."	2:8–9 8:20 14:21 16:8 17:5 18:23 19:17 20:26 21:13, 15 22:2, 8–9, 16 28:3, 8, 15, 21, 27 29:4, 7, 13–14 30:14
Repentance	**10:17:** "Whoever heeds instruction is on the path to life, but he who rejects reproof leads others astray." **28:13:** "Whoever conceals his transgressions will not prosper, but he who confesses and forsakes them will obtain mercy." **29:1:** "He who is often reproved, yet stiffens his neck, will suddenly be broken beyond healing."	3:7 4:27 14:9 16:6

Topics	Proverbs	Others
Conse-quences	**3:7–8:** "Be not wise in your own eyes; fear the Lord, and turn away from evil. It will be healing to your flesh and refreshment to your bones." **9:11:** "By me your days will be multiplied, and years will be added to your life." **11:19:** "Whoever is steadfast in righteousness will live, but he who pursues evil will die." **14:12:** "There is a way that seems right to a man, but its end is the way to death."	3:4 4:12 11:3 12:14, 28 14:27, 32 17:13, 20 19:5, 9, 16 21:16 22:5 28:10, 17 29:6
Discipline	**6:31:** "If he is caught, he will pay sevenfold; he will give all the goods of his house." **11:21:** "Be assured, an evil person will not go unpunished, but the offspring of the righteous will be delivered." **11:31:** "If the righteous is repaid on earth, how much more the wicked and the sinner!" **12:1:** "Whoever loves discipline loves knowledge, but he who hates reproof is stupid." **13:18:** "Poverty and disgrace come to him who ignores instruction, but whoever heeds reproof is honored." **19:29:** "Condemnation is ready for scoffers, and beating for the backs of fools." **26:3:** "A whip for the horse, a bridle for the donkey, and a rod for the back of fools."	1:26–28 3:11–12 5:23 6:23 10:13, 17 11:27 15:5, 10–12 17:10–11 19:19, 25 20:30 21:11 24:12 29:1, 19

CHARACTER		
Topics	**Proverbs**	**Others**
Love/ Kindness **Hebrew:** ***chesed******	**3:3*:** "Let not steadfast love and faithfulness forsake you; bind them around your neck; write them on the tablet of your heart." **10:12:** "Hatred stirs up strife, but love covers all offenses." **11:17*:** "A man who is kind benefits himself, but a cruel man hurts himself." **19:22*:** "What is desired in a man is steadfast love, and a poor man is better than a liar." **21:21*:** "Whoever pursues righteousness and kindness will find life, righteousness, and honor." **31:26*:** "She opens her mouth with wisdom, and the teaching of kindness is on her tongue."	3:12 5:19 8:17 9:8 13:24 14:22* 15:9, 17 17:9, 17 19:8 20:6*, 28* 27:5
Commitment	**14:22:** "Do they not go astray who devise evil? Those who devise good meet steadfast love and faithfulness." **16:6:** "By steadfast love and faithfulness iniquity is atoned for, and by the fear of the Lord one turns away from evil." **20:6:** "Many a man proclaims his own steadfast love, but a faithful man who can find?" **25:13:** "Like the cold of snow in the time of harvest is a faithful messenger to those who send him; he refreshes the soul of his masters."	3:3 12:22 13:13, 17 14:5 17:17 20:28 28:9, 20

Topics	Proverbs	Others
Joy	**10:28:** "The hope of the righteous brings joy, but the expectation of the wicked will perish." **15:13:** "A glad heart makes a cheerful face, but by sorrow of heart the spirit is crushed." **17:22:** "A joyful heart is good medicine, but a crushed spirit dries up the bones." **21:15:** "When justice is done, it is a joy to the righteous but terror to evildoers."	12:20, 25 13:12, 19 14:10, 13 15:15, 21, 23, 30 17:21 23:24–25 29:3
Peacemak-ing	**12:20:** "Deceit is in the heart of those who devise evil, but those who plan peace have joy." **16:7:** "When a man's ways please the Lord, he makes even his enemies to be at peace with him." **17:1:** "Better is a dry morsel with quiet than a house full of feasting with strife."	3:2, 17–18 14:30 29:9, 11
Patience	**19:2:** "Desire without knowledge is not good, and whoever makes haste with his feet misses his way." **19:11:** "Good sense makes one slow to anger, and it is his glory to overlook an offense." **25:15:** "With patience a ruler may be persuaded, and a soft tongue will break a bone."	14:29 15:18 16:32 18:14 21:5

Topic	Proverbs	Other
Goodness	**4:23:** "Keep your heart with all vigilance, for from it flow the springs of life." **11:27:** "Whoever diligently seeks good seeks favor, but evil comes to him who searches for it." **12:2:** "A good man obtains favor from the Lord, but a man of evil devices he condemns." **14:14:** "The backslider in heart will be filled with the fruit of his ways, and a good man will be filled with the fruit of his ways."	2:20–21 10:9 11:5 13:6, 22 14:19, 22, 34 20:9, 11 21:3, 21 22:1, 11
Gentleness	**15:4:** "A gentle tongue is a tree of life, but perverseness in it breaks the spirit." **17:27:** "Whoever restrains his words has knowledge, and he who has a cool spirit is a man of understanding."	12:18 15:1 18:21 25:11, 15
Self-Control	**13:3:** "Whoever guards his mouth preserves his life; he who opens wide his lips comes to ruin." **16:32:** "Whoever is slow to anger is better than the mighty, and he who rules his spirit than he who takes a city." **25:28:** "A man without self-control is like a city broken into and left without walls."	17:27–28 21:23 23:20–21 24:10 25:16, 27 27:8 28:7

Topic	Proverbs	Other
Pride	**11:2:** "When pride comes, then comes disgrace, but with the humble is wisdom." **16:18:** "Pride goes before destruction, and a haughty spirit before a fall." **18:12:** "Before destruction a man's heart is haughty, but humility comes before honor." **29:23:** "One's pride will bring him low, but he who is lowly in spirit will obtain honor."	6:17 8:13 13:10 15:25 16:5, 19 17:19 21:4, 24 26:12 30:12–13, 29–31
Humility	**3:34:** "Toward the scorners he is scornful, but to the humble he gives favor." **16:19:** "It is better to be of a lowly spirit with the poor than to divide the spoil with the proud." **22:4:** "The reward for humility and fear of the Lord is riches and honor and life."	11:2 13:10 15:33 18:12 29:23

WEALTH		
Topic	**Proverbs**	**Others**
Money	**10:15:** "A rich man's wealth is his strong city; the poverty of the poor is their ruin." **11:4:** "Riches do not profit in the day of wrath, but righteousness delivers from death." **12:9:** "Better to be lowly and have a servant than to play the great man and lack bread." **17:18:** "One who lacks sense gives a pledge and puts up security in the presence of his neighbor." **19:4:** "Wealth brings many new friends, but a poor man is deserted by his friend." **22:2:** "The rich and the poor meet together; the Lord is the Maker of them all." **30:8:** "Remove far from me falsehood and lying; give me neither poverty nor riches; feed me with the food that is needful for me."	3:14, 16 8:18–19 10:4, 16, 22 11:7, 24–25, 28 13:7–8, 11, 22 14:20, 24 15:6, 16 18:11, 23 19:6–7, 14 20:21 22:1, 4, 7, 16 3:4–8 24:4 27:24 28:6, 11, 20, 22
Dishonest Gain	**11:1:** "A false balance is an abomination to the Lord, but a just weight is his delight." **20:17:** "Bread gained by deceit is sweet to a man, but afterward his mouth will be full of gravel." **21:6:** "The getting of treasures by a lying tongue is a fleeting vapor and a snare of death." **23:10–11:** "Do not move an ancient landmark or enter the fields of the fatherless, for their Redeemer is strong; he will plead their cause against you." **28:6:** "Better is a poor man who walks in his integrity than a rich man who is crooked in his ways."	1:19 10:2 11:18 15:27 16:11 17:8 20:10, 14, 23 21:14 22:1, 16 28:8, 16 30:8

Topic	Proverbs	Others
Greed	**1:19:** "Such are the ways of everyone who is greedy for unjust gain; it takes away the life of its possessors." **13:11:** "Wealth gained hastily will dwindle, but whoever gathers little by little will increase it." **15:27:** "Whoever is greedy for unjust gain troubles his own household, but he who hates bribes will live." **27:20:** "Sheol and Abaddon are never satisfied, and never satisfied are the eyes of man."	1:13 20:21 22:16 23:4 28:20, 22, 25 30:7–9, 14–16
Debt	**22:7:** "The rich rules over the poor, and the borrower is the slave of the lender." **22:26–27:** "Be not one of those who give pledges, who put up security for debts. If you have nothing with which to pay, why should your bed be taken from under you?"	3:27–28 6:1–5 11:15 27:13
Laziness	**6:9–11:** "How long will you lie there, O sluggard? When will you arise from your sleep? A little sleep, a little slumber, a little folding of the hands to rest, and poverty will come upon you like a robber, and want like an armed man." **10:26:** "Like vinegar to the teeth and smoke to the eyes, so is the sluggard to those who send him." **13:4:** "The soul of the sluggard craves and gets nothing, while the soul of the diligent is richly supplied." **19:24:** "The sluggard buries his hand in the dish and will not even bring it back to his mouth."	6:6–8 10:4–5 12:24, 27 15:19 18:9 19:15 20:4, 13 21:17, 25 22:13 24:30–34 26:13–16

Topic	Proverbs	Others
Work	**12:11:** "Whoever works his land will have plenty of bread, but he who follows worthless pursuits lacks sense." **12:24:** "The hand of the diligent will rule, while the slothful will be put to forced labor." **14:4:** "Where there are no oxen, the manger is clean, but abundant crops come by the strength of the ox." **14:23:** "In all toil there is profit, but mere talk tends only to poverty." **22:29:** "Do you see a man skillful in his work? He will stand before kings; he will not stand before obscure men."	6:6–8 10:4–5 16:26 21:5 24:27 27:23–27 28:19 31:13–27, 31
Plans	**16:9:** "The heart of man plans his way, but the Lord establishes his steps." **19:21:** "Many are the plans in the mind of a man, but it is the purpose of the Lord that will stand." **21:5:** "The plans of the diligent lead surely to abundance, but everyone who is hasty comes only to poverty."	5:21 6:18 15:22 16:1, 3, 33 20:18, 24 21:1
Generosity	**3:9–10:** "Honor the Lord with your wealth and with the firstfruits of all your produce; then your barns will be filled with plenty, and your vats will be bursting with wine." **11:24–25:** "One gives freely, yet grows all the richer; another withholds what he should give, and only suffers want. Whoever brings blessing will be enriched, and one who waters will himself be watered." **19:17:** "Whoever is generous to the poor lends to the Lord, and he will repay him for his deed." **22:9:** "Whoever has a bountiful eye will be blessed, for he shares his bread with the poor."	

Notes

CHAPTER 1: WISDOM

1. Scott Sorokin, "Thriving in a World of 'Knowledge Half-Life,'" CIO, April 5, 2019, cio.com/article/219940/thriving-in-a-world-of-knowledge-half-life.html.
2. Another four times Solomon writes in the plural, "O sons," but his intent seems to have been to pass his wisdom to his successor, Rehoboam.

CHAPTER 3: MENTORS

1. *Britannica,* "Thomas Edison," last updated April 21, 2025, britannica.com/biography/Thomas-Edison/Menlo-Park; "The Electric Light System," National Park Service, last updated February 26, 2015, home.nps.gov/edis/learn/kidsyouth/the-electric-light-system-phonograph-motion-pictures.htm; *Britannica,* "Joseph Swan," last updated October 27, 2024, britannica.com/biography/Joseph-Wilson-Swan.
2. Robert D. Putnam, *Bowling Alone: The Collapse and Revival of American Community* (Simon & Schuster, 2000), 438–439.
3. "Living Arrangements of Children: 1970–2023," Office of Juvenile Justice and Delinquency Prevention, March 15, 2024, ojjdp.gov/ojstatbb//population/qa01201.asp?qaDate=2023&text=yes.
4. Richard Florida, "Singles Now Make Up More Than Half the U.S. Adult Population. Here's Where They All Live," Bloomberg, September 15, 2014, bloomberg.com/news/articles/2014-09-15/singles-now-make-up-more-than-half-the-u-s-adult-population-here-s-where-they-all-live.
5. Vivek H. Murthy, "Letter from the Surgeon General," in *Our Epidemic of Loneliness and Isolation: The U.S. Surgeon General's Advisory on the Healing Effects of Social Connection and Community* (Office of the U.S. Surgeon General, 2023), 4, hhs.gov/sites/default/files/surgeon-general-social-connection-advisory.pdf.

6. Jean M. Twenge and W. Keith Campbell, *The Narcissism Epidemic: Living in the Age of Entitlement* (Free Press, 2009), 34.

CHAPTER 5: WICKED

1. Delroy L. Paulhus and Kevin M. Williams, "The Dark Triad of Personality: Narcissism, Machiavellianism, and Psychopathy," *Journal of Research in Personality* 36, no. 6 (2002): 556–63, doi.org/10.1016/S0092-6566(02)00505-6.
2. "What Is Narcissistic Personality Disorder?," American Psychiatric Association, January 30, 2024, psychiatry.org/news-room/apa-blogs/what-is-narcissistic-personality-disorder.
3. "Machiavellianism," ScienceDirect, sciencedirect.com/topics/psychology/machiavellianism.
4. "Understanding Psychopaths," UC Irvine News, June 18, 2012, https://news.uci.edu/2012/06/18/understanding-psychopaths.
5. "Psychology's Dark Triad." In Dark Minds, Deadly Deeds. csi.pressbooks.pub/darkmindsdeadlydeeds/chapter/psychologys-dark-triad.

CHAPTER 6: RIGHTEOUS

1. Vivian Hunt et al., "Diversity Matters Even More: The Case for Holistic Impact," McKinsey & Company, December 5, 2023, mckinsey.com/featured-insights/diversity-and-inclusion/diversity-matters-even-more-the-case-for-holistic-impact.
2. Sarah Treuhaft, Justin Scoggins, and Jennifer Tran, *The Equity Solution: Racial Inclusion Is Key to Growing a Strong New Economy* (PolicyLink, October 22, 2014), 2, dornsife.usc.edu/eri/wp-content/uploads/sites/41/2023/02/2014_Equity_Solution_FINAL.pdf.
3. Laura Anderko et al., "Promoting Prevention Through the Affordable Care Act: Workplace Wellness," *Preventing Chronic Disease* 9 (2012), doi.org/10.5888/pcd9.120092.

CHAPTER 7: TRUTH

1. Jordan B. Peterson, *12 Rules for Life: An Antidote to Chaos* (Random House Canada, 2018), 203–32. We are focusing in this chapter on truth, but Proverbs also has much to say about lies. Here are some of the dominant proverbs

dealing with deception: Proverbs 4:24; 6:16–17; 10:18; 20:17; 21:6; 25:18; 26:18–19, 24–26. A deeper look at these passages will offer beneficial insight if you are dealing with a deceptive child, friend, colleague, or boss.

CHAPTER 10: QUARRELING

1. "War of the Stray Dog: The Incident at Petrich 1925," Balkan Military History, balkanhistory.org/war-of-the-stray-dog.html.

CHAPTER 12: BOASTING

1. Irene Scopelliti, "Why Do People Brag?," TEDx Talks, posted February 2, 2016, YouTube, youtube.com/watch?v=pNTyl_nUOVo.
2. "The Psychology of Bragging," *Counselling Connection* (blog), Australian Institute of Professional Counsellors, November 14, 2019, counsellingconnection.com/index.php/2019/11/14/the-psychology-of-bragging.
3. Scopelliti, "Why Do People Brag?"

CHAPTER 14: ENCOURAGEMENT

1. Malcolm Gladwell, host, *Revisionist History,* podcast, season 2, episode 6, "The King of Tears," Pushkin Industries, July 20, 2017, pushkin.fm/podcasts/revisionist-history/the-king-of-tears.

CHAPTER 15: PARENTS

1. "Historical Living Arrangements of Children: Table CH-1," United States Census Bureau, November 2024, census.gov/data/tables/time-series/demo/families/children.html.
2. "Major Depression," National Institute of Mental Health, last updated July 2023, nimh.nih.gov/health/statistics/major-depression.
3. "Drug Overdose Deaths," National Institute on Drug Abuse, nida.nih.gov/research-topics/trends-statistics/overdose-death-rates#Fig3.
4. U.S. Department of Health and Human Services, Office of Population Affairs, Treatment for Pediatric Gender Dysphoria: Review of Evidence and Best Practices (Washington, D.C.: HHS, 2025), opa.hhs.gov/sites/default/files/2025-05/gender-dysphoria-report.pdf (see Figure 4.1, page 57).

CHAPTER 17: SPOUSES

1. *The American Family Survey: 2022 Report* (Deseret News and Center for the Study of Elections and Democracy, 2022), 92, media.deseret.com/media/misc/pdf/afs/2022-american-family-survey.pdf.
2. D'Vera Cohn et al., "Barely Half of U.S. Adults Are Married—a Record Low," Pew Research Center, December 14, 2011, pewresearch.org/social-trends/2011/12/14/barely-half-of-u-s-adults-are-married-a-record-low.
3. Chad Cook and Alessandra N. Garcia, "Post-Randomization Bias," *Journal of Manual and Manipulative Therapy* 28, no. 2 (2020): 69–71, doi.org/10.1080/10669817.2020.1739153; Robert Taibbi, "5 Risks for People Marrying a Second or Third Time," *Psychology Today,* February 22, 2024, psychologytoday.com/us/blog/fixing-families/202401/5-dangers-and-opportunities-for-second-and-third-marriages. Admittedly, there is variation in the estimates of divorce, since how the studies are carried out will provide differing results. Yet the point remains that marriage stands on increasingly shaky ground.
4. Paul R. Amato, "Children of Divorce in the 1990s: An Update of the Amato and Keith (1991) Meta-Analysis," *Journal of Family Psychology* 15, no. 3 (2001): 355–70, pubmed.ncbi.nlm.nih.gov/11584788.
5. Jay L. Zagorsky, "Marriage and Divorce's Impact on Wealth," *Journal of Sociology* 41, no. 4 (2005): 406–24, doi.org/10.1177/1440783305058478.
6. Rodney Stark, *The Rise of Christianity: How the Obscure, Marginal Jesus Movement Became the Dominant Religious Force in the Western World in a Few Centuries* (HarperSanFrancisco, 1996), 95–128.

CHAPTER 18: FRIENDS

1. Robin I. M. Dunbar, "Neocortex Size as a Constraint on Group Size in Primates," *Journal of Human Evolution* 22, no. 6 (1992): 469–93, doi.org/10.1016/0047-2484(92)90081-J.
2. Daniel A. Cox, "Men's Social Circles Are Shrinking," Survey Center on American Life, June 29, 2021, americansurveycenter.org/why-mens-social-circles-are-shrinking.
3. Daniel A. Cox, "The State of American Friendship: Change, Challenges, and Loss," Survey Center on American Life, June 8, 2021, americansurveycenter.org/research/the-state-of-american-friendship-change-challenges-and-loss.
4. Tegan Cruwys et al., "Social Group Memberships Protect Against Future De-

pression, Alleviate Depression Symptoms, and Prevent Depression Relapse," *Social Science & Medicine* 98 (December 2013): 179–86, sciencedirect.com/science/article/abs/pii/S0277953613005194; Zara Abrams, "The Science of Why Friendships Keep Us Healthy," *Monitor on Psychology* 54, no. 4 (June 2023), apa.org/monitor/2023/06/cover-story-science-friendship.

CHAPTER 19: INFLUENCERS

1. Lauren Young, "Watch These Awkward Elevator Rides from an Old Episode of Candid Camera," Atlas Obscura, September 30, 2016, atlasobscura.com/articles/watch-these-awkward-elevator-rides-from-an-old-episode-of-candid-camera.
2. Solomon Asch, "Studies of Independence and Conformity: I. A Minority of One Against a Unanimous Majority," *Psychological Monographs: General and Applied* 70, no. 9 (1956): 1–70, doi.org/10.1037/h0093718.
3. Lucy Freeman, "Teenage Elephants Need a Father Figure," BBC Earth, bbcearth.com/news/teenage-elephants-need-a-father-figure; "The Delinquents," CBS News, August 22, 2000, cbsnews.com/news/the-delinquents.
4. Rodney Stark and William Sims Bainbridge, "Networks of Faith: Interpersonal Bonds and Recruitment to Cults and Sects," *American Journal of Sociology* 85/6 (May 1980): 1376–1395.

CHAPTER 21: ENEMIES

1. K. Allan Blume, "'Guilty as Charged,' Cathy Says of Chick-fil-A's Stand on Biblical and Family Values," Baptist Press, July 16, 2012, baptistpress.com/resource-library/news/guilty-as-charged-cathy-says-of-chick-fil-as-stand-on-biblical-family-values.
2. Chris Good, "Chick-fil-A CEO and Gay Activist Are Now Friends," ABC News, January 28, 2013, abcnews.go.com/blogs/politics/2013/01/chick-fil-a-ceo-and-gay-activist-are-now-friends.

CHAPTER 22: GOD

1. Robert A. Hummer et al., "Religious Involvement and U.S. Adult Mortality," *Demography* 36, no.26 (May 1999): 273–85, doi.org/10.2307/2648114. See also Laura E. Wallace et al., "Does Religion Stave Off the Grave? Religious

Affiliation in One's Obituary and Longevity," *Social Psychological and Personality Science* 10, no. 5 (2018): 662–70, doi.org/10.1177/1948550618779820.

2. Brian J. Grim and Melissa E. Grim, "Belief, Behavior, and Belonging: How Faith Is Indispensable in Preventing and Recovering from Substance Abuse," *Journal of Religion and Health* 58, no. 5 (2019): 1713–50, doi.org/10.1007/s10943-019-00876-w.
3. Raphael Bonelli et al., "Religious and Spiritual Factors in Depression: Review and Integration of the Research," Depression Research and Treatment (2012), doi.org/10.1155/2012/962860.
4. Andrew Houser, "The Impact of Church Attendance on Child Development and Family Life," Acton Institute, September 19, 2021, rlo.acton.org/archives/122459-the-impact-of-church-attendance-on-child-development-and-family-life.html.
5. Leviticus 19:14, 32; 25:17; Deuteronomy 4:10; 6:2, 13, 24; 8:6; 10:12, 20; 13:4; 14:23; 17:19; 28:58; 31:12–13; Joshua 4:24; 24:14; 1 Samuel 12:14, 24; 2 Kings 17:28, 36, 39; 1 Chronicles 16:25; 2 Chronicles 19:7, 9; Job 28:28; Psalm 2:11; 15:4; 19:9; 33:8; 34:9; 47:2; 96:4; 111:10; 112:1; 115:11, 13; 118:4; 128:1, 4; 135:20; Proverbs 1:7; 2:5; 3:7; 8:13; 9:10; 10:27; 14:26–27; 15:16, 33; 16:6; 19:23; 22:4; 23:17; 24:21; 28:14; Isaiah 8:13; 11:2–3; 33:6; Jeremiah 5:24; Hosea 3:5; Jonah 1:9; Habakkuk 3:2; Acts 9:31; 2 Corinthians 5:11; Colossians 3:22.

CHAPTER 23: LEADERSHIP

1. James M. Kouzes and Barry Z. Posner, *The Leadership Challenge: How to Make Extraordinary Things Happen in Organizations,* 7th ed. (Wiley, 2023), 19–21.

CHAPTER 24: ADULTERY

1. Justin J. Lehmiller, "Does Infidelity Peak After 7 Years of Marriage?," *Psychology Today,* last updated October 5, 2023, psychologytoday.com/us/blog/the-myths-of-sex/202308/does-infidelity-peak-in-the-seventh-year-of-marriage.
2. Gary Chapman, *The 5 Love Languages: The Secret to Love That Lasts* (Northfield, 2015).

CHAPTER 25: DRINKING

1. Caroline J. Easton, "The Role of Substance Abuse in Intimate Partner Violence," *Psychiatric Times* 25, no. 1 (January 2006), psychiatrictimes.com/view/role-substance-abuse-intimate-partner-violence.
2. Center for Substance Abuse Treatment, *Substance Abuse Treatment and Domestic Violence,* no. 25 (SAMHSA, 2012), 3, library.samhsa.gov/sites/default/files/SMA12-3390_508.pdf.
3. John Pritchard, "Crime and Substance Abuse," EBSCO, 2022, ebsco.com/research-starters/law/crime-and-substance-abuse.
4. Anne Beck and Andreas Heinz, "Alcohol-Related Aggression: Social and Neurobiological Factors," *Deutsches Ärzteblatt* 110, no. 42 (2013): 711, doi.org/10.3238/arztebl.2013.0711.
5. Nedeljko Golubovic et al., "The Effects of Substance Use on Public Perceptions of Rape Crimes," *Journal of Addiction & Addictive Disorders* 8 (2021), doi.org/10.24966/AAD-7276/100063.

CHAPTER 26: SCHEMING

1. Robert M. Sapolsky, *Why Zebras Don't Get Ulcers,* 3rd ed. (Henry Holt, 2004), 4–7; Kevin Ritzenthaler, "Why Zebras Don't Get Ulcers (and Why Humans Do)," Innovative Health, innovativehealthclinic.com/functional-medicine-weston/why-zebras-dont-get-ulcers-and-why-humans-do; Craig Holdrege, "The Intertwined Worlds of Zebra and Lion," The Nature Institute, 2020, natureinstitute.org/article/craig-holdrege/intertwined-worlds-of-lion-and-zebra; Anping Chen et al., "Increased Vigilance of Plains Zebras (*Equus quagga*) in Response to More Bush Coverage in a Kenyan Savanna," *Climate Change Ecology* 1 (July 2021), doi.org/10.1016/j.ecochg.2021.100001.
2. "Chronic Stress Puts Your Health at Risk," Mayo Clinic, August 1, 2023, mayoclinic.org/healthy-lifestyle/stress-management/in-depth/stress/art-20046037.

CHAPTER 27: ANGER

1. "Anger Management: 10 Tips to Tame Your Temper," Mayo Clinic, October 4, 2024, mayoclinic.org/healthy-lifestyle/adult-health/in-depth/anger-management/art-20045434.

CHAPTER 28: REVENGE

1. *Britannica,* "Hatfields and McCoys," last updated April 24, 2025, britannica.com/topic/Hatfields-and-McCoys; "The Hatfield's and McCoy's," Hatfield & McCoy Foundation and Museum, hatfieldmccoyfoundation.org/the-hatfields-mccoys.

CHAPTER 29: PRUDENCE

1. M. Tullius Cicero, *Cato Major; or, A Treatise on Old Age,* trans. James Logan, 4th ed. (Philadelphia, 1758), 51.
2. Thomas Aquinas, *The Summa Theologica,* trans. Fathers of the English Dominican Province, vol. 2, *Questions 47–79* (Burns, Oates & Washbourne, 1929), 14.

CHAPTER 30: MODERATION

1. Simon Kemp, "Digital 2023: Global Overview Report," DataReportal, January 26, 2023, datareportal.com/reports/digital-2023-global-overview-report; Simon Kemp, "Digital 2025: Global Overview Report," DataReportal, February 5, 2025, datareportal.com/reports/digital-2025-global-overview-report.
2. "FastStats: Sleep in Adults," Centers for Disease Control and Prevention, May 15, 2024, cdc.gov/sleep/data-research/facts-stats/adults-sleep-facts-and-stats.html.
3. "Only 1 in 10 Adults Get Enough Fruits or Vegetables," Centers for Disease Control and Prevention, November 16, 2017, archive.cdc.gov/#/details?url=https://www.cdc.gov/media/releases/2017/p1116-fruit-vegetable-consumption.html.
4. "Get the Facts: Added Sugars," Centers for Disease Control and Prevention, January 5, 2024, cdc.gov/nutrition/php/data-research/added-sugars.html; "How Much Sugar Is Too Much?," American Heart Association, September 23, 2024, heart.org/en/healthy-living/healthy-eating/eat-smart/sugar/how-much-sugar-is-too-much.
5. Marie Ng et al., "National-Level and State-Level Prevalence of Overweight and Obesity Among Children, Adolescents, and Adults in the USA, 1990–2021, and Forecasts up to 2050," *The Lancet* 404 (December 2024): 2278–98, doi.org/10.1016/S0140-6736(24)01548-4; Craig M. Hales et al., "Prevalence of Obesity and Severe Obesity Among Adults: United States,

2017–2018," Centers for Disease Control and Prevention, February 2020, cdc.gov/nchs/products/databriefs/db360.htm.

6. "Adult Activity: An Overview," Centers for Disease Control and Prevention, December 20, 2023, cdc.gov/physical-activity-basics/guidelines/adults.html; "Exercise or Physical Activity," Centers for Disease Control and Prevention, September 24, 2024, cdc.gov/nchs/fastats/exercise.htm.
7. "Mental Illness," National Institute of Mental Health, last updated September 2024, nimh.nih.gov/health/statistics/mental-illness.
8. Emily P. Terlizzi and Tina Norris, "Mental Health Treatment Among Adults: United States, 2020," Centers for Disease Control and Prevention, October 2021, cdc.gov/nchs/products/databriefs/db419.htm.
9. Gregory A. Smith et al., "8. Religious Attendance and Congregational Involvement," Religious Landscape Study, Pew Research Center, February 26, 2025, pewresearch.org/religion/2025/02/26/religious-attendance-and-congregational-involvement.

CHAPTER 31: SOCIAL JUSTICE

1. *Global Estimates of Modern Slavery: Forced Labour and Forced Marriage* (International Labour Organization, Walk Free, and International Organization for Migration, 2022), 2, 4, ilo.org/sites/default/files/wcmsp5/groups/public/%40ed_norm/%40ipec/documents/publication/wcms_854733.pdf.
2. Steve Corbett and Brian Fikkert, *When Helping Hurts: How to Alleviate Poverty Without Hurting the Poor . . . and Yourself* (Moody, 2012).

CHAPTER 32: REPENTANCE

1. Flavius Josephus, *The Life of Flavius Josephus,* in *The Works of Josephus: Complete and Unabridged,* rev. ed., trans. William Whiston (Hendrickson, 1987), 7.
2. Many translations render this "faith in Jesus" rather than "Jesus's faithfulness." Both are possible, yet the implication is inevitable that Jesus's faithfulness to God's assignment allowed our entrance into the kingdom through repentance.

CHAPTER 33: CONSEQUENCES

1. Robert Frost, "The Road Not Taken," 1915, Poetry Foundation, poetryfoundation.org/poems/44272/the-road-not-taken.

2. Andy Stanley, *The Principle of the Path: How to Get from Where You Are to Where You Want to Be* (Thomas Nelson, 2008), 14.

CHAPTER 34: DISCIPLINE

1. For example, Robert D. Sege et al., "Effective Discipline to Raise Healthy Children," *Pediatrics* 142, no. 6 (2018): doi.org/10.1542/peds.2018-3112.
2. Thomas Lickona, "4 Parenting Styles: How They Relate to a Child's Character," *Psychology Today,* June 18, 2020, psychologytoday.com/us/blog/raising-kind-kids/202006/4-parenting-styles-how-they-relate-childs-character.

CHAPTER 35: LOVE

1. "Pat's Story," Pat Tillman Foundation, pattillmanfoundation.org/the-foundation/pats-story.
2. You might notice that we will touch on all the fruit of the Spirit in the following chapters, except kindness. That's because there isn't a separate word for "kindness" in the Hebrew language. It's subsumed in the word "love." For example, Proverbs 11:17: "A man who is kind benefits himself, but a cruel man hurts himself." Or Proverbs 21:21: "Whoever pursues righteousness and kindness will find life, righteousness, and honor."
3. Johnny Lee, "Lookin' for Love," track 1 on *Lookin' for Love,* Elektra Entertainment, 1980.

CHAPTER 36: COMMITMENT

1. Matthew 13:44–46, 52; 18:23–35; 20:1–16; 21:33–41; 24:45–51; 25:14–30; Luke 7:41–42; 10:29–37; 11:5–8; 12:16–21; 15:8–32; 16:1–9, 19–31; 18:2–8.

CHAPTER 37: JOY

1. "Feel-Good Hormones: How They Affect Your Mind, Mood, and Body," Harvard Health Publishing, health.harvard.edu/mind-and-mood/feel-good-hormones-how-they-affect-your-mind-mood-and-body.

CHAPTER 38: PEACEMAKING

1. Topical Lexicon, s.v. "7965. *shalom,*" Bible Hub, biblehub.com/hebrew/7965.htm. "Go in peace": Exodus 4:18; Judges 18:6; 1 Samuel 1:17; 20:42; 25:35;

2 Samuel 15:9; 2 Kings 5:19; Mark 5:34; Luke 7:50; 8:48; Acts 16:36; James 2:16. See also Judges 6:23; 1 Samuel 25:5–6; 2 Samuel 3:21–22; 1 Kings 22:27–28; 2 Chronicles 18:16, 26–27; 19:1; Matthew 10:13; Luke 10:5–6; 24:36; John 20:19, 21, 26.

2. 1 Samuel 16:4–5, NIV; 1 Kings 2:13. Also "Is it peace?": 2 Kings 9:17–19, 22, 31. See also 2 Samuel 20:9; 1 Chronicles 12:17–18.

CHAPTER 39: PATIENCE

1. Cai Ellis and Robert Brandl, "Website Loading Time Statistics (2025)," Tooltester, April 9, 2024, tooltester.com/en/blog/website-loading-time-statistics.
2. "The Three Second Social Media Rule," Marketing Essentials Lab, December 2, 2021, marketingessentialslab.com/%E2%80%A8the-three-second-social-media-rule.
3. Rachita Kauldhar, "Understanding Short-Form Videos and Its Potential," *African Journal of Biological Sciences* 6, no. 7 (2024), afjbs.com/issue-content/understanding-short-form-videos-and-its-potential-4377.

CHAPTER 40: GOODNESS

1. *Britannica,* "Fred Rogers," last updated April 25, 2025, britannica.com/biography/Fred-Rogers; Daryl Austin, "The Sad Story Behind Mr. Rogers' Hallmark Empathy," *Reader's Digest,* August 11, 2021, rd.com/article/mr-rogers; "About Fred Rogers," Mister Rogers' Neighborhood, misterrogers.org/about-fred-rogers.

CHAPTER 41: GENTLENESS

1. *Britannica,* "Ulysses S. Grant," last updated May 9, 2025, britannica.com/biography/Ulysses-S-Grant; Joan Waugh, "Ulysses S. Grant: Family Life," Miller Center, millercenter.org/president/grant/family-life; "The Surrender Meeting," National Park Service, last updated April 15, 2025, nps.gov/apco/learn/historyculture/the-surrender-meeting.htm.

CHAPTER 42: SELF-CONTROL

1. Sharon Hodde Miller, *The Cost of Control: Why We Crave It, the Anxiety It Gives Us, and the Real Power God Promises* (Baker Books, 2022), 37–38, 113–32, 142, 168–69, 176.

CHAPTER 43: PRIDE

1. Herodotus, *The Histories,* trans. Aubrey de Sélincourt (Penguin Books, 1964), 8.56–96.

CHAPTER 44: HUMILITY

1. LeBron James, in "Flashback: LeBron James Makes His Decision to Join Miami," ESPN, espn.com/video/clip/_/id/19904298.
2. "Reflective LeBron Admits He Was Immature Last Year," NBC Sports, nbcsports.com/nba/news/reflective-lebron-admits-he-was-immature-last-year.
3. "I Promise School," The LeBron James Family Foundation, lebronjamesfamilyfoundation.org/i-promise-school; Sarah Jones, "What LeBron Can Prove About Public Education," *The New Republic,* August 7, 2018, newrepublic.com/article/150478/lebron-can-prove-public-education.

CHAPTER 45: MONEY

1. Margaret Wood, "In God We Trust," *In Custodia Legis* (blog), Library of Congress, April 22, 2013, blogs.loc.gov/law/2013/04/in-god-we-trust.

CHAPTER 46: DISHONEST GAIN

1. *Britannica,* "Enron scandal," last updated April 25, 2025, britannica.com/event/Enron-scandal; Adam Hayes, "What Was Enron? What Happened and Who Was Responsible?," Investopedia, last updated December 4, 2024, investopedia.com/terms/e/enron.asp; "Enron," FBI, fbi.gov/history/famous-cases/enron.
2. *Britannica,* "financial crisis of 2007–08," britannica.com/money/financial-crisis-of-2007-2008; John Fraedrich et al., *Countrywide Financial: The Subprime Meltdown* (Auburn University, 2014), harbert.auburn.edu/binaries/documents/center-for-ethical-organizational-cultures/cases/countrywide.pdf.
3. "Apple Fined for Slowing Down Old iPhones," BBC, February 7, 2020, bbc.com/news/technology-51413724.
4. "Sensa and Three Other Marketers of Fad Weight-Loss Products Settle FTC Charges in Crackdown on Deceptive Advertising," Federal Trade Commission, January 7, 2014, ftc.gov/news-events/news/press-releases/2014/01/sensa-three-other-marketers-fad-weight-loss-products-settle-ftc-charges-crackdown-deceptive.

5. "Nine FIFA Officials and Five Corporate Executives Indicted for Racketeering Conspiracy and Corruption," U.S. Department of Justice, May 27, 2015, justice.gov/archives/opa/pr/nine-fifa-officials-and-five-corporate-executives-indicted-racketeering-conspiracy-and.
6. Daniel Kahneman and Angus Deaton, "High Income Improves Evaluation of Life but Not Emotional Well-Being," *Proceedings of the National Academy of Sciences of the United States of America* 107, no. 38 (2010): 16489–93, doi.org/10.1073/pnas.1011492107.

CHAPTER 47: GREED

1. Angelica Leicht, "Here's How Much Credit Card Debt the Average American Has (and How to Pay It Off)," CBS News, last updated April 26, 2024, cbsnews.com/news/heres-how-much-credit-card-debt-the-average-american-has-and-how-to-pay-it-off.
2. "Auto Loan Debt Statistics: 2025 Roundup," LendingTree.com, lendingtree.com/auto/debt-statistics.
3. "Student Loan Debt Statistics," EducationData.org, educationdata.org/student-loan-debt-statistics.
4. "How Much Is a Phone Bill in 2025?" T-Mobile.com, t-mobile.com/dialed-in/wireless/average-phone-bill-per-month.
5. Todd Spangler, "Americans Now Spend $69 per Month on Video Streaming—and Nearly Half Think It's Too Much," *Variety,* March 25, 2025, variety.com/2025/digital/news/streaming-survey-cost-monthly-value-deloitte-1236342738.
6. Jean M. Twenge, *Generation Me: Why Today's Young Americans Are More Confident, Assertive, Entitled—and More Miserable Than Ever Before,* rev. ed. (Atria Books, 2014), 175.

CHAPTER 48: DEBT

1. Richard Sandomir, "Tyson's Bankruptcy Is a Lesson in Ways to Squander a Fortune," *New York Times,* August 5, 2003, nytimes.com/2003/08/05/sports/tyson-s-bankruptcy-is-a-lesson-in-ways-to-squander-a-fortune.html.
2. Carlin Miller, "Nicolas Cage Says He'll Pay $14 Million Debt to IRS; Finances in Ruin," CBS News, January 19, 2010, cbsnews.com/news/nicolas

-cage-says-hell-pay-14-million-debt-to-irs-finances-in-ruin; Emmie Martin, "How Nicolas Cage Blew $150 Million on Mansions, a Private island—and a Real Dinosaur Skull," CNBC, last updated May 11, 2017, cnbc.com/2017/05/10/craziest-things-nicholas-cage-bought-with-150-million.html.

3. "MC Hammer Files for Bankruptcy," Music History Calendar, Songfacts, calendar.songfacts.com/april/1/17530.
4. Dave Ramsey (@DaveRamsey), "If you will live like no one else now, later you can live and give like no one else!," Facebook, April 14, 2018, facebook.com/daveramsey/posts/if-you-will-live-like-no-one-else-now-later-you-can-live-and-give-like-no-one-el/10155492350110886.

When Mark E. Moore isn't chasing his seven grandkids or trying to convince them he's still cool, you'll find him onstage as a teaching pastor at Christ's Church of the Valley (CCV), with multiple locations all across the Phoenix metro area (where hell is not a theology but a shared experience from June through September).

Before trading his professor's tweed for a pastoral role, Moore spent twenty-two years shaping young minds at Ozark Christian College in Joplin, Missouri—long enough to baptize his Bible teaching in dad jokes. He later compiled that teaching into bestsellers like *Core 52* and *Quest 52*. These days, he and his bride, Barbara, beam with pride watching their two adult children follow their own callings in ministry.

Mark E. Moore's life mission is to make Jesus famous through teaching biblical wisdom. If you've found this book helpful, he's made a treasure trove of his teachings freely available at markmoore.org.

ABOUT THE TYPE

This book was set in Garamond, a typeface originally designed by the Parisian type cutter Claude Garamond (c. 1500–61). This version of Garamond was modeled on a 1592 specimen sheet from the Egenolff-Berner foundry, which was produced from types assumed to have been brought to Frankfurt by the punch cutter Jacques Sabon (c. 1520–80).

Claude Garamond's distinguished romans and italics first appeared in *Opera Ciceronis* in 1543–44. The Garamond types are clear, open, and elegant.

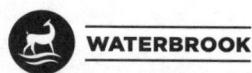